Java EE 6 Development with NetBeans 7

Develop professional enterprise Java EE applications
quickly and easily with this popular IDE

David R. Heffelfinger

PUBLISHING

BIRMINGHAM - MUMBAI

Java EE 6 Development with NetBeans 7

First published: June 2011

Production Reference: 1130611

Published by Packt Publishing Ltd.
32 Lincoln Road
Olton
Birmingham, B27 6PA, UK.

ISBN 978-1-849512-70-1

www.packtpub.com

Cover Image by Asher Wishkerman (wishkerman@hotmail.com)

Credits

Author
David R. Heffelfinger

Reviewers
Allan Bond

Arun Gupta

Bruno Vernay

Acquisition Editor
Douglas Patterson

Development Editor
Kartikey Pandey

Technical Editor
Pallavi Kachare

Project Coordinator
Shubhanjan Chatterjee

Proofreader
Mario Cecere

Indexer
Hemangini Bari

Production Coordinator
Adline Swetha Jesuthas

Cover Work
Adline Swetha Jesuthas

About the Author

David R. Heffelfinger is the Chief Technology Officer of Ensode Technology, LLC, a software consulting firm based in the greater Washington DC area. He has been architecting, designing, and developing software professionally since 1995. He has been using Java as his primary programming language since 1996. He has worked on many large scale projects for several clients including IBM, Accenture, Lockheed Martin, Fannie Mae, Freddie Mac, the US Department of Homeland Security, and the US Department of Defense. He has a Masters degree in Software Engineering from Southern Methodist University. David is an editor in chief of Ensode.net (http://www.ensode.net), a web site about Java, Linux, and other technology topics.

I would like to thank everyone whose help made this book a reality. I would like to thank the Development Editors, Kartikey Pandey and Tariq Rakhange; and the Project Coordinator, Shubhanjan Chatterjee.

I would also like to thank the technical reviewers, Allan Bond, Arun Gupta, and Bruno Vernay for their insightful comments and suggestions.

Additionally, I would like to thank the NetBeans team at Oracle for developing such an outstanding IDE.

Finally, I would like to thank my wife and daughter, for putting up with the long hours of work that kept me away from the family.

About the Reviewers

Allan Bond is a software developer who has been active in the IT industry for over 10 years. His primary focus is systems development using Java and related technologies. He has worked and consulted for a variety of organizations ranging from small businesses to Fortune 500 companies and government agencies. Allan holds a Masters degree in Information Systems Management from Brigham Young University.

> I would like to thank my wife and children for their patience during the nights (and sometimes weekends) I needed to complete the review of this book.

Arun Gupta is a Java EE and GlassFish evangelist working at Oracle. Arun has over 15 years of experience in the software industry working in the Java(TM) platform and several web-related technologies. In his current role, he works to create and foster the community around Java EE and GlassFish. He has been with the Java EE team since its inception and contributed to all Java EE releases. Arun has extensive world wide speaking experience on a myriad of topics and loves to engage with the community, customers, partners, and Java User Groups everywhere to spread the goodness of Java.

He is a prolific blogger at `http://blogs.oracle.com/arungupta` with over 1200 blog entries and frequent visitors from all around the world with cumulative page visits > 1.2 million. He is a passionate runner and always up for running in any part of the world. You can catch him at `@arungupta`.

Bruno Vernay has been through Database and Web development, Network & Security, Messaging and Rule Engines, Data Mining, Portal, SSO and Federation. All this with Java, Linux, and Open Source. He is still asking for more after almost 13 years. He enjoys the "human adventure", engages with the community globally and locally and also participates in the group AlpesJUG.FR. He likes new technologies as much as getting rid of old unneeded ones. He tries to take the time to learn new stuff by reading books. He likes to be useful.

www.PacktPub.com

Support files, eBooks, discount offers and more

You might want to visit www.PacktPub.com for support files and downloads related to your book.

Did you know that Packt offers eBook versions of every book published, with PDF and ePub files available? You can upgrade to the eBook version at www.PacktPub.com and as a print book customer, you are entitled to a discount on the eBook copy. Get in touch with us at service@packtpub.com for more details.

At www.PacktPub.com, you can also read a collection of free technical articles, sign up for a range of free newsletters and receive exclusive discounts and offers on Packt books and eBooks.

http://PacktLib.PacktPub.com

Do you need instant solutions to your IT questions? PacktLib is Packt's online digital book library. Here, you can access, read and search across Packt's entire library of books.

Why Subscribe?

- Fully searchable across every book published by Packt
- Copy and paste, print and bookmark content
- On demand and accessible via web browser

Free Access for Packt account holders

If you have an account with Packt at www.PacktPub.com, you can use this to access PacktLib today and view nine entirely free books. Simply use your login credentials for immediate access.

Table of Contents

Preface

Java EE 6, the latest version of the Java EE specification, adds several new features to simplify enterprise application development. New versions of existing Java EE APIs have been included in this latest version of Java EE. JSF 2.0 greatly simplifies web application development. JPA 2.0 features a new criteria API and several other enhancements. EJB session beans have been enhanced to support asynchronous method calls as well as a few other enhancements. Servlet 3.0 adds several new features such as additional method calls and making the web.xml deployment descriptor optional. Additionally, few new APIs have been added to Java EE, including JAX-RS, which simplifies RESTful web service development, and CDI, which helps integrate the different layers in a typical enterprise application.

NetBeans has been updated to support all features of Java EE 6, making development of Java EE 6 compliant application even quicker and simpler. This book will guide you through all the NetBeans features that make development of enterprise Java EE 6 applications a breeze.

What this book covers

Chapter 1, Getting Started with NetBeans provides an introduction to NetBeans, giving time saving tips and tricks that will result in more efficient development of Java applications.

Chapter 2, Developing Web Applications with Servlets and JSPs covers how NetBeans aids in the development of web applications using the servlet API and JavaServer Pages.

Chapter 3, Enhancing JSP Functionality with JSTL and Custom Tags shows how NetBeans can help us create maintainable web applications by taking advantage of **JavaServer Pages Standard Tag Library (JSTL)**, and it also covers how to write our own custom JSP tags.

Chapter 4, Developing Web Applications using JavaServer Faces 2.0 explains how NetBeans can help us easily develop web applications that take advantage of the JavaServer Faces 2.0 framework.

Chapter 5, Elegant Web Applications with PrimeFaces covers how to develop elegant web applications with full Ajax functionality by taking advantage of the PrimeFaces JSF component library bundled with NetBeans.

Chapter 6, Interacting with Databases through the Java Persistence API explains how NetBeans allows us to easily develop applications taking advantage of the **Java Persistence API (JPA)**, including how to automatically generate JPA entities from existing schemas. This chapter also covers how complete web-based applications can be generated with a few clicks from an existing database schema.

Chapter 7, Implementing the Business Tier with Session Beans discusses how NetBeans simplifies EJB 3.1 session bean development.

Chapter 8, Contexts and Dependency Injection (CDI) discusses how the new CDI API introduced in Java EE 6 can help us integrate the different layers of our application.

Chapter 9, Messaging with JMS and Message Driven Beans addresses Java EE messaging technologies such as **the Java Messaging Service (JMS)** and **Message Driven Beans (MDB)**, covering NetBeans features that simplify application development taking advantage of these APIs.

Chapter 10, SOAP Web Services with JAX-WS explains how NetBeans can help us easily develop SOAP web services based on the Java API for XML Web Services (JAX-WS) API.

Chapter 11, RESTful Web Services with JAX-RS covers JAX-RS, a new addition to the Java EE specification that simplifies development of RESTful web services.

Appendix A, Debugging Enterprise Applications with the NetBeans Debugger provides an introduction to the NetBeans debugger, and how it can be used to discover defects in our application.

Appendix B, Identifying Performance Issues with the NetBeans Profiler covers the NetBeans profiler, explaining how it can be used to analyze performance issues in our applications.

What you need for this book

You need Java Development Kit (JDK) version 1.6 or newer and NetBeans 7.0, Java EE Edition.

Who this book is for

The book is aimed at three different types of developers:

- Java developers (not necessarily familiar with NetBeans) wishing to become proficient in Java EE 6, and who wish to use NetBeans for Java EE development.
- NetBeans users wishing to find out how to use their IDE of choice to develop Java EE 6 applications.
- Experienced Java EE 6 developers wishing to find out how NetBeans can make their Java EE 6 development easier.

Conventions

In this book, you will find a number of styles of text that distinguish between different kinds of information. Here are some examples of these styles, and an explanation of their meaning.

Code words in text are shown as follows: "We simply copied the form from `login.jsp` and pasted it into the JSP fragment."

A block of code is set as follows:

```
<head>
<meta http-equiv="Content-Type" content="text/html; charset=UTF-8">
<title>Login</title>
</head>
```

When we wish to draw your attention to a particular part of a code block, the relevant lines or items are set in bold:

```
<body>
<p>Please enter your username and password to access the application</p>
<%@ include file="WEB-INF/jspf/loginform.jspf" %>
</body>
```

New terms and **important words** are shown in bold. Words that you see on the screen, in menus or dialog boxes for example, appear in the text like this: "To create a JSP fragment in NetBeans, we simply need to go to **File | New File**, select **Web** as the category".

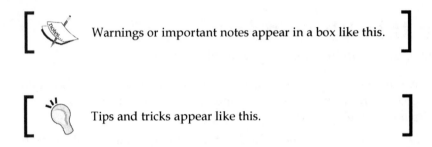

Warnings or important notes appear in a box like this.

Tips and tricks appear like this.

Reader feedback

Feedback from our readers is always welcome. Let us know what you think about this book—what you liked or may have disliked. Reader feedback is important for us to develop titles that you really get the most out of.

To send us general feedback, simply send an e-mail to feedback@packtpub.com, and mention the book title via the subject of your message.

If there is a book that you need and would like to see us publish, please send us a note in the **SUGGEST A TITLE** form on www.packtpub.com or e-mail suggest @packtpub.com.

If there is a topic that you have expertise in and you are interested in either writing or contributing to a book, see our author guide on www.packtpub.com/authors.

Customer support

Now that you are the proud owner of a Packt book, we have a number of things to help you to get the most from your purchase.

Downloading the example code

You can download the example code files for all Packt books you have purchased from your account at http://www.PacktPub.com. If you purchased this book elsewhere, you can visit http://www.PacktPub.com/support and register to have the files e-mailed directly to you.

Errata

Although we have taken every care to ensure the accuracy of our content, mistakes do happen. If you find a mistake in one of our books—maybe a mistake in the text or the code—we would be grateful if you would report this to us. By doing so, you can save other readers from frustration and help us improve subsequent versions of this book. If you find any errata, please report them by visiting http://www.packtpub. com/support, selecting your book, clicking on the **errata submission form** link, and entering the details of your errata. Once your errata are verified, your submission will be accepted and the errata will be uploaded on our website, or added to any list of existing errata, under the Errata section of that title. Any existing errata can be viewed by selecting your title from http://www.packtpub.com/support.

Piracy

Piracy of copyright material on the Internet is an ongoing problem across all media. At Packt, we take the protection of our copyright and licenses very seriously. If you come across any illegal copies of our works, in any form, on the Internet, please provide us with the location address or website name immediately so that we can pursue a remedy.

Please contact us at copyright@packtpub.com with a link to the suspected pirated material.

We appreciate your help in protecting our authors, and our ability to bring you valuable content.

Questions

You can contact us at questions@packtpub.com if you are having a problem with any aspect of the book, and we will do our best to address it.

1
Getting Started with NetBeans

In this chapter, we will cover how to get started with NetBeans; topics covered in this chapter include:

- Introduction
- Obtaining NetBeans
- Installing NetBeans
- Starting NetBeans for the first time
- Configuring NetBeans for Java EE development
- Deploying our first application
- NetBeans tips for effective development

Introduction

NetBeans is an **Integrated Development Environment (IDE)** and platform. Although initially the NetBeans IDE could only be used to develop Java applications, as of version 6 NetBeans supports several programming languages, either by built-in support or by installing additional plugins. Programing languages natively supported by NetBeans include Java, JavaFX, C, C++ and PHP. Groovy, Scala, Ruby and others are supported via additional plugins

In addition to being an IDE, NetBeans is also a platform. Developers can use NetBeans' APIs to create both NetBeans plugins and standalone applications.

For a brief history of Netbeans, see `http://netbeans.org/about/history.html`.

Although the NetBeans IDE supports several programming languages, because of its roots as a Java only IDE it is a lot more popular with this language. As a Java IDE, NetBeans has built-in support for Java SE (Standard Edition) applications, which typically run in the user's desktop or notebook computer; Java ME (Micro Edition), which typically runs in small devices such as cell phones or PDAs; and for Java EE (Enterprise Edition) applications, which typically run on "big iron" servers and can support thousands of concurrent users.

In this book, we will be focusing on the Java EE development capabilities of NetBeans, and how to take advantage of NetBeans features to help us develop Java EE applications more efficiently.

Some of the features we will cover include how NetBeans can help us speed up web application development using JSF or the Servlet API and JSPs by providing a starting point for these kind of artifacts, and how we can use the NetBeans palette to drag and drop code snippets into our JSPs, including HTML and JSP markup. We will also see how NetBeans can help us generate JPA entities from an existing database schema (JPA is the Java Persistence API, the standard Object-Relational mapping tool included with Java EE).

In addition to web development, we will also see how NetBeans allows us to easily develop Enterprise JavaBeans (EJBs); and how to easily develop web services. We will also cover how to easily write both EJB and web service clients by taking advantage of some very nice NetBeans features.

Before taking advantage of all of the above NetBeans features, we of course need to have NetBeans installed, as covered in the next section.

Obtaining NetBeans

NetBeans can be obtained by downloading it from `http://www.netbeans.org`.

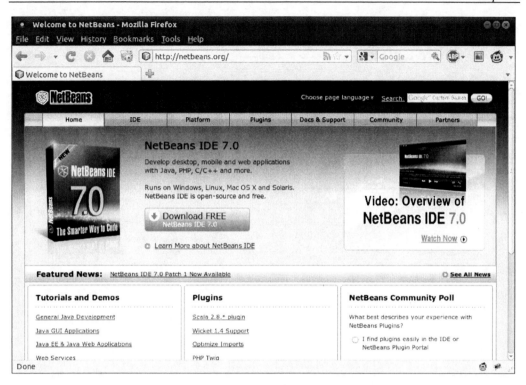

To download NetBeans, we need to click on the button labeled **Download Free NetBeans IDE 7.0** (the exact name of the button may vary depending on the current version of NetBeans). Clicking on this button will take us to a page displaying all of NetBeans download bundles.

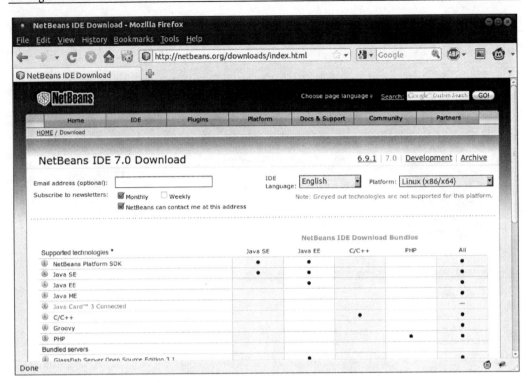

NetBeans download includes different NetBeans bundles that provide different levels of functionality. The following table summarizes the different available NetBeans bundles and describes the functionality they provide:

NetBeans bundle	Description
Java SE	Allows development of Java desktop applications.
Java EE	Allows development of Java Standard Edition (typically desktop applications), and Java Enterprise Edition (enterprise application running on "big iron" servers) applications.
C/C++	Allows development of applications written in the C or C++ languages.
PHP	Allows development of web applications using the popular open source PHP programming language.
All	Includes functionality of all NetBeans bundles.

To follow the examples on this book, either the **Java EE** or the **All** bundle is needed.

The screenshots in this book were taken with the **Java EE** bundle. NetBeans may look slightly different if the **All** Pack is used, particularly, some additional menu items may be seen.

The following platforms are officially supported:

- Windows 7/Vista/XP/2000
- Linux x86
- Linux x64
- Solaris x86
- Solaris x64
- Mac OS X

Additionally, NetBeans can be executed in any platform containing Java 6 or newer. To download a version of NetBeans to be executed in one of these platforms, an OS independent version of NetBeans is available for download.

 Although the OS independent version of NetBeans can be executed in all of the supported platforms, it is recommended to obtain the platform-specific version of NetBeans for your platform.

The NetBeans download page should detect the operating system being used to access it, and the appropriate platform should be selected by default. If this is not the case, or if you are downloading NetBeans with the intention of installing it in another workstation on another platform, the correct platform can be selected from the drop down labeled, appropriately enough, **Platform**.

Once the correct platform has been selected, we need to click on the appropriate **Download** button for the NetBeans bundle we wish to install. For Java EE development, we need either the **Java EE** or the **All** bundle. NetBeans will then be downloaded to a directory of our choice.

 Java EE applications need to be deployed to an application server. Several application servers exist in the market, both the **Java EE** and the **All** NetBeans bundles come with GlassFish and Tomcat bundled. Tomcat is a popular open source servlet container, it can be used to deploy applications using the Servlets, JSP and JSF, however it does not support other Java EE technologies such as EJBs or JPA. GlassFish is a 100 percent Java EE-compliant application server. We will be using the bundled GlassFish application server to deploy and execute our examples.

Installing NetBeans

NetBeans requires a **Java Development Kit (JDK)** version 6.0 or newer to be available before it can be installed.

 Since this book is aimed at experienced Java Developers, we will not spend much time explaining how to install and configure the JDK, since we can safely assume the target market for the book more than likely has a JDK installed. Installation instructions for JDK 6 can be found at http://www.oracle.com/technetwork/java/javase/index-137561.html.

Readers wishing to use Mac OS X can get installation instructions and the JDK download for their platform at http://developer.apple.com/java/.

NetBeans installation varies slightly between the supported platforms. In the following few sections we explain how to install NetBeans on each supported platform.

Microsoft Windows

For Microsoft Windows platforms, NetBeans is downloaded as an executable file named something like **netbeans-7.0-ml-java-windows.exe**, (exact name depends on the version of NetBeans and the NetBeans bundle that was selected for download). To install NetBeans on Windows platforms, simply navigate to the folder where NetBeans was downloaded and double-click on the executable file.

Mac OS X

For Mac OS X, the downloaded file is called something like **netbeans-7.0-ml-java-macosx.dmg** (exact name depends on the NetBeans version and the NetBeans bundle that was selected for download). In order to install NetBeans, navigate to the location where the file was downloaded and double-click on it.

The Mac OS X installer contains four packages, NetBeans, GlassFish, Tomcat, and OpenESB, these four packages need to be installed individually, They can be installed by simply double-clicking on each one of them. Please note that GlassFish must be installed before OpenESB.

Linux and Solaris

For Linux and Solaris, NetBeans is downloaded in the form of a shell script. The name of the file will be similar to **netbeans-7.0-ml-java-linux.sh**, **netbeans-7.0-ml-java-solaris-x86.sh**, or **netbeans-7.0-ml-java-solaris-sparc.sh**, depending on the version of NetBeans, the selected platform and the selected NetBeans bundle.

Before NetBeans can be installed in these platforms, the downloaded file needs to be made executable. This can be done in the command line by navigating to the directory where the NetBeans installer was downloaded and executing the following command:

```
chmod +x ./filename.sh
```

Substitute **filename.sh** with the appropriate file name for the platform and the NetBeans bundle.

Once the file is executable it can be installed from the command line:

```
./filename.sh
```

Again substitute **filename.sh** with the appropriate file name for the platform and the NetBeans bundle.

Other platforms

For other platforms, NetBeans can be downloaded as a platform-independent zip file. The name of the zip file will be something like **netbeans-7.0-201007282301-ml-java.zip** (exact file name may vary, depending on the exact version of NetBeans downloaded and the NetBeans bundle that was selected).

To install NetBeans on one of these platforms, simply extract the zip file to any suitable directory.

Installation procedure

Even though the way to execute the installer varies slightly between platforms, the installer behaves in a similar way between most of them.

One exception is the Mac OS X installer, under Mac OS X, each individual component (NetBeans, GlassFish, Tomcat, and OpenESB) comes with its own installer and must be installed individually. GlassFish must be installed before OpenESB.

Another exception is the platform-independent zip file. In this case there is essentially no installer, installing this version of NetBeans consists of extracting the zip file to any suitable directory.

After executing the NetBeans installation file for our platform, we should see a window similar to the one illustrated in the following screenshot:

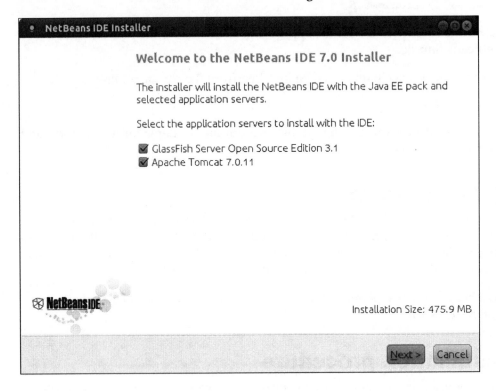

The packs shown may vary depending on the NetBeans bundle that was downloaded; the above screen shot is for the "Java EE" bundle.

At this point we should click on the button labeled **Next>** to continue the installation.

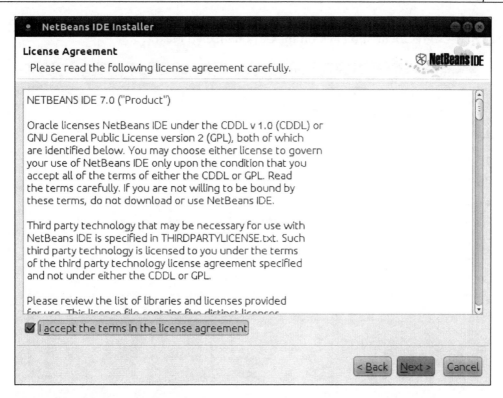

NetBeans is dual licensed, licenses for NetBeans include the **GNU Public License (GPL)** version 2 with CLASSPATH exception, and the **Common Development and Distribution License (CDDL)**. Both of these licenses are approved by the **Open Source Initiative (OSI)**.

To continue installing NetBeans, click on the checkbox labeled **I accept the terms in the license agreement** and click on the button labeled **Next>**.

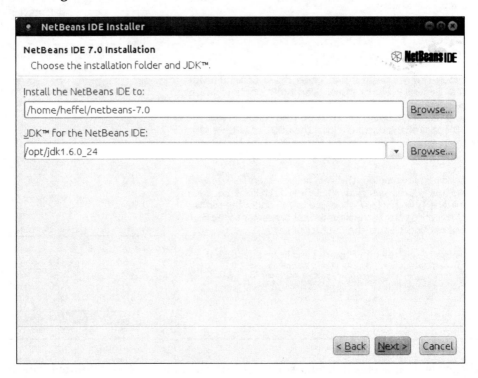

We need to either accept the terms of the JUnit license at this point or choose not to install JUnit

At this point the installer will prompt us for a NetBeans installation directory, and for a JDK to use with NetBeans. We can either select new values for these or take the provided defaults.

Once we have selected the appropriate installation directory and JDK, we need to click on the button labeled **Next>** to continue the installation.

 NetBeans uses the JAVA_HOME environment variable to populate the JDK directory location.

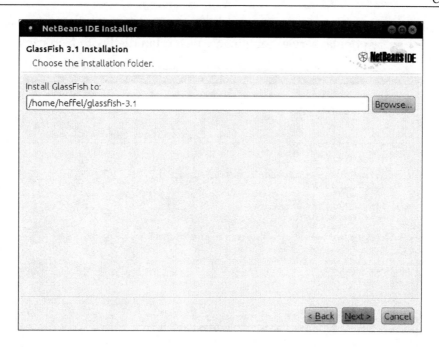

The installer will now prompt us for an installation directory for the GlassFish application server; we can either enter a directory or take the default.

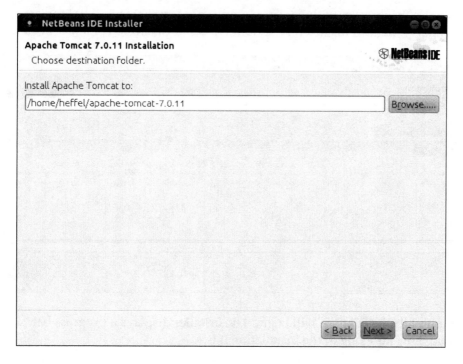

In the next step in the wizard, the installer will prompt us for an installation directory for Tomcat, a very popular servlet container, which is bundled with NetBeans.

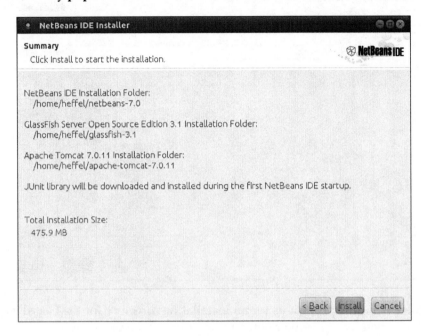

At this point the installer will display a summary of our choices. After reviewing the summary, we need to click on the button labeled **Install** to begin the installation.

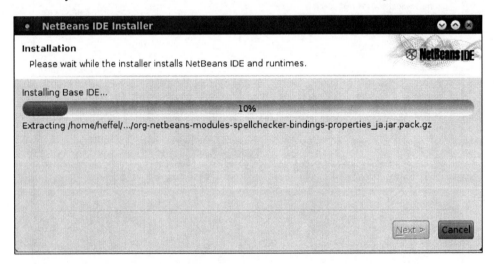

At this point the installation will begin. The installer displays a progress bar indicating how far along in the installation it is.

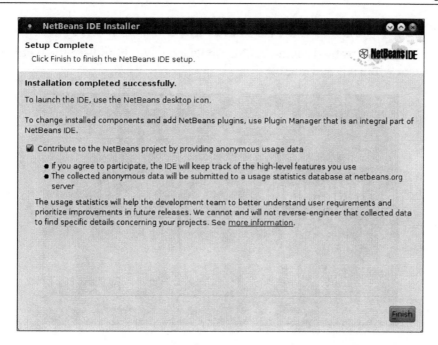

After NetBeans and all related components have been installed, the installer indicates a successful installation, giving us the option to contribute anonymous usage data. After making our selection we can simply click on the **Finish** button to exit the installer.

On most platforms, the installer places a NetBeans icon on the desktop, the icon should look like the following image:

Starting NetBeans for the first time

We can start NetBeans by double-clicking on its icon, we should see the NetBeans splash screen while it is starting up.

Once NetBeans starts, we should see a page with links to demos, tutorials, sample projects, etc.

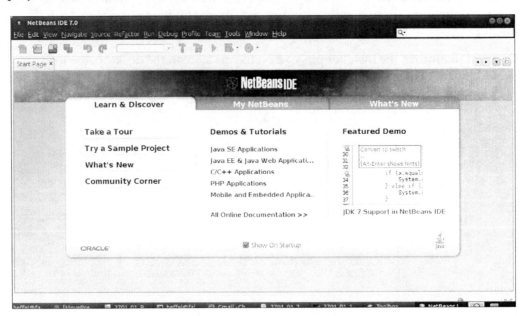

NetBeans defaults to showing this start page every time it is started, if we don't wish for this page to be displayed automatically every time NetBeans is started, we can disable this behavior by un-checking the checkbox labeled **Show on Startup** at the bottom of the page. We can always get the start page back by going to **Help | Start Page**.

Configuring NetBeans for Java EE development

NetBeans comes preconfigured with the GlassFish 3 application server, and with the JavaDB RDBMS. If we wish to use the included GlassFish 3 and JavaDB RDBMS, there is nothing we need to do to configure NetBeans.

We can, however, integrate NetBeans with other Java EE application servers such as JBoss, Weblogic, or WebSphere and with other Relational Database Systems such as MySQL, PostgreSQL, Oracle, or any RDBMS supported by JDBC, which pretty much means any RDBMS.

Integrating NetBeans with a third party application server

Integrating NetBeans with an application server is very simple, to do so, we need to follow the following steps:

 In this section we will illustrate how to integrate NetBeans with JBoss, the procedure is very similar for other application servers or servlet containers.

1. First, we need to click on **Window | Services**.

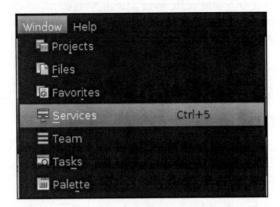

2. Next, we need to right-click on the node labeled **Servers** in the tree inside the **Services** window, and select **Add Server...** from the resulting pop up menu.

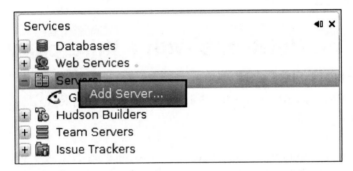

3. Then we need to select the server to install from the list in the resulting window, and click on the button labeled **Next>**.

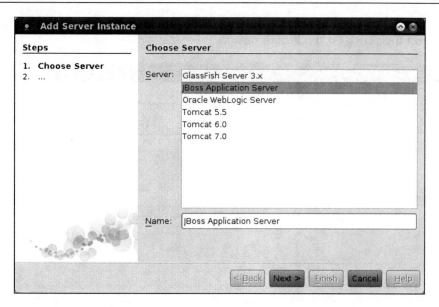

4. We then need to enter a location in the file system where the application server is installed and click **Next>**.

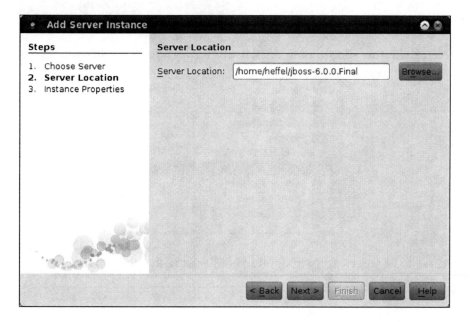

5. Finally, we need to select a domain, host, and port for our application server, and then click on the **Finish** button.

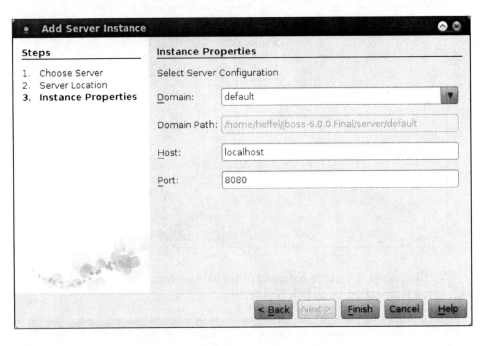

The **Services** window should now display our newly added application server.

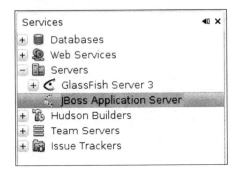

That's it! We have successfully integrated NetBeans with a third party application server.

Integrating NetBeans with a third party RDBMS

NetBeans comes with built-in integration with the JavaDB RDBMS system. Additionally, it comes with JDBC drivers for other RDBMS systems such as MySQL and PostgreSQL. It also comes with the JDBC-ODBC bridge driver to connect to RDBMS systems that don't natively support JDBC or for which a JDBC driver is not readily available.

Although using the JDBC-ODBC bridge allows us to connect to most RDBMS systems without having to obtain a JDBC driver, it is usually a better idea to obtain a JDBC driver for our RDBMS. The JDBC-ODBC bridge does not offer the best performance and there are JDBC drivers available for the vast majority of RDBMS systems.

In this section, we will create a connection to HSQLDB, an open source RDBMS written in Java. The idea is illustrate how to integrate NetBeans with a third party RDBMS, the procedure is very similar for other RDBMS systems such as Oracle, Sybase, SQL Server, and so on.

Adding a JDBC driver to NetBeans

Before we can connect to a third party RDBMS, we need to add its JDBC driver to NetBeans. To add the JDBC driver, we need to right-click on the **Drivers** node under the **Databases** node in the **Services** tab.

We then need to select a JAR file containing the JDBC driver for our RDBMS, NetBeans guesses the name of the driver class containing the JDBC driver. If more than one driver class is found in the JAR file, the correct one can be selected from the drop down menu labeled **Driver Class**. We need to click on the **OK** button to add the driver to NetBeans.

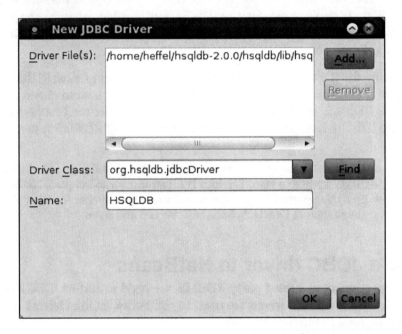

Once we have followed the above procedure, our new JDBC driver is displayed in the list of registered drivers.

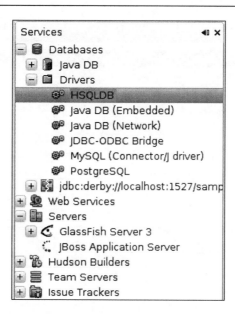

Connecting to a third party RDBMS

Once we have added the JDBC driver for our RDBMS to NetBeans, we are ready to connect to the third party RDBMS.

To connect to our third party RDBMS, we need to right click on its driver on the Services tab, then click on **Connect Using...** on the resulting pop up menu.

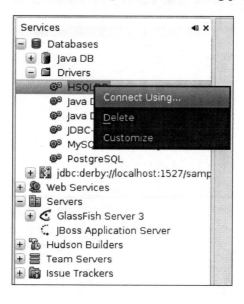

Then we need to enter the JDBC URL, username, and password for our database.

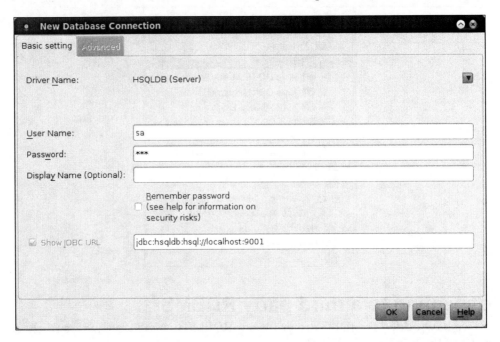

After clicking on the **OK** button, NetBeans may ask us to select a database schema.

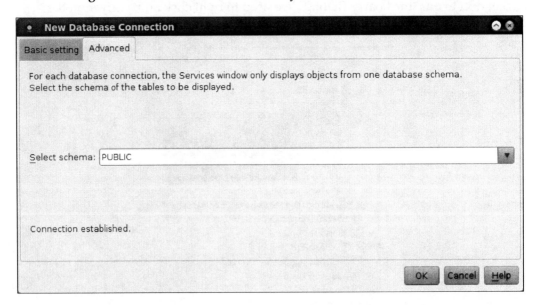

After selecting the schema and clicking on the **OK** button, our database is shown in the list of databases in the **Services** window. We can connect to it by right-clicking on it, selecting **Connect** from the resulting pop up, then entering our username and password for the database (we can choose not to allow NetBeans to "remember" the password when we add the database).

We have now successfully connected NetBeans to a third party RDBMS.

Deploying our first application

NetBeans comes pre-configured with a number of sample applications. To make sure everything is configured correctly, we will now deploy one of the sample applications to the integrated GlassFish application server that comes bundled with NetBeans.

To open the sample project, we need to go to **File | New Project**, then select **Samples | Java Web** from the categories list in the resulting pop up window. Once we have selected **Java Web** from the categories list, a list of projects is displayed in the **Projects** list, for this example we need to select the **Servlet Stateless** project. This sample is a simple project, it uses both a servlet and a stateless session bean, which gives us a chance to use both the GlassFish servlet container and its EJB container.

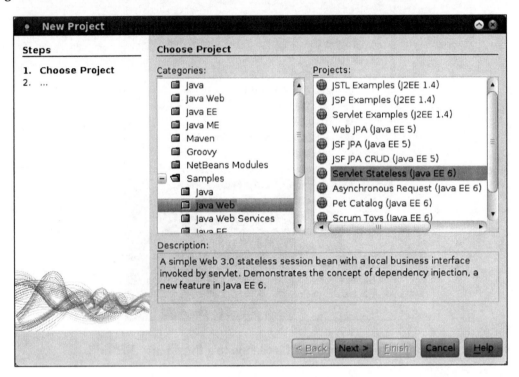

After clicking on the **Next>** button, we are prompted to enter a project name and location, the default values are sensible.

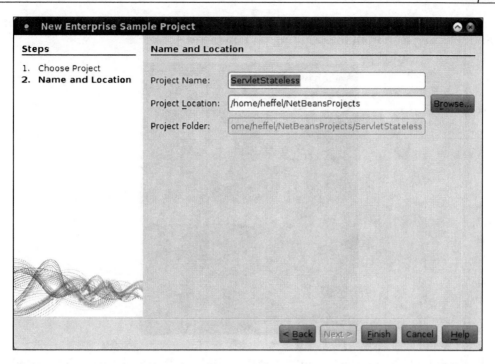

Once we click on the **Finish** button, our new project is displayed in the **Projects** window.

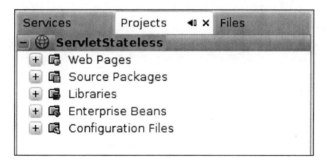

We can compile, package, and deploy our project all in one shot by right-clicking on it and selecting **Run** from the resulting pop up menu.

At this point we should see the output of the build script. Also both the integrated GlassFish application server and the integrated JavaDB RDBMS system should automatically start.

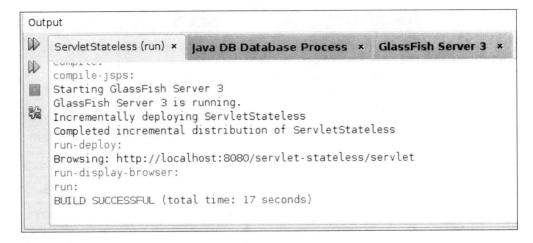

As soon as our application is deployed, a new browser window or a tab automatically starts, displaying the default page for our sample application.

The sample web application we just deployed is a simple application that demonstrates a nice feature that was introduced in Java EE 6, namely the ability to use dependency injection on a stateless session bean without the need to implement a business interface for said bean like it was required in Java EE 5, or without needing to use a home interface to obtain an instance of the session bean as we had to do back in the days of J2EE.

If our browser is displaying a page similar to the one above, then we can be certain that NetBeans and GlassFish are working properly and we are ready to start developing our own Java EE applications.

NetBeans tips for effective development

Although NetBeans offers a wide array of features that make Java EE development easier and faster, it also has a lot of features that ease Java development in general. In the following few sections we cover some of the most useful features.

Code completion

The NetBeans code editor includes very good code completion, for example, if we wish to create a private variable, we don't need to type the whole "private" word. We can simply write the first three letters ("pri"), then hit *Ctrl+space*, and NetBeans will complete the word "private" for us.

Code completion also works for variable types and method return values, for example, if we want to declare a variable of type `java.util.List` , we simply need to type the first few characters of the type, then hit *Ctrl+space*, NetBeans will try to complete with types in any packages we have imported in our class. To make NetBeans attempt to complete with any type in the CLASSPATH, we need to hit *Ctrl+space* again.

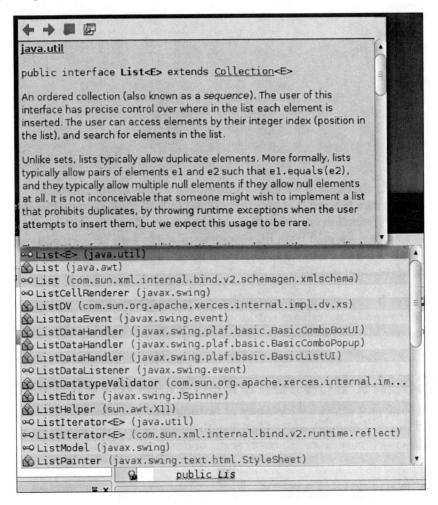

As we can see in the above screenshot, NetBeans displays JavaDoc for the class we selected from the code completion options. Another time-saving feature is that the class we select from the options is automatically imported into our code.

Once we have the type of our variable, we can hit *Ctrl+Space* again right after the variable and NetBeans will suggest variable names.

```
    */
    public class  □ l
                 □ list
        public List |

        /**
         * @param args the command line arguments
         */
        public static void main(String[] args) {
            // TODO code application logic here
        }
```

When we want to initialize our variable to a new value, we can simply hit *Ctrl+space* again and a list of valid types is shown as options for code completions.

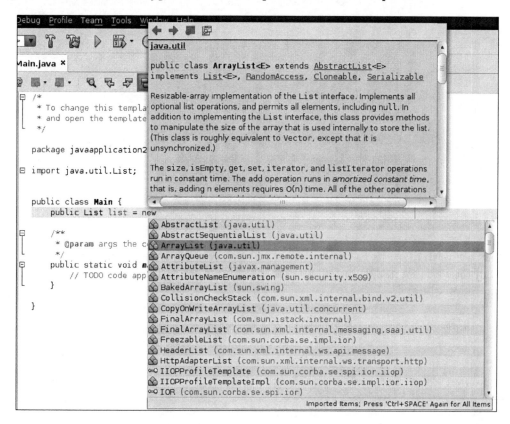

In our example, our type (`java.util.List`) is an interface, therefore all classes implementing this interface are shown as possible candidates for code completion. Had our type been a class, both our class and all of its subclasses would have been shown as code completion candidates.

When we are ready to use our variable, we can simply type the first few characters of the variable name, then hit *Ctrl+Space*.

When we wish to invoke a method in our object, we simply type the dot at the end of the variable name, and all available methods are displayed as code completion options.

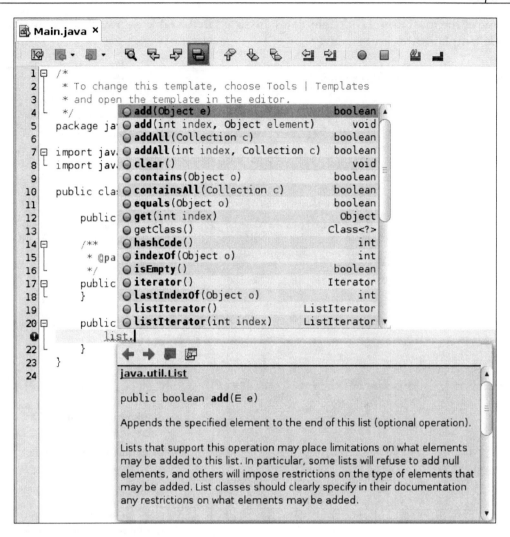

Notice how the JavaDoc for the selected method is automatically displayed.

Code templates

Code templates are abbreviations for frequently used code snippets. To use a code template, we simply type it into the editor and hit the *Tab* key to expand the abbreviations into the full code snippet it represents.

For example, typing sout and pressing the *Tab* key will expand into System.out. println("");, with the caret placed between the two double quotes.

Some of the most useful code templates are listed in the table below, please note that code templates are case sensitive.

Abbreviation	Example expanded text	Description
`Psf`	`public static final`	Useful when declaring public static final variables.

`forc`	`for (Iterator it = list.iterator();`
	
	`    it.hasNext();) {`
	
	`    Object object = it.next();`
	
	`}`
		Use a standard for loop to iterate through a collection.

`fore`	`for (Object object : list) {` `}`	Use the enhanced for loop to iterate through a collection.

`ifelse`	`if (boolVar) {`
	
	`} else {`
	
	`}`
		Generate an if-else conditional.

`psvm`	`public static void main(String[] args) {`
	
	`}`
		Generate a main method for our class.

`soutv`	`System.out.println("boolVar = "`
	`+`
	`            boolVar);`
		Generate a `System.out.println()` statement displaying the value of a variable.

`trycatch`	`try {`
	
	`} catch (Exception exception) {`
	`}`
		Generate a try/catch block.

`whileit`	`while (iterator.hasNext()) {`
	`        Object object = iterator.next();`
	`    }`
		Generate a while loop to iterate through an Iterator.

To see the complete list of code templates, click on **Tools | Options**, click on the **Editor** icon, then on the **Code Templates** tab.

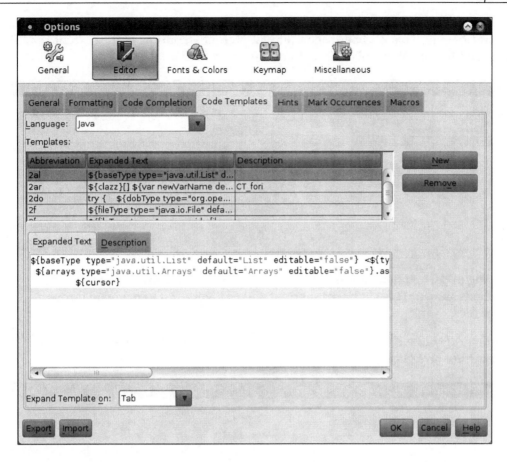

We can add our own templates by clicking on the **New** button, we will be prompted for the template's abbreviation. Once we enter it our new template will be added to the template list and will automatically be selected. We can then enter the expanded text for our template in the **Expanded Text** tab.

It would be good to mention that code templates exist not only for Java but for HTML, CSS, and all other editors in NetBeans.

Keyboard shortcuts

NetBeans offers several keyboard shortcuts that allow very fast navigation between source files. Memorizing these keyboard shortcuts allow us to develop code a lot more effectively than relying on the mouse. Some of the most useful NetBeans keyboard shortcuts are listed in this section, but this list is by no means exhaustive, the complete list of NetBeans keyboard shortcuts can be found online at http://netbeans.org/projects/www/downloads/download/shortcuts.pdf.

One useful keyboard shortcut that allows us to quickly navigate within a large Java file is *Ctrl+F12*. This keyboard shortcut will present an outline of the current Java file in the editor and show all of its methods and member variables.

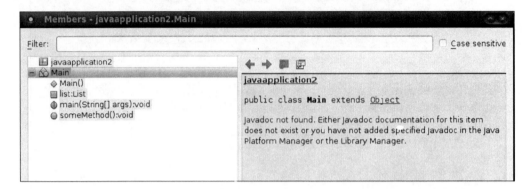

Typing in the text field labeled **Filter** narrows the list of member variables and methods shown. This keyboard shortcut makes it very fast to navigate through large files.

Hitting *Alt+F12* will result in a pop up window outlining the class hierarchy of the current Java class.

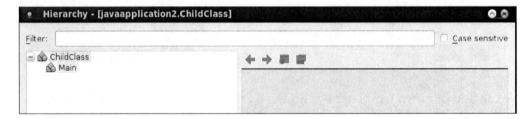

We can use the above shortcut to quickly navigate to a superclass or a subclass of the current class.

Another useful keyboard shortcut is *Alt+Insert*, this keyboard shortcut can be used to generate frequently used code such as constructors, getter, and setter methods, etc.

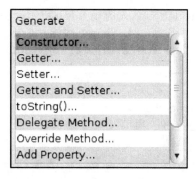

The code will be generated at the current location of the caret.

Additionally, when the caret is right next to an opening or closing brace, clicking Ctrl+[results in the caret being placed in the matching brace. This shortcut works for curly braces, parenthesis, and square brackets. Hitting *Ctrl+Shift+[* has a similar effect, but this key combination not only places the caret in the matching brace, it also selects the code between the two carets.

```java
public void displayListItems(List list) {
    for (Object object : list) {
        System.out.println(object);
    }
}
```

Sometimes, we would like to know all the places in our project where a specific method is invoked. Hitting *Alt+F7* while the method is highlighted allows us to easily find out this information.

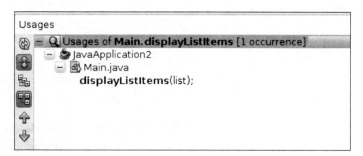

The above keyboard shortcut works with variables as well.

NetBeans will indicate compilation errors in our code by underlining the offending line with a squiggly red line. Placing the caret over the offending code and hitting *Alt+Enter* will allow us to select from a series of suggestions to fix our code.

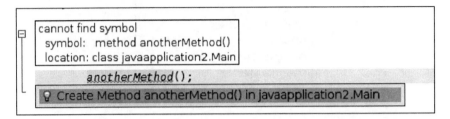

Sometimes navigating through all the files in a project can be a bit cumbersome, especially if we know the name of the file we want to open but we are not sure of its location. Luckily, NetBeans provides the *Shift+Alt+O* keyboard shortcut that allows us to quickly open any file in our project.

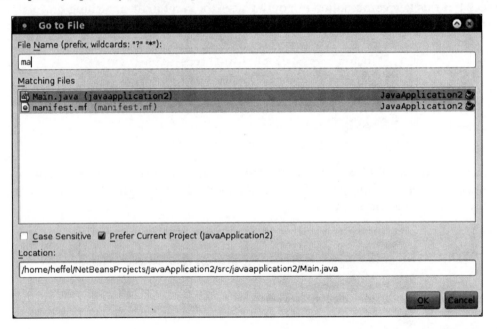

Additional useful keyboard shortcuts include *Shift+Alt+F*, this shortcut quickly formats our code; *Ctrl+E* erases the current line, much faster than highlighting the line and hitting backspace. Sometimes we import a class into our code and later decide not to use it, some of us delete the lines where the class is used but forget to delete the import line at the top of the source file, NetBeans will generate a warning about the unused import, hitting *Ctrl+Shift+I* will delete all unused imports in one fell swoop, plus it will attempt to add any missing imports.

One last thing worth mentioning, even though it is not strictly a keyboard shortcut, a very useful feature of the NetBeans editor is that left-clicking on a method or variable while pressing *Ctrl* will turn the method or variable into a hyper link. Clicking on that hyper link will result in NetBeans taking us to the method or variable declaration.

Understanding NetBeans visual cues

In addition to offering keyboard shortcuts, code templates, and code completion, NetBeans offers a number of visual cues that allow us to better understand our code at a glance. Some of the most useful are illustrated in the following screenshot:

```java
package com.ensode.netbeansfeaturesdemo;

import java.util.Collection;

/**
 *
 * @author heffel
 */
public class Secondary extends Main implements SomeInterface {

    public static int someInt = 3;
    public int anotherInt=4;

    @Override
    public void someMethod() {
        anotherInt = 5;
        super.someMethod();
    }

    public void doSomething() {
        int j = 2;
        foo = 3;
    }
}
```

When there is a warning in our code NetBeans will alert us in two ways, it will underline the offending line with a squiggly yellow line, and it will place the icon shown below in the left margin of the offending line.

The light bulb in the icon indicates that NetBeans has a suggestion on how to fix the problem, moving the caret to the offending line and hitting *Alt+Enter* as discussed in the previous section will result in NetBeans offering one or more ways of fixing the problem.

Similarly, when there is a compilation error, NetBeans will underline the offending line with a red squiggly line, and place the icon shown below on the left margin of said line.

Again the light bulb indicates that NetBeans has suggestions on how to fix the problem, hitting *Alt+Enter* in the offending line will allow us to see the suggestions that NetBeans has.

NetBeans not only provides visual cues for errors in our code, it also provides other cues, for example, placing the caret next to an opening or closing brace will highlight both the opening and closing brace, as shown in the doSomething() method in the above screenshot.

If one of our methods overrides a method from a parent class, the icon shown below will be placed in the left margin next to the method declaration.

The icon is an upper case "O" inside a circle, the **O**, of course, stands for **override**.

Similarly, when one of our methods is an implementation of one of the interfaces that our class implements, the icon shown below will be placed in the left margin of the method declaration.

The icon is an uppercase **I** inside a green circle, which stands for **implements**.

NetBeans also provides visual cues in the form of fonts and font colors. For example, static methods and variables are shown in *italics*, member variables are shown in green, and Java reserved keywords are shown in blue, all of the above cues can be seen in the screenshot at the beginning of this section.

Another nice feature of the NetBeans editor is that highlighting a method or variable highlights it everywhere it is used in the current open file.

Summary

In this chapter, we provided a brief history of how Java EE came into existence. We also explained how to obtain and install NetBeans for the different platforms it supports.

Additionally, we explained how to set up NetBeans with third party Java EE application servers and with third party Relational Database Systems, including how to register a JDBC driver for the RDBMS in question.

We also built and deployed our first Java EE application by using one of the sample projects included by NetBeans.

Finally we covered some of the NetBeans features such as code completion, code templates, keyboard shortcuts, and visual cues that allow us to do our job as software developers more effectively.

2

Developing Web Applications with Servlets and JSPs

In this chapter we will be covering how to develop Java EE web applications taking advantage of the Servlet API. We will also see how to develop **Java Server Pages (JSPs)** to better separate application business logic from presentation. Some of the topics covered in this chapter include:

- Developing JavaServer Pages for display of dynamic web content
- Developing servlets for server-side processing of Java web applications
- Securing Web Applications
- Extracting common markup into JSP fragments

Creating our first web application

NetBeans provides a web category for web applications. To create a new web application, we need to create a new project; click on **File | New Project** (or press *ctrl+shift+N* simultaneously), then select **Java Web** as the project category, and **Web Application** under **Projects**.

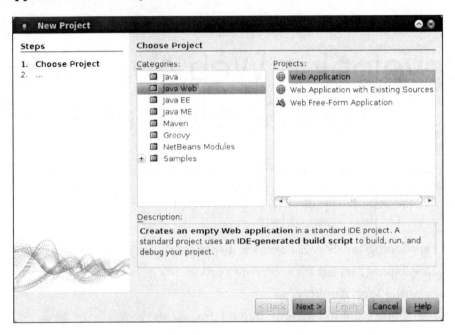

After clicking **Next>**, we need to select a project name for our project. As we type the name for our project, the project location, project folder, and context path are updated automatically. Although we can override default values for these fields if we wish, it is always a good idea to use them since this makes our projects more maintainable as developers familiar with NetBeans defaults will know the values for these fields without having to look them up.

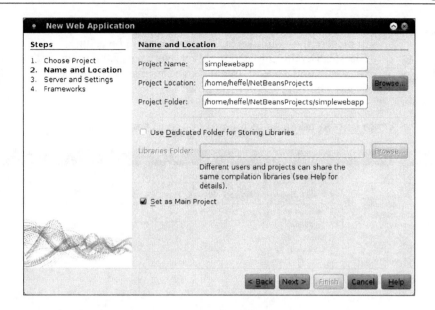

Clicking on the **Next>** button takes us to the next page in the New Web Application wizard.

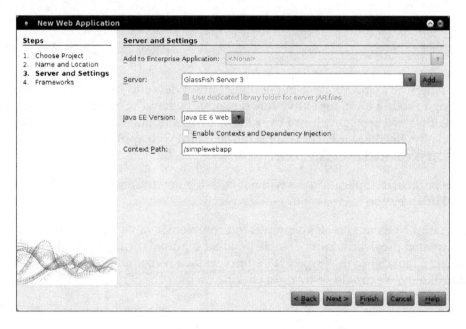

At this stage in the wizard we select what server our application will be deployed to, as well as the Java EE version to use and the context path (the "root" URL) for our application. Default values are usually sensible.

In most of the examples in this book, we will be using GlassFish as the application server. NetBeans 7.0 bundles both GlassFish and Tomcat. In the above screenshot we selected GlassFish in the **server** drop down.

Clicking the **Next>** button takes us to the next page in the wizard.

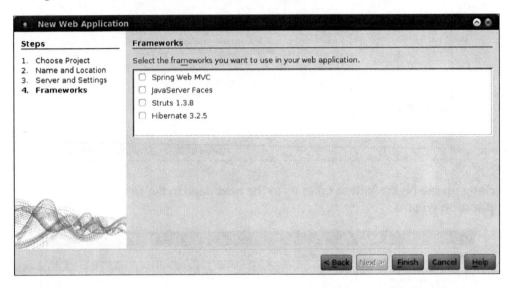

Developing web applications using nothing but servlets and JSPs typically results in having to code a lot of repetitive functionality "by hand". Several web application frameworks have been developed over the years to automate a lot of the repetitive functionality. **JavaServer Faces (JSF)** is the standard web application framework for Java EE. It is covered in detail in *Chapter 4*.

For this particular application we will not be using any framework, we should click on the **Finish** button to create our new project.

At this point NetBeans creates a simple, but complete Java web application. The newly created project contains a single JSP, that is automatically opened in the NetBeans editor. Since the project is a complete Java web application, we can deploy it immediately, we can do so by right clicking on the project name and selecting **Run** from the resulting pop up menu.

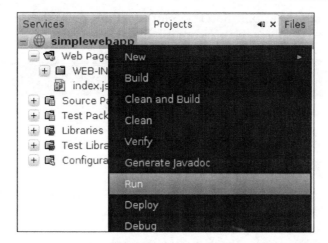

At this point the integrated GlassFish application server and the integrated JavaDB RDBMS are automatically started. Tabs for both of them, plus another tab for the build process to execute our project are created in the NetBeans output window. The **Java DB** tab will display the contents of the database's log file, similarly, the **GlassFish** tab will display the contents of the application server's log file, and the build process tab will display the output of the NetBeans generated build script for our application.

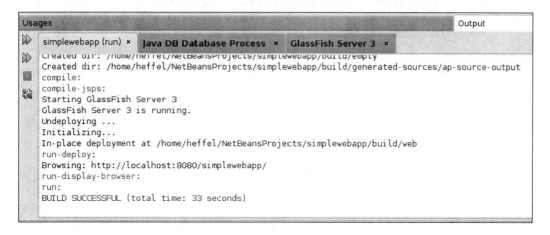

A few seconds later, the application is deployed; at this point the default web browser opens and displays the project's JSP file.

The generated JSP is very simple, if we examine its source we can see that it consists almost entirely of standard HTML tags.

```
<%--
    Document    : index
    Created on  : Aug 20, 2010, 9:23:43 PM
    Author      : heffel
--%>
<%@page contentType="text/html" pageEncoding="UTF-8"%>
<!DOCTYPE HTML PUBLIC "-//W3C//DTD HTML 4.01 Transitional//EN"
    "http://www.w3.org/TR/html4/loose.dtd">

<html>
    <head>
        <meta http-equiv="Content-Type" content="text/html;
charset=UTF-8">
        <title>JSP Page</title>
    </head>
    <body>
        <h1>Hello World!</h1>
    </body>
</html>
```

The `<%--` and `--%>` tags delineate JSP comments, therefore everything between those two tags is ignored by the JSP compiler. These types of comments will not be rendered on the page. Additionally, we can use standard HTML comments, delineated by `<!--` and `-->`, these type of comments will be placed on the rendered page and, just like with standard HTML pages, they will only be visible by viewing the source of the rendered page.

The next line we see that isn't standard HTML is a JSP page directive. JSP page directives define attributes that apply to the entire page. A JSP page can have more than one page directive, and each directive defines one or more page attributes. The `contentType` attribute sets the mime type and, optionally, the character set for the page. The `pageEncoding` attribute sets the character encoding the page uses to render itself.

We can see all valid attributes (and their descriptions) for the page directive by typing < %@page and then hitting *ctrl+space*; rather than repeating this information here, readers are encouraged to see it "live" in NetBeans by performing this action.

We will now write our own web application using NetBeans' generated code and markup as a base.

Modifying NetBeans' generated code

In this section we will develop a simple web application. The application will be a simple survey asking software developers what programming languages they are familiar with. We need to develop two pages, an input page where the information from the user will be collected, and an output page where the information entered by the user will be displayed. The output page will serve as a confirmation page where the user can verify that his or her input was collected properly.

Developing the input page

NetBeans has a palette where we can drag and drop many HTML and JSP elements into the page. For all HTML and JSP elements, regardless of whether they are available in the palette or not, NetBeans offers code completion.

We need to modify our page so that it has an appropriate header and title and some instructions for the user.

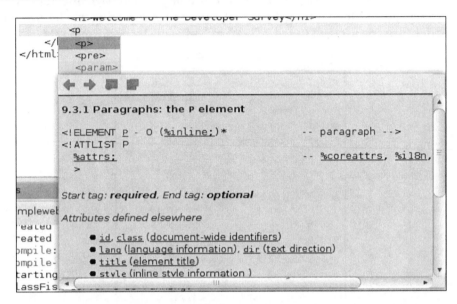

Changing the title and header is trivial; we simply need to modify the body of the tags that were already in the page. We would like to display the instructions inside an HTML <p> tag. We can of course type the tag directly or we can type the opening angle bracket and hit *Ctrl+space* to invoke code completion, we can then select the tag from the list.

At this point the page should look like this:

```
<%--
    Document    : index
    Created on  : Aug 20, 2010, 9:23:43 PM
    Author      : heffel
--%>
<%@page contentType="text/html" pageEncoding="UTF-8"%>
<!DOCTYPE HTML PUBLIC "-//W3C//DTD HTML 4.01 Transitional//EN"

    "http://www.w3.org/TR/html4/loose.dtd">

<html>
```

```
<head>
    <meta http-equiv="Content-Type" content="text/html;
charset=UTF-8">
    <title>Developer Survey</title>
</head>
<body>
    <h1>Welcome To The Developer Survey</h1>
    <p>Please indicate which programming languages you are
familiar with.</p>
</body>
</html>
```

Modifications to the page are highlighted. As most readers are probably aware, all HTML input fields need to be nested inside an HTML form, therefore we need to add a form tag to our page. We can either type the HTML directly into the page, or we can drag and drop the form from the NetBeans palette into the page.

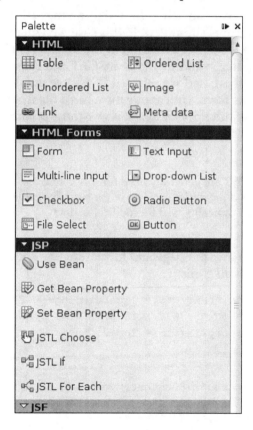

After dragging the form element from the palette and dropping it into the page the following window pops up:

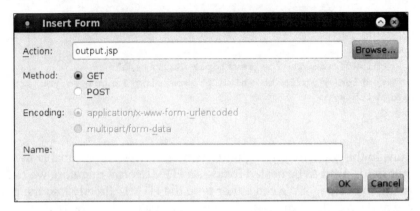

At this point we need to enter an action for the form, the action is the URL that will be executed when the form is submitted. In this case we will execute a JSP called **output.jsp**. We also need to select a method to use for the HTTP request generated when our form is submitted; valid methods are GET and POST. In this case we will use the default **GET** method; had we selected POST, we would also have had to select an encoding for the form. Unless our form has a file upload field, the encoding should always be the default application/x-www-form-urlencoded. One more field we can optionally enter is the name for our form.

 GET and POST are generally used for different reasons; GET methods are typically used for retrieving data or for bookmarkable pages and POST methods are typically used for modifying data.

After dropping the form into the page and formatting the code (shift+alt+F), its markup should now look like this:

```
<%@page contentType="text/html" pageEncoding="UTF-8"%>
<!DOCTYPE HTML PUBLIC "-//W3C//DTD HTML 4.01 Transitional//EN"
    "http://www.w3.org/TR/html4/loose.dtd">

<html>
    <head>
        <meta http-equiv="Content-Type" content="text/html;
charset=UTF-8">
        <title>Developer Survey</title>
    </head>
    <body>
```

```
        <h1>Welcome To The Developer Survey</h1>
        <p>Please indicate which programming languages you are
familiar with.</p>
        <form action="output.jsp">
        </form>
    </body>
</html>
```

The easiest way to lay out input fields in an HTML form is to place them in a table. HTML table is one of the elements that can be dragged and dropped from the NetBeans palette to the page, after doing so the following window pops up:

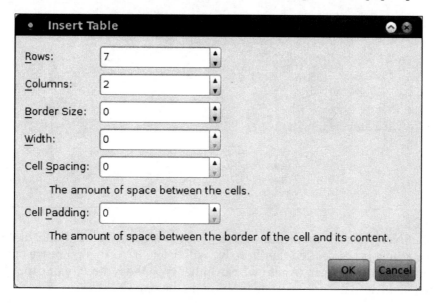

In the previous screenshot we can select the properties for our table. In this case we want a table with seven rows, two columns, a border size of zero, default width, and cell spacing and cell padding of zero.

After selecting the table properties and clicking **OK**, the markup for our table is placed in the location where we dropped it.

```
index.jsp ×

html  body  form
15  ├          </head>
16  ├          <body>
17                 <h1>Welcome To The Developer Survey</h1>
18                 <p>Please indicate which programming languages you are familiar with.</p
19  ├             <form action="output.jsp">
20  ├                 <table border="0">
21  ├                     <thead>
22  ├                         <tr>
23                              <th></th>
24                              <th></th>
25  ├                         </tr>
26  ├                     </thead>
27  ├                     <tbody>
28  ├                         <tr>
29                              <td></td>
30                              <td></td>
31  ├                         </tr>
32  ├                         <tr>
33                              <td></td>
34                              <td></td>
35  ├                         </tr>
36  ├                         <tr>
```

Notice that NetBeans automatically adds a `<thead>` element to our table. In this particular case it is not needed therefore we will delete it. At this point we need to add input fields to our form. Again we can either type them directly or drop them from the palette into the appropriate location on the page.

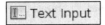

After dragging an HTML Text Input element and dropping it into the appropriate location in the page the following window pops up:

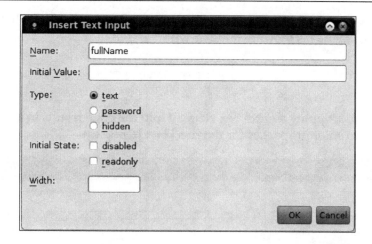

In this window we can enter a name for our field (entering a name is a good practice since that name will later be used to retrieve the value of the field). We can optionally enter an initial value for the field. Additionally we can select the type of the input field, our options are: text (for standard text fields), password (for password fields, fields of this type will not display characters as they are typed into the field, instead either asterisks or dots will be shown, depending on the browser), and hidden (fields that are not displayed on the rendered page but are part of the page's markup).

Additionally, we can set the initial state of our field to either disabled or read only, plus we can select a width for our input field. Initial state and width are only applicable when the type is either text or password.

After dropping our component into its proper place in the page, selecting its properties and clicking on the **OK** button, and then entering some text in the adjacent table cell to be used as a label for our field, the markup for our page now looks like this:

```
index.jsp ×

html  body  form  table  tbody  tr  td
15          </head>
16          <body>
17              <h1>Welcome To The Developer Survey</h1>
18              <p>Please indicate which programming languages you are familiar with.</p
19              <form action="output.jsp">
20                  <table border="0">
21                      <tbody>
22                          <tr>
23                              <td>Full Name:</td>
24                              <td><input type="text" name="fullName" value="" /></td>
25                          </tr>
26                          <tr>
27                              <td></td>
28                              <td></td>
29                          </tr>
```

At this point we need to add checkboxes for our developers to select what programming languages they are familiar with.

Unsurprisingly, dropping a checkbox element into the page results in a window prompting us to enter properties for the checkbox to pop up.

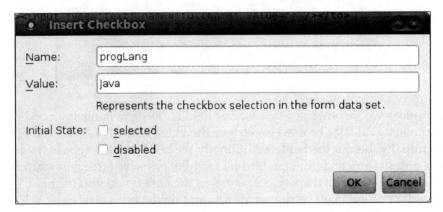

Again we should enter a name for our checkbox, since this name will be used to get the value of the checkbox after the form is submitted. We should also enter a value for the checkbox, this value will only be present in the request object created when the form is submitted and if the checkbox is selected when submitting the form.

After adding additional checkboxes for different programming languages and entering their corresponding labels, the markup for the page should now look like this:

```
19    <form action="output.jsp">
20        <table border="0">
21            <tbody>
22                <tr>
23                    <td>Full Name:</td>
24                    <td><input type="text" name="fullName" value="" /></td>
25                </tr>
26                <tr>
27                    <td>Java</td>
28                    <td><input type="checkbox" name="progLang" value="Java" /></td>
29                </tr>
30                <tr>
31                    <td>Groovy</td>
32                    <td><input type="checkbox" name="progLang" value="Groovy" /></td>
33                </tr>
34                <tr>
35                    <td>Scala</td>
36                    <td><input type="checkbox" name="progLang" value="Scala" /></td>
37                </tr>
38                <tr>
39                    <td>C#</td>
40                    <td><input type="checkbox" name="progLang" value="C_Sharp" /></td>
41                </tr>
42                <tr>
43                    <td>Ruby</td>
44                    <td><input type="checkbox" name="progLang" value="Ruby" /></td>
45                </tr>
46                <tr>
47                    <td></td>
48                    <td></td>
49                </tr>
50            </tbody>
51        </table>
52    </form>
```

Notice that the name for each checkbox is the same. The reason for this is that when the page is submitted, the values of all selected checkboxes will be retrieved as an array of Strings from the HTTP request. We will talk about this in detail when we discuss the output page.

The last thing we need to do is to add a submit button to our page. After dropping the button element from the palette into the page, we are prompted to enter properties for the button.

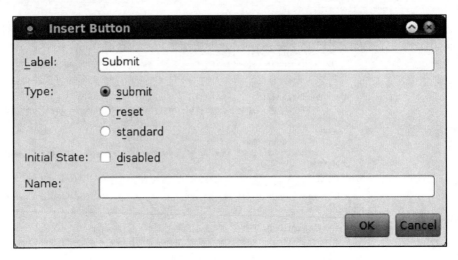

In this window we can enter the button's label.

We can also select a type: **submit** buttons submit a form, **reset** buttons reset a form's values to what they were when the page was loaded, **standard** buttons are typically used to fire JavaScript events. Since our button will be used to submit a form, the appropriate type for our button is **submit**.

We can also set the button's initial state to be disabled, doing this would result in the button being grayed out and the users would be unable to submit the form.

We could optionally enter a name for our button, in most cases this is not necessary for submit buttons. The only case where entering a name for a **submit** button would be useful would be if a form had more than one **submit** button, and different actions needed to take place depending on what button was pressed. In a case like this, each button would have the same name, this name would then become a parameter in the HTTP request, the value for this parameter would be the label of the button that was pressed to submit the form.

We now have a fully functional (although admittedly not too elegant) page.

```
 index.jsp ×
18      <p>rtease indicate which programming tanguages you are familiar with.</p>
19          <form action="output.jsp">
20              <table border="0">
21                  <tbody>
22                      <tr>
23                          <td>Full Name:</td>
24                          <td><input type="text" name="fullName" value="" /></td>
25                      </tr>
26                      <tr>
27                          <td>Java</td>
28                          <td><input type="checkbox" name="progLang" value="Java" /></td>
29                      </tr>
30                      <tr>
31                          <td>Groovy</td>
32                          <td><input type="checkbox" name="progLang" value="Groovy" /></td>
33                      </tr>
34                      <tr>
35                          <td>Scala</td>
36                          <td><input type="checkbox" name="progLang" value="Scala" /></td>
37                      </tr>
38                      <tr>
39                          <td>C#</td>
40                          <td><input type="checkbox" name="progLang" value="C_Sharp" /></td>
41                      </tr>
42                      <tr>
43                          <td>Ruby</td>
44                          <td><input type="checkbox" name="progLang" value="Ruby" /></td>
45                      </tr>
46                      <tr>
47                          <td></td>
48                          <td><input type="submit" value="Submit" /></td>
49                      </tr>
50                  </tbody>
51              </table>
52          </form>
```

With this our input page is ready, we can view the way it is displayed in the browser by right-clicking on it and selecting **Run File** (or by pressing *Shift+F6*).

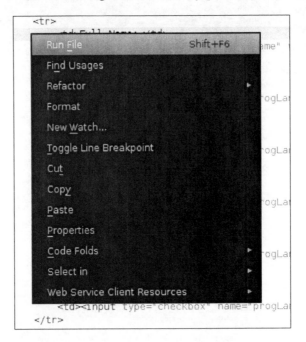

At this point both GlassFish and JavaDB start up if they weren't already started, our application is automatically deployed and our page is displayed in the browser. If GlassFish was already started, all we need to do is reload the page on the browser, the modifications are automatically deployed in the background as we work.

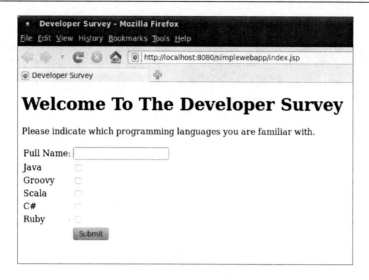

The page now renders properly in the browser. Before the form input can be processed successfully, we need to develop a page that will process it and display an appropriate message.

Developing the output page

In order to develop our output page, we need to create a new JSP file, NetBeans can assist us by providing a file we can use as a starting point. To create a new JSP, we can right click on the project and select **New | JSP**.

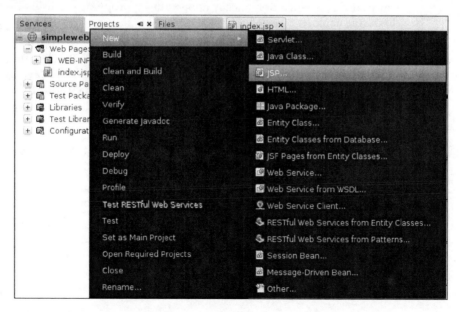

We are then prompted to enter additional information for our page.

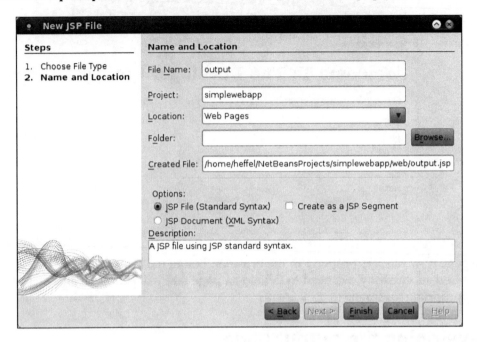

In this particular case we only need to enter the **File Name** and accept all the defaults.

 Notice that we shouldn't enter the file name extension for our JSP since NetBeans will automatically append the appropriate extension to the file name.

We could optionally enter additional information for our page such as what project to use (provided we had more than one web project open, which isn't the case in our example), a folder to place our page (the selected folder must be under the Web Pages folder, in our example there are no folders in this location, therefore we are unable to select a folder).

The **Created File** field is not editable and is automatically populated based on the choices we made on the previous fields.

We are then given the option of creating a JSP file using standard syntax (default), a JSP using XML syntax, or a JSP fragment. In our experience, most JSPs are developed using standard syntax, and NetBeans provides us with a lot more help if we choose this syntax. An alternative syntax for JSP files is the XML syntax, this syntax is less popular than standard syntax and, other than code completion, NetBeans doesn't offer a lot of help when working with this syntax, for this reason we chose to use standard syntax for our pages.

We are also given the option of creating a JSP segment. JSP segments (or fragments) are pages containing common markup that is contained in many pages in an application. JSP fragments typically contain navigation menus, header information, and so on. They can then be included dynamically into JSPs in the application. The advantage of JSP fragments is that these common markups can be maintained separately instead of having to update several JSPs in the application. We will cover JSP fragments later in this chapter.

After entering all appropriate data in the **New JSP File** pop up window, NetBeans generates a JSP file which we can use as a starting point. We need to modify this file so that it displays the data that was entered in the previous page.

```
11  <html>
12      <head>
13          <meta http-equiv="Content-Type" content="text/html; charset=UTF-8">
14          <title>Thank You!</title>
15      </head>
16      <body>
17          <h2>Thanks for taking our survey</h2>
18          <p>
19              <%= request.getParameter("fullName")%>,
20              you indicated you are familiar with the following
21              programming languages:</p>
22          <ul>
23              <%
24                      String[] selectedLanguages =
25                          request.getParameterValues("progLang");
26                  if (selectedLanguages != null) {
27                      for (int i = 0; i < selectedLanguages.length;
28                          i++) {
29              %>

31              <li>
32                  <%= selectedLanguages[i]%>
33              </li>

35              <%}
36                      }
37              %>
38          </ul>
39      </body>
40  </html>
41
```

As we can see, this page is composed of both static HTML elements and JSP expressions and scriptlets. As can be seen in the above screenshot, NetBeans automatically highlights both JSP expressions and scriptlets, making it easy to spot the dynamic parts of our JSP at a glance.

JSP expressions are enclosed in `<%=` and `%>` delimiters. Inside these delimiters we can place any valid Java expression returning a value. The value is automatically converted to a `String` and displayed on the page. To simplify expressions, JSPs contain a number of implicit objects. One of these implicit objects is `request`, this object contains the HTTP request that was generated when navigating to the page. The first JSP expression on our output page uses the implicit request object. It is used to retrieve the value of the request parameter named "fullName". Notice that the String we passed to this method matches the name of the text input field used to collect the user's full name in the previous page. When that page is submitted, a request parameter is automatically generated with this name and the user entered input as its value. Invoking this method allows us to retrieve the data that the user entered.

Hitting *Ctrl+space* between `<%=` and `%>` or `<%` and `%>` delimiters results in all implicit objects available to JSP pages being displayed.

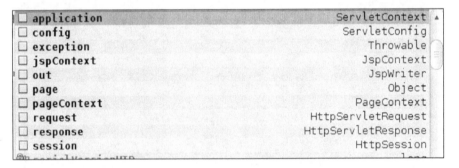

The following table briefly describes all implicit JSP objects.

Implicit Object	Implicit Object Type	Implicit Object Description
application	javax.servlet. ServletContext	This object can have attributes attached that are visible across user sessions.
config	javax.servlet. ServletConfig	Typically used to obtain initialization parameters.

Implicit Object	Implicit Object Type	Implicit Object Description
exception	java.lang.Throwable	Provides access to the exception that was thrown that led to the page being invoked. This implicit object is only accessible if the page directive's isErrorPage attribute is set to true.
jspContext	javax.servlet.jsp. JspContext	Provides methods for setting, retrieving, and removing attributes from the different scopes (page, request, session, application).
out	javax.servlet.jsp. JspWriter	Used to output text on the page.
page	java.lang.Object	Returns a reference to the current JSP. This implicit object is not typically used by JSP page authors.
pageContext	javax.servlet.jsp. PageContext	Provides all functionality provided by jspContext plus additional methods specific to a servlet environment.
request	javax.servlet. ServletRequest	Commonly used to obtain HTTP request parameters and attributes.
response	javax.servlet. ServletResponse	Contains several methods to manipulate the HTTP response sent to the browser. Can be used to add HTTP headers, cookies, etc.
session	javax.servlet.http. HttpSession	Typically used to set and retrieve attributes that are specific to each user session.

After typing an implicit object followed by a dot, NetBeans will present a list of all available methods for that object, along with a description of each method.

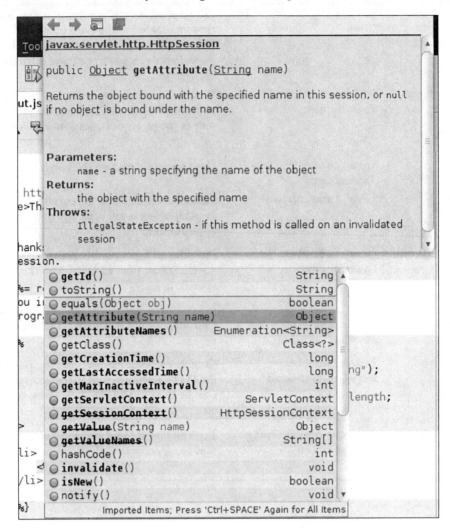

This feature can be used both as a learning tool so that we can see what functionality is available, and as a reference for more experienced developers.

In addition to JSP expressions, our page contains JSP scriptlets. Scriptlets can contain any arbitrary Java code and have access to all implicit objects. In our example, the first scriptlet obtains the values of the request parameter named "progLang", this is the name we used on the input JSP for all checkboxes. Using the same name for several checkboxes has the effect of creating a request parameter whose value is an array of String objects containing the values of the checkboxes that were checked. Our JSP obtains this array and assigns it to a variable named `selectedLanguages`, it then iterates through this array and outputs the value to the page as an unordered list (bullet points).

Notice that the scriptlets can be "interrupted", to add static content or expressions inside them. In our example, there is both a conditional and a loop started in the first scriptlet, then there is some static markup to generate an item in the list and an expression to display the current element in the list. The next scriptlet closes both the conditional and the loop.

At this point, we are ready to test the new page, one very nice feature of NetBeans is that it deploys our code in the background automatically as we work, therefore there is no need to redeploy our application, it should be now "ready to go" without any action on our part. After we enter some data in the input page and hit **submit**, we should see the output page rendered in the browser.

Assuming the user entered **David Heffelfinger** as the full name and selected **Java** and **Groovy** from the checkboxes, the following data should be displayed on the screen:

We have now completed a simple but complete application using JSPs.

Servlet development

Although the application developed in the previous section was fairly easy to develop, the resulting code isn't very maintainable. One of the JSPs has both business logic and presentation logic embedded in it. It is considered a best practice for JSPs to have only presentation logic, and keep the business logic elsewhere.

One common way to approach this problem is to use the **Model-View-Controller (MVC)** design pattern. This pattern provides a clean separation of concerns, providing artifacts that solely act as data (model), while other artifacts are solely responsible for displaying the data (view) and another artifact or artifacts is responsible for manipulating the data and transferring control to the view (controller). In Java web applications, JSPs typically act as view, servlets act as controllers, and custom JavaBeans act as the model.

In this section we will modify the application we developed previously so that it follows this pattern.

Adding a Servlet to our Application

NetBeans provides functionality that allows us to easily create a servlet. In order to create our servlet, we need to go to **File | New File**, choose **Web** from the **Categories** list, then **Servlet** from the **File Types** list.

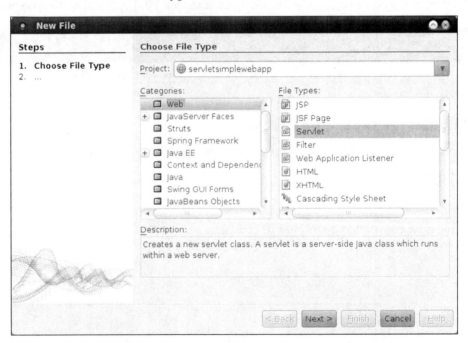

When we click on **Next>**, we should enter a class name and package for our servlet.

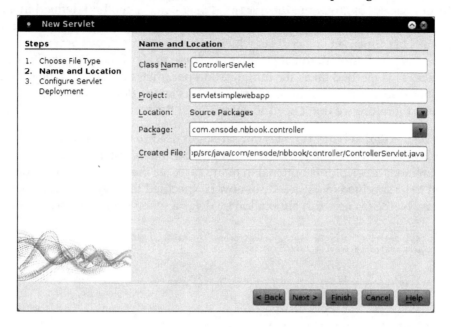

In the next page in the servlet wizard, we are given the opportunity to specify a logical name for our servlet, as well as an URL pattern that will be used to execute our servlet.

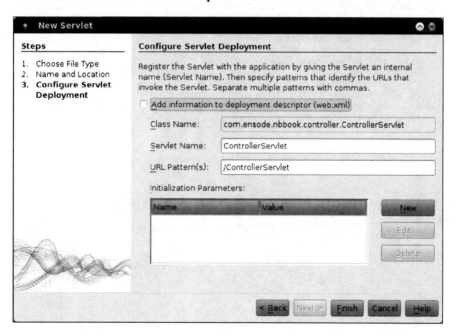

We can also add initialization parameters for our servlets, these parameters can be read by our servlet by invoking the `getInitParameter()` method defined in the `javax.servlet.GenericServlet` class. All servlets in a web application extend `javax.servlet.http.HttpServlet`, which in turn extends `javax.servlet.GenericServlet`, therefore this method is available to all of our servlets through inheritance. This method takes the initialization parameter as a `String` object and returns its value as a `String`. In our particular servlet we don't need initialization parameters therefore we don't need to enter any in the NetBeans servlet wizard.

Clicking on the **Finish** button creates our servlet. It used to be the case that every Java web application had to contain a `web.xml` deployment descriptor. As of Java EE 6, this deployment descriptor is optional in many cases, as the configuration information that used to be specified in `web.xml` can now be specified through the `@WebServlet` annotation, NetBeans uses this annotation by default when generating servlets.

```java
@WebServlet(name="ControllerServlet", urlPatterns={"/ControllerServlet"})
public class ControllerServlet extends HttpServlet {

    /**
     * Processes requests for both HTTP <code>GET</code> and <code>POST</code> methods.
     * @param request servlet request
     * @param response servlet response
     * @throws ServletException if a servlet-specific error occurs
     * @throws IOException if an I/O error occurs
     */
    protected void processRequest(HttpServletRequest request, HttpServletResponse response)
    throws ServletException, IOException {
        response.setContentType("text/html;charset=UTF-8");
        PrintWriter out = response.getWriter();
        try {
            /* TODO output your page here
            out.println("<html>");
            out.println("<head>");
            out.println("<title>Servlet ControllerServlet</title>");
            out.println("</head>");
            out.println("<body>");
            out.println("<h1>Servlet ControllerServlet at " + request.getContextPath () + "</h1>"
            out.println("</body>");
            out.println("</html>");
            */
        } finally {
            out.close();
        }
    }

    HttpServlet methods. Click on the + sign on the left to edit the code.

}
```

NetBeans creates a servlet using the class name and package we specified in the wizard. The generated servlet contains a `processRequest()` method that will be executed every time the servlet receives an HTTP GET or an HTTP POST request from the browser. This method takes an instance of `javax.servlet.http.HttpServletRequest` and an instance of `javax.servlet.HttpServletResponse` as parameters. These parameters are equivalent to the request and response implicit objects in JSPs.

The `processRequest()` method is a NetBeans specific method that is generated when we use the NetBeans servlet wizard to create a method. The reason this method is created is because in most cases we would like the servlet to execute the same code regardless of if the servlet received an HTTP GET or an HTTP POST request from the browser. These two requests are handled by the `doGet()` and `doPost()` methods, respectively, these methods are inherited from the `javax.servlet.http.HttpServlet` class, which is the parent class of all the servlets in a Java web application.

Notice at the bottom of our class we can see that there is some code in our servlet that has collapsed (using NetBeans code folding feature). By clicking on the plus sign next to the collapsed code we can expand it and examine it.

```java
// <editor-fold defaultstate="collapsed" desc="HttpServlet methods. Click on th
/**
 * Handles the HTTP <code>GET</code> method.
 * @param request servlet request
 * @param response servlet response
 * @throws ServletException if a servlet-specific error occurs
 * @throws IOException if an I/O error occurs
 */
@Override
protected void doGet(HttpServletRequest request, HttpServletResponse response)
throws ServletException, IOException {
    processRequest(request, response);
}

/**
 * Handles the HTTP <code>POST</code> method.
 * @param request servlet request
 * @param response servlet response
 * @throws ServletException if a servlet-specific error occurs
 * @throws IOException if an I/O error occurs
 */
@Override
protected void doPost(HttpServletRequest request, HttpServletResponse response)
throws ServletException, IOException {
    processRequest(request, response);
}

/**
 * Returns a short description of the servlet.
 * @return a String containing servlet description
 */
@Override
public String getServletInfo() {
    return "Short description";
}// </editor-fold>

}
```

As we can see, the doPost() and doGet() methods for our servlet simply invoke the generated processRequest() method, passing along the request and response parameters. If we wish our servlet to handle only POST request, we should delete the generated doGet() method; similarly, if we wish the servlet to handle only GET request, the doPost() method should be deleted.

We need our servlet to process the data entered by the user in the application's input page, then invoke the output page, which will be modified to obtain its data from an attribute in the HTTP request.

```
protected void processRequest(HttpServletRequest request, HttpServletResponse response)
        throws ServletException, IOException {
    SurveyData surveyData = new SurveyData();
    surveyData.setFullName(request.getParameter("fullName"));
    surveyData.setProgLangList(request.getParameterValues("progLang"));
    request.setAttribute("surveyData", surveyData);

    request.getRequestDispatcher("output.jsp").forward(request, response);
}
```

In our example we modified the processRequest() method of our servlet so that it creates an instance of a JavaBean called SurveyData and populates it with values from the request parameters.

SurveyData is a very simple JavaBean with two private properties and corresponding getters and setters. Since it is so simple, it is not shown, it is part of this book's code download. This bean's role is to be the model in our MVC architecture.

The instance of SurveyData is then stored as a request attribute by invoking the setAttribute() method in the request object. Request attributes are visible as long as no new HTTP request is generated from the application.

We can navigate to other pages by forwarding the request and its attributes will be preserved. Redirecting the HTTP response through the sendRedirect() method in the HttpServletResponse() interface, clicking on a link, submitting a page, or entering an URL directly in the browser's location field are all actions that generate a new request, causing previous request attributes to be lost.

The URL used as a parameter to sendRedirect() can be a page on any server, Forwarding, on the other hand, is limited to pages or resources in the same server as the one where the servlet or JSP doing the forwarding is deployed.

Objects can also be stored by a servlet as attributes at the session or application scope. Had we wished to store the `SurveyData` instance as a session attribute, we would have added the following line to the `processRequest()` method:

```
request.getSession().setAttribute("surveyData", surveyData);
```

The `getSession()` method of the `javax.servlet.http.HttpServletRequest` interface returns an instance of `javax.servlet.http.HttpSession` representing the user's session. Session attributes are visible to all pages in a user's session, and are preserved across requests.

Storing the instance of `SurveyData` at the application scope would have been accomplished by the following line in the `processRequest()` method:

```
getServletContext().setAttribute("surveyData", surveyData);
```

The `getServletContext()` method is defined in `javax.servlet.GenericServlet`, which is the parent class of `javax.servlet.http.HttpServlet`, that in turn is the parent class of every servlet in a web application. This method returns an instance of `javax.servlet.ServletContext`. Storing an object as an attribute of the servlet context makes it visible across user sessions; therefore all users in the application have access to the attribute.

Request, session, and application attributes can be retrieved by invoking the `getAttribute()` method. This method exists in `HttpServletRequest`, `HttpSession`, and `ServletContext`. In all instances it takes a String parameter indicating the name of the attribute to obtain, and returns an instance of `java.lang.Object`, which then needs to be cast to the appropriate type. If there is no attribute of the specified name, the method returns null.

The last thing we need to do in our example is to forward the request to the output JSP, this is accomplished by obtaining an instance of `javax.servlet.RequestDispatcher`, this instance is obtained by invoking the `getRequestDispatcher()` method of `javax.servlet.http.HttpServletRequest`, this method has a single parameter, which is a String indicating the relative or absolute URL of the page or servlet we wish to navigate to. In our example we are using the relative URL of `output.jsp`, we know the URL is relative because all absolute URLs begin with a forward slash (/). Once we have an instance of `javax.servlet.RequestDispatcher`, we simply invoke its `forward()` method to navigate to the desired page.

We need to make one minor modification to the input JSP page so that it invokes our servlet when its form is submitted.

The line:

```
<form action="output.jsp">
```

Needs to be modified as follows:

```
<form action="ControllerServlet" method="post">
```

What we did was change the value of the action attribute of the HTML `<form>` element to be the URL of our servlet. We defined this URL in the servlet wizard when we were creating our servlet, it is defined as the value of the `urlPatterns` attribute of the generated `@WebServlet` annotation.

```
@WebServlet(name = "ControllerServlet", urlPatterns = {"/
ControllerServlet"})
public class ControllerServlet extends HttpServlet {
...
}
```

Additionally, we added a method attribute to the `<form>` element, and gave it a value of `post`. This step wasn't strictly necessary, however, by default a form uses a `get` method, and HTTP GET requests have a disadvantage, parameter names and values are shown in the browser's location text field, and malicious users might attempt to break our application by modifying the displayed URL by giving invalid values to the request parameters. HTTP POST requests have no such disadvantage; therefore it is a good idea to use POST requests whenever possible.

We also need to make a few modifications to the output JSP so that it retrieves values from the JavaBean that is stored.

The first thing we need to do is to add a `<jsp:useBean>` tag to our JSP. This tag can be either typed in directly, or can be dragged from the palette and dropped into the page. Dragging and dropping the tag into the page results in the following window to popping up:

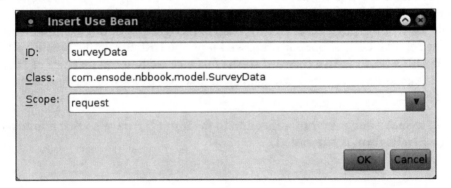

The value of the **ID** field must match the value that was used to store the bean as a request attribute. The value of the **Class** field must be the fully qualified name of the bean's type. The value of the **Scope** field must be the scope we wish to retrieve the bean from; valid values include page, request, session, or application. The scope where the bean is placed affects when and where the bean can be accessed, the following table summarizes all valid scopes.

Scope	Description
page	Bean is only accessible in the current page, including any JSP page fragments included in the page.
request	Bean is only accessible within a single HTTP request, usually from the page to be displayed after the request is processed.
session	Bean is accessible across requests in a single HTTP session, typically this means there is a single instance of the bean per user of the application.
application	Bean is accessible across HTTP sessions, typically this means there is a single instance of the bean accessible to all users of the application.

After filling out all fields, NetBeans inserts the following markup code in the location where we dropped the component:

```
<jsp:useBean id="surveyData" scope="request"
        class="com.ensode.nbbook.model.SurveyData" />
```

The next thing we need to do is replace the JSP expression retrieving the "fullName" request parameter with the `<jsp:getProperty>` tag. This tag retrieves the value of a JSP property. Again we can either type the tag in the appropriate location, or drag it from the palette and drop it into the page. As usual, NetBeans pops up a window when the tag is dropped into the page.

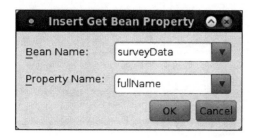

The **Bean Name** drop-down options show all valid beans in the page, the value for this field must match the bean's ID from the `<jsp:useBean>` tag. After we select one the **Property Name** drop-down is populated with all properties in the bean. Once we select the appropriate bean and property, NetBeans generates the following markup code:

```
<jsp:getProperty name="surveyData" property="fullName" />
```

The value of the `name` attribute matches the value we selected in the **Bean Name** drop-down, and the value of the `property` attribute matches the values selected in the **Property Name** drop-down.

The last change we need to make to the page is to modify the scriptlet so that the array containing the programming languages selected by the user is obtained from the bean instead of directly from the HTTP request.

To accomplish this, the line:

```
String[] selectedLanguages =
        request.getParameterValues("progLang");
```

Needs to be changed to:

```
String[] selectedLanguages =
        surveyData.getProgLangList();
```

Notice that the bean's ID (surveyData, in our case) can be used in scriptlets as a variable name.

After implementing all of the above changes, our output page now looks like this:

```
<%@page contentType="text/html" pageEncoding="UTF-8"%>
<!DOCTYPE HTML PUBLIC "-//W3C//DTD HTML 4.01 Transitional//EN"
"http://www.w3.org/TR/html4/loose.dtd">
<jsp:useBean id="surveyData" type="com.ensode.nbbook.model.SurveyData"
        scope="request"/>
<html>
    <head>
        <meta http-equiv="Content-Type" content="text/html;
            charset=UTF-8">
        <title>Thank You!</title>
    </head>
    <body>
        <h2>Thanks for taking our survey</h2>

        <p>
            <jsp:getProperty name="surveyData"
```

```
                    property="fullName"/>
            ,you indicated you are familiar with the
    following programming languages:</p>
        <ul>
            <%
            String[] selectedLanguages =
                    surveyData.getProgLangList();
            if (selectedLanguages != null) {
                for (int i = 0; i < selectedLanguages.length;
                i++) {
            %>

            <li>
                <%= selectedLanguages[i] %>
            </li>
            <%}
            }
            %>
        </ul>
    </body>
</html>
```

We can execute our application by right-clicking on the project and selecting **Run**
(or simply by reloading the page), at this point the application will be deployed and
opened automatically in the default browser.

With one minor exception, it should behave exactly like it did before we introduced
the servlet. The one exception is that the URL displayed on the browser's location
text field when the form is submitted is the servlet's URL. The reason for this is
that the URL displayed in the browser does not change when the HTTP request is
forwarded, like we did in our servlet.

We have now successfully re-architected our application to use the industry standard
Model-View-Controller design pattern. We followed standard practices in Java web
applications of having JavaBeans serve as the model, JSPs serving as the view, and a
servlet serving as the controller.

Securing web applications

It is a common requirement to only allow certain users to access certain pages in a web application. Before a web application can be secured, a **security realm** needs to be set up in the application server where the application will be deployed. Security realms are essentially collections of users and security groups.

Each security realm allows the application server to obtain security information from some sort of permanent storage. This security information could be stored in a simple flat file, a relational database, an LDAP repository, or any other kind of persistent storage. Configuring the application server to obtain the security information from any kind of persistent storage allows us as application developers not to have to worry about the specific implementation. We simply configure our application to use a defined security realm for authentication.

Each user can belong to one or more security groups. Secured pages in a web application are only accessible by certain security groups.

The procedure of setting up a security realm varies from application server to application server. In this section we will use a pre-configured GlassFish security realm called file. Consult your application server documentation for information on how to configure security realms.

There are four different ways we can authenticate a user. When accessing a page using **Basic Authentication**, a browser pop up window is displayed asking the user to enter his credentials.

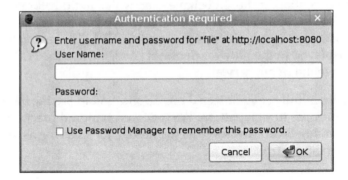

The advantage of this approach is that it is the easiest to implement. Disadvantages of this approach include the fact that by default passwords are not encrypted, and that the login page is not very elegant. Another disadvantage of this approach is that there is no way for the user to log out, other than closing the browser window.

The second approach we can use for authentication is to use **Digest Authentication**, this approach works much like basic authentication, with the exception that passwords are encrypted when sent to the server.

 Digest authentication is not in widespread use, and many application servers do not support it, therefore its use is discouraged.

The third approach we can use to authenticate users is to use a **client side certificate**. These certificates are issued by certificate authorities such as Verisign or Thawte. Client side certificates are essentially a file in the user's hard drive. The user's browser needs to be configured to use the client side certificate for authentication. Although applications using client-side certificates tend to be very secure, they are not very common due to the expense and lack of convenience of issuing client-side certificates.

The fourth and most common approach to user authentication is to use **form-based authentication**. When using this type of authentication, we need to develop a JSP or HTML page used to collect user credentials. The advantages of this approach include the ability to make login pages as elaborate or as simple as we wish; additionally, the user name and password can be easily encrypted by setting up the page to use the HTTPS (HTTP over SSL).

Implementing form-based authentication

To implement form-based authentication, a few steps need to be followed:

1. A login page needs to be created.
2. A login error page needs to be created, this page will be displayed when a user enters incorrect credentials.
3. The web application needs to be configured to use a security realm for authentication.

Implementing the login page

The first step to follow to implement form-based authentication is to create a login page. A fairly simple and "bare bones" login page is shown in the following listing:

```
<%@ page language="java" contentType="text/html; charset=UTF-8"
  pageEncoding="UTF-8"%>
<!DOCTYPE html PUBLIC "-//W3C//DTD HTML 4.01 Transitional//EN"
"http://www.w3.org/TR/html4/loose.dtd">
<html>
```

```
<head>
<meta http-equiv="Content-Type" content="text/html; charset=UTF-8">
<title>Login</title>
</head>
<body>
<p>Please enter your username and password to access the application</
p>
<form method="POST" action="j_security_check">
<table cellpadding="0" cellspacing="0" border="0">
  <tr>
    <td align="right">Username: </td>
    <td>
      <input type="text" name="j_username">
    </td>
  </tr>
  <tr>
    <td align="right">Password: </td>
    <td>
      <input type="password" name="j_password">
    </td>
  </tr>
  <tr>
    <td></td>
    <td><input type="submit" value="Login"></td>
  </tr>
</table>
</form>
</body>
</html>
```

Every login page created for form-based authentication must contain an HTML
form with a method of POST and an action of j_security_check. Every Java
EE-compliant application server will have a security servlet already deployed on
installation, this servlet is mapped to the j_security_check URL, as such, its
doPost() method is executed when the form is submitted.

Each form-based authentication login page must also have two additional fields:
a text field named j_username, and a password field named j_password. The
security servlet will then check that these values match those in the security realm
when the form is submitted. Needless to say, the form needs a **submit** button so
that user-entered credentials can be sent to the servlet.

We need a way to display an authentication error if the user enters incorrect
credentials.

Implementing a login error page

The next step we need to do to implement form-based authentication is to develop a page to be displayed when login fails. A common practice is to allow the user to attempt to log in again from the error page, this practice is followed in our login error page.

```
<%@ page language="java" contentType="text/html; charset=UTF-8"
         pageEncoding="UTF-8"%>
<!DOCTYPE html PUBLIC "-//W3C//DTD HTML 4.01 Transitional//EN"
"http://www.w3.org/TR/html4/loose.dtd">
<html>
  <head>
    <meta http-equiv="Content-Type" content="text/html;
    charset=UTF-8">
    <title>Login Error</title>
  </head>
  <body>
    There was an error logging in. Please try again.
    <br />
    <form method="POST" action="j_security_check">
      <table cellpadding="0" cellspacing="0" border="0">
        <tr>
          <td align="right">Username: </td>
          <td>
           <input type="text" name="j_username">
          </td>
        </tr>
        <tr>
          <td align="right">Password: </td>
          <td><input type="password" name="j_password"></td>
        </tr>
        <tr>
          <td></td>
          <td><input type="submit" value="Login"></td>
        </tr>
      </table>
    </form>
  </body>
</html>
```

If a user enters incorrect credentials when attempting to log in to our application, he/she will automatically be directed to this page. In our particular implementation of the login error page, we chose to display an error message and allow the user to try to log in again, a fairly common practice.

Configuring our application for form-based authentication

When an unauthenticated user attempts to access a secured page, our application must redirect the user to the login page. Once the user has successfully authenticated through the application's security realm, the user is presented with the page he/she was trying to access. If the user does not successfully authenticate, the application must direct the user to our login error page. All of this needs to be configured in the application's web.xml deployment descriptor.

As previously mentioned, the Servlet 3.0 specification introduces several annotations that minimize the need for a web.xml deployment descriptor, however web.xml is still needed for securing web applications. To add a web.xml deployment descriptor to our application, we need to right-click on the project then select **New | Other**, then select the **Web** category and **Standard Deployment Descriptor (web.xml)** from the **File Types** list.

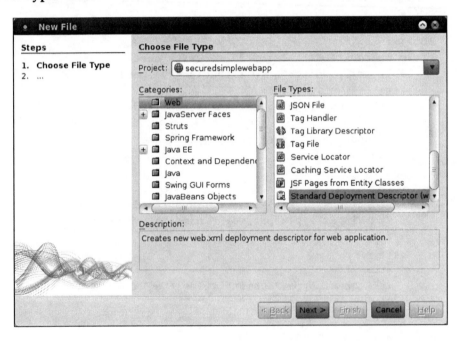

After clicking **Next >**, and then **Finish** to select all the defaults the file will be created for us.

By default, NetBeans immediately opens the web.xml deployment descriptor in a visual editor. After clicking the **Security** button in the toolbar, we can enter security information for our application.

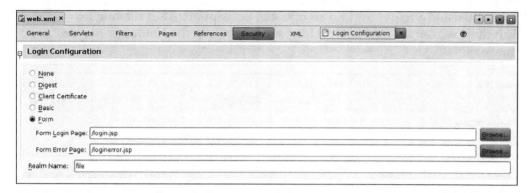

In the **Login Configuration** section, we need to choose the type of authentication the application will use. For form-based authentication, we also need to indicate the login and login error pages.

In the **Security Roles** section, we add security roles for our web application.

Security roles can be added by clicking on the **Add...** button.

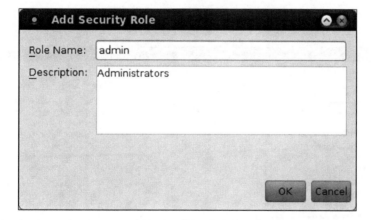

We can then add a role name and an optional description. After clicking the **OK** button, we can see our newly added security role in the NetBeans web.xml visual editor.

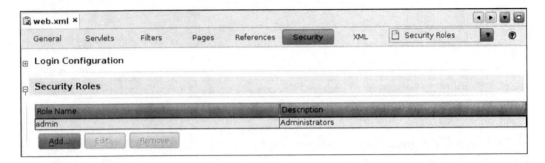

 Our application requires two security roles, admin and user, the procedure to add each security role is identical, therefore adding the user role is not shown.

Next, we need to specify what roles have access to what pages. We can do this by clicking on the **Add Security Constraint** button.

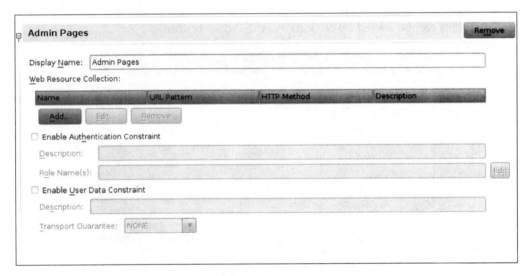

It is recommended to modify the default for the **Display Name** field, giving it a descriptive value. We then need to specify the pages that belong to our security constraint, we do this by clicking on the **Add...** button under the **Web Resource Collection** section.

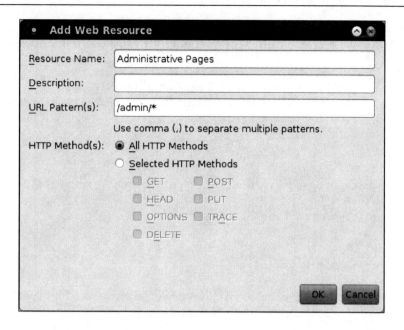

We then need to provide a **Resource Name**, an optional **Description** and **URL Pattern(s)** for the pages belonging to our security constraint. A common practice is to group all pages belonging to a security constraint under a sub folder of the Web Pages folder, a practice we followed in our example, all administrative pages are under the `admin` folder, therefore the URL pattern to access them is `/admin/*`, meaning any URL beginning with `/admin`, after the context root of our application.

In order to allow only authorized users to view our protected pages, we need to check the **Enable Authentication Constraint** checkbox and enter the role(s) that are authorized to view the page in the **Role Name(s)** field.

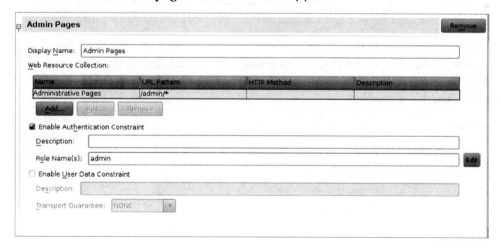

In our application we will have a single JSP named `admin.jsp` in the `admin` folder, this JSP will only be accessible after the user enters a valid username/password combination.

```
<%@page contentType="text/html" pageEncoding="UTF-8"%>
<!DOCTYPE HTML PUBLIC "-//W3C//DTD HTML 4.01 Transitional//EN"
    "http://www.w3.org/TR/html4/loose.dtd">

<html>
    <head>
        <meta http-equiv="Content-Type" content="text/html;
charset=UTF-8">
        <title>Admin Page</title>
    </head>
    <body>
        <h2>Admin Page</h2>
        <p>
            Had this been a real admin page, you would have been able
            to administer the system from here!
        </p>
    </body>
</html>
```

GlassFish Specific Security Configuration

The configuration presented in the previous section is part of the Java EE specification, and, as such, must take place regardless of what application server we are using to deploy our application. Application server vendors may optionally require additional steps. In this section we will cover the steps needed to deploy on GlassFish, the Java EE application server bundled with NetBeans; consult your application server documentation for additional security configuration information.

When deploying our application to GlassFish, we need to modify glassfish-web. xml, a GlassFish-specific deployment descriptor. We can create this deployment descriptor by going to **File | New**, selecting the **GlassFish** category and the **GlassFish Descriptor** file type.

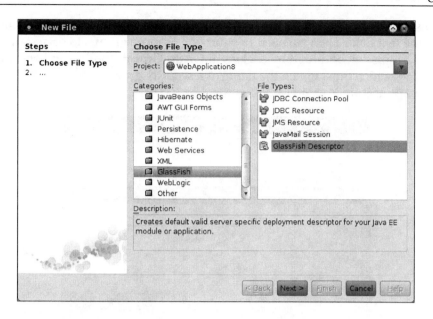

glassfish-web.xml can be found under the **Configuration Files** folder in our project. The file opens in the NetBeans visual glassfish-web.xml editor. After opening this file and clicking on the **Security** tab, we can modify the security role mappings for our application.

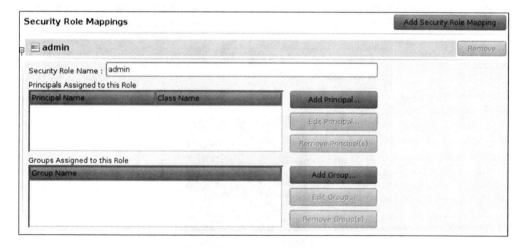

NetBeans automatically detects the security role names in web.xml and fills **Security Role Name** text field. Then we need to enter one or more groups to be assigned to this role. Groups can be added by clicking the **Add Group...** button and entering the group name, which must match the name of a security group defined in the security realm our application is using for authentication.

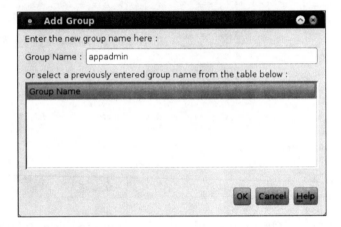

The last thing we need to do to finish configuring application security, is to create our users and groups in the security realm used by our application. To do this with the pre-configured file realm in GlassFish, we need to open the GlassFish admin console by going to the **Services** window, expanding the **Servers** node, then right-clicking on the **GlassFish Server 3**, and selecting **View Admin Console**.

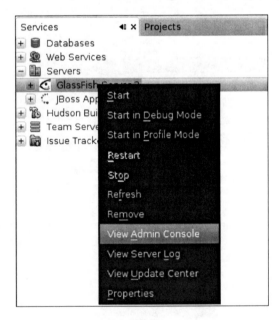

In the GlassFish console, we need to expand the **Configuration** node, followed by **Security**, followed by **Realms**, then click on the **file** realm.

We can add users by clicking on the **Manage Users** button.

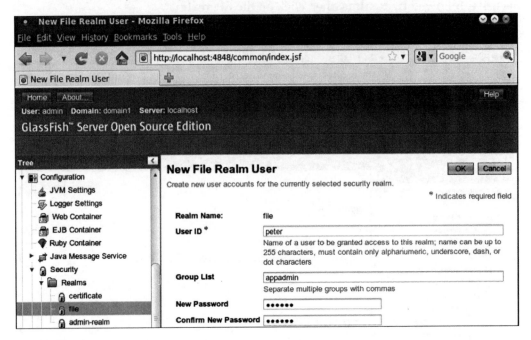

We need to enter the following information for our user, a **User ID**, one or more groups, and a password. The groups our user belongs to must match one of the group names we used in the application's sun-web.xml deployment descriptor. After entering this data and clicking on the **OK** button, we are now ready to test our application's security.

After deploying our application and pointing the browser to a protected page (http://localhost:8080/simplewebapp/admin/admin.jsp in our example), the user is automatically directed to the application's login page.

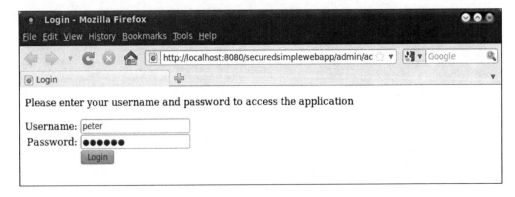

After entering the correct credentials we are allowed to access the protected page.

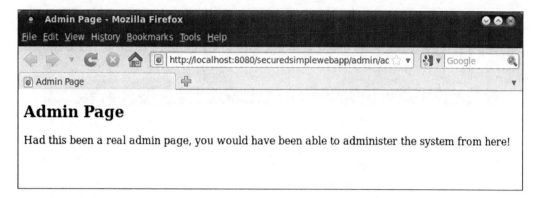

JSP fragments

In a typical web application, most pages share certain common areas such as a navigation menu, a header, footer, and so forth. Since these areas must be identical across pages, maintaining them can be a tedious process since every change in one of these areas must be done in each and every page in the application. To avoid this situation in Java web applications, we can create JSP fragments that can be included in every page. This way if we need to make a change, we only need to do it in the JSP fragment.

In the previous section, we created a login form on both the `login.jsp` and `loginerror.jsp` pages. If we wish to change the look of this login form, we would have to do it twice, once in each page. This form is a perfect candidate to be extracted to a JSP fragment.

Creating a JSP fragment in NetBeans

To create a JSP fragment in NetBeans, we simply need to go to **File | New File**, select **Web** as the category, then **JSP** as the file type. We then fill out all the information in the **New JSP File** window as usual, making sure to check the **Create as JSP Segment** checkbox.

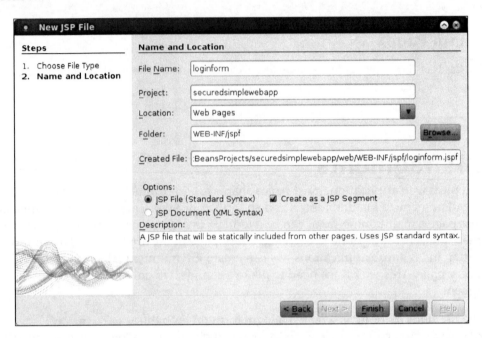

NetBeans suggests placing the JSP fragment under `WEB-INF/jspf`, the reason for this is that any files under the `WEB-INF` folder are not directly accessible via the web browser. Since JSP fragments are not full JSPs, most of the time they won't render properly in a web browser by themselves, therefore it is a good idea to follow NetBeans' suggestion.

 NetBeans will automatically create the `WEB-INF/jspf` folder for us if it doesn't already exist.

At this point, NetBeans generates our page with some trivial content meant to be replaced with something else.

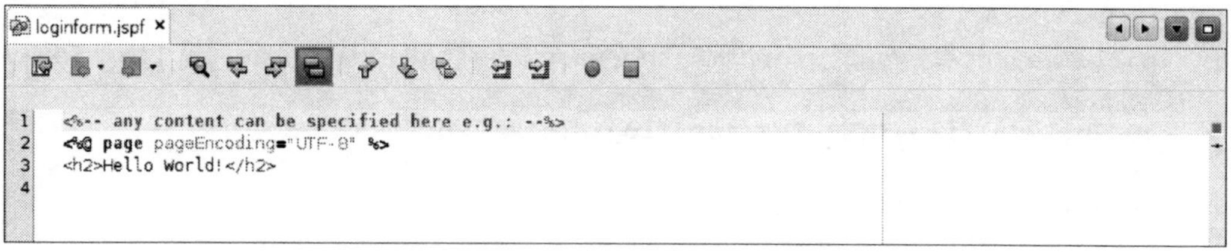

In our case what we want to do is extract the form used in both `login.jsp` and `loginerror.jsp` into the page fragment.

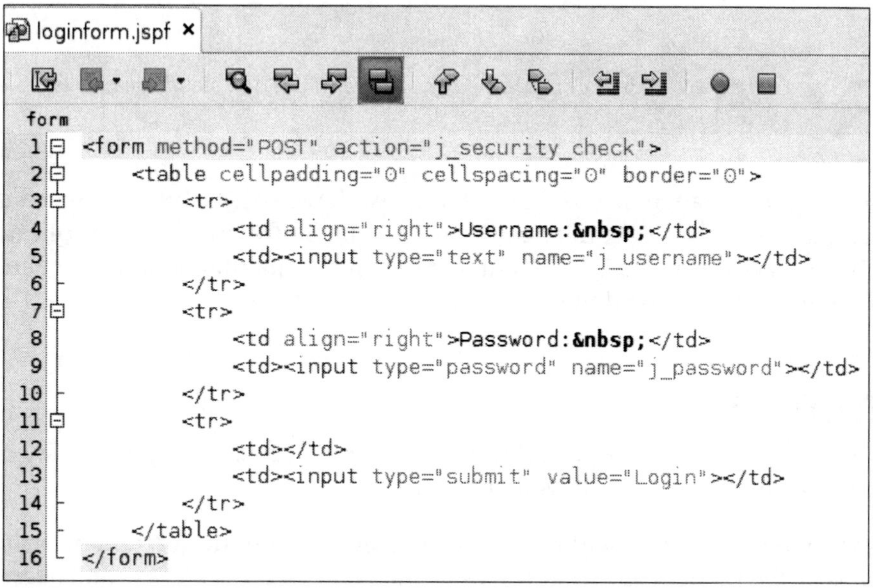

We simply copied the form from `login.jsp` and pasted it into the JSP fragment.

The next thing we need to do is modify `login.jsp` and `loginerror.jsp` to use the JSP fragment by replacing the HTML form with a JSP include directive. The modified version of `login.jsp` is shown next.

```
<%@ page language="java" contentType="text/html; charset=UTF-8"
  pageEncoding="UTF-8"%>
<!DOCTYPE html PUBLIC "-//W3C//DTD HTML 4.01 Transitional//EN"
"http://www.w3.org/TR/html4/loose.dtd">
<html>
<head>
<meta http-equiv="Content-Type" content="text/html; charset=UTF-8">
<title>Login</title>
</head>
```

```
<body>
<p>Please enter your username and password to access the application</
p>
<%@ include file="WEB-INF/jspf/loginform.jspf" %>
</body>
</html>
```

The include directive inserts the contents of the JSP fragment into our page. The value of its file attribute is a relative path to the file we want to include. When the page is rendered in the browser, the contents of the included `file` are placed where we placed our include directive.

 Ctrl+space code completion works between the double quotes for the file attribute.

After making this change in `loginerror.jsp`, we have successfully extracted the common markup between both pages in to a single JSP fragment. Our application will behave exactly as it did before, but it is now more maintainable since changes to the HTML form have to be done only once.

Summary

In this chapter we covered how to develop JavaServer Pages (JSPs) to display both static and dynamic content in a web browser.

We also saw how to implement the Model-View-Controller design pattern by using JavaBeans as the model component, JSPs as the view and servlets as controllers.

Additionally, we learned how to secure web applications via form-based authentication. We also covered how to extract common markup across pages into a single JSP fragment, easing maintenance of web applications.

3
Enhancing JSP Functionality with JSTL and Custom Tags

In the previous chapter, we covered how to write applications using Servlets and JSPs using NetBeans. In this chapter we will see how NetBeans allows us to easily use the **JSP Standard Tag Library** (JSTL) to build JSPs that are readable and maintainable, by relying less on JSP scriptlets.

The topics covered in this chapter include:

- NetBeans support for Core JSTL tags that, among other things, allows to implement conditional logic and loops in JSPs without resorting to scriptlets

- NetBeans support for SQL JSTL tags that allow us to insert, retrieve, or update data in a relational database

- Using NetBeans to create JSP tags that can help us create more maintainable JSPs by abstracting common markup into a single file

The **Java Standard Tag Library (JSTL)** allows us to add functionality to our pages without having to rely on scriptlets, that tend to create pages that are hard to maintain.

Core JSTL tags allow us to control how pages are displayed, for example, by conditionally rendering segments of the page or iterating through a collection of objects to dynamically generate markup from said collection.

SQL JSTL tags allow us to access a database and run SQL queries by simply adding some tags to our JSPs.

Since using JSTL allows us to avoid scriptlets, our pages become more maintainable and easier to read. NetBeans allows us to use both Core JSTL tags and SQL JSTL tags by simply dragging items from the NetBeans palette into our JSPs.

Core JSTL tags

NetBeans allows us to easily use three core JSTL tags:

- The `<c:if>` tag, used to conditionally render segments of a page
- The `<c:choose>` tag, that allows us to render part of a page differently based on a Boolean condition
- The `<c:forEach>` tag, that allows us to iterate through an instance of a class implementing `java.util.Collection` or through an array

These tags can be dragged from the NetBeans palette into our page.

By convention, the prefix of `c` is used for JSTL core tags. The value of the `uri` attribute is a **Unique Resource Identifier (URI)** that will let our page know where to find the custom tags. Each tag library defines its URI in a tag library descriptor file. For JSTL core tags, the value of the `uri` attribute must always be `http://java.sun.com/jsp/jstl/core`.

Conditionally displaying part of a page with the <c:if> tag

The JSTL `<c:if>` tag allows us to conditionally display or hide part of a page, based on a Boolean condition. With NetBeans, all we need to do to add a JSTL `<c:if>` tag to one of our JSP pages is to drag the **JSTL If** item from the palette to the location in our page where we wish to place the tag.

After dragging the **JSTL If** item to our page, NetBeans prompts us for additional information.

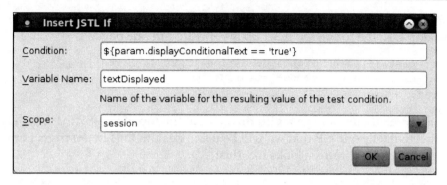

The value of the **Condition** field must be enclosed in ${ }, this denotes this value as a **JSTL expression**. In our particular example, we are looking for a request parameter named displayConditionalText, whose value is true. If (and only if) the request parameter is present and has the expected value, the text inside the <c:if> tag will be rendered in the generated HTML page from our JSP.

In the above screenshot, param is a **JSTL implicit object** to obtain the value of a request parameter, param.displayConditionalText is equivalent to request. getParameter("displayConditionalText"), as we can see, using the implicit object allows us to save quite a bit of typing, and it makes our expression a lot more readable. There are a lot of JSTL implicit objects, the most common ones are param, applicationScope, sessionScope, requestScope, and pageScope. As we already saw, param allows us to easily retrieve request parameters, the others in the list allow us to retrieve attributes in the application, session, request, and page scopes, respectively, they all use the dot notation we saw in the param implicit object, with the key used to store the attribute following the dot, and return the object attached to the appropriate scope with the said key.

To see all implicit JSTL objects, simply invoke code completion (*Ctrl+space*) between the two curly braces in a JSTL expression (${ }) in the NetBeans JSP editor.

Back to our example, the **Variable Name** field is optional; if entered, it will be used to store the value of the conditional expression in a Boolean variable. The **Scope** field is also optional, if a value is selected, this will be the scope of the variable entered in the **Variable Name** field; if no value is selected for the **Scope** field, and a value is entered for the **Variable Name** field, then the variable will have a default scope of page.

After filling out the fields in the **Insert JSTL If** window as shown in the screenshot and clicking **OK**, the following markup is generated in our page.

```
<c:if test="${param.displayConditionalText == 'true'}"
var="textDisplayed" scope="session">
</c:if>
```

Additionally, NetBeans adds a **taglib directive** at the top of the JSP markup. The taglib directive tells our JSP that we will be using custom tags in the page. For core JSTL tags, the taglib directive looks like this:

```
<%@ taglib prefix="c" uri="http://java.sun.com/jsp/jstl/core" %>
```

We, of course need to add some markup between the `<c:if>` and `</c:if>` tags, whatever we add between these two tags will only be rendered if the condition inside the `test` attribute is true.

After adding some markup both before, inside and after the `<c:if>` tag, the body of our page now looks like this:

```
<body>
        <h2>Hello World!</h2>
        <p>
            This paragraph will always be displayed.
        </p>
        <c:if test="${param.displayConditionalText == 'true'}"
var="textDisplayed" scope="session">
            <p>
                This paragraph will only be displayed if the request
parameter named "displayConditionalText" has a value  of "true".
            </p>
        </c:if>
        <p>
            This paragraph will also always be displayed.
        </p>
</body>
```

We can see how the page is displayed in the browser by right-clicking on it and selecting **Run File** from the resulting pop up menu.

 Please note that if we haven't deployed our project, NetBeans may complain about the JSTL libraries not being present. To solve this issue, we simply need to right-click on our project and click **Deploy**.

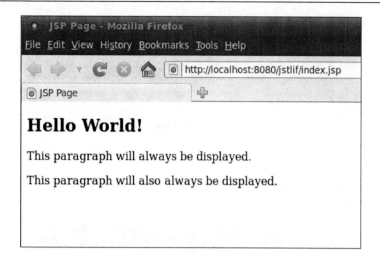

Since the request parameter used in the `<c:if>` tag condition was not present, the markup in its body was not rendered. Modifying the URL so that the parameter is there and has the expected value results in the conditional markup being rendered.

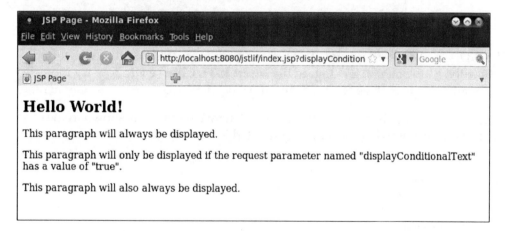

Displaying mutually exclusive markup with the <c:choose> tag

One disadvantage of the `<c:if>` JSTL tag discussed in the previous section is that there is no way to display markup if (and only if) the expression in its `test` attribute evaluates to false. If we need this kind of functionality, we need the JSTL `<c:choose>` tag.

Just as with the `<c:if>` tag, we can drag and drop the **JSTL Choose** item from the NetBeans palette into our page.

After dropping the **JSTL Choose** item into the appropriate location in our page, we are prompted for additional information.

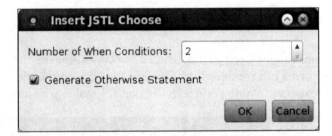

The JSTL `<c:choose>` tag needs to have one or more nested `<c:when>` tags, and optionally, a `<c:otherwise>` tag. In the **Insert JSTL Choose** window we indicate how many `<c:when>` tags we need, and if we need a `<c:otherwise>` statement.

After filling out the fields in the **Insert JSTL Choose** window as shown in the screenshot, the following markup is generated in our page:

```
<c:choose>
    <c:when test="">
    </c:when>
    <c:when test="">
    </c:when>
    <c:otherwise>
    </c:otherwise>
</c:choose>
```

We of course need to fill the body and the value of the test attribute for each `<c:when>` tag, and the body of the `<c:otherwise>` tag. After doing just that and adding some additional markup both before and after the `<c:choose>` tag, the body of our page now looks like this:

```
<body>
    <h2>Hello World!</h2>
```

```
<p>
   This paragraph will always be displayed.
</p>
<p>
   <c:choose>
     <c:when
         test="${param.displayConditionalText == '1'}">
         This paragraph will only be displayed if the request
         parameter named "displayConditionalText" has a value
         of "1".
     </c:when>
     <c:when
         test="${param.displayConditionalText == '2'}">
         This paragraph will only be displayed if the request
         parameter named "displayConditionalText" has a value
         of "2".
     </c:when>
     <c:otherwise>
         This paragraph will only be displayed if the request
         parameter named "displayConditionalText" is either not
         present or has a value different from "1" or
         "2".
     </c:otherwise>
   </c:choose>
</p>
<p>
   This paragraph will also always be displayed.
</p>
</body>
```

When executing the JSP by right-clicking on it and selecting Run File, no request parameter is added to the URL, therefore we see the text inside the `<c:otherwise>` tag displayed in the rendered page.

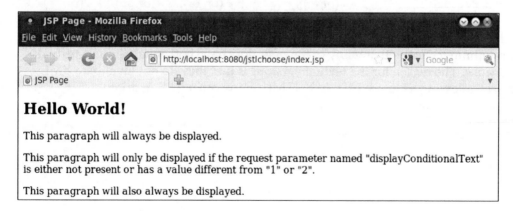

Modifying the URL so that it has the `displayConditionalText` request parameter and one of the expected values results in the corresponding markup being rendered in the page.

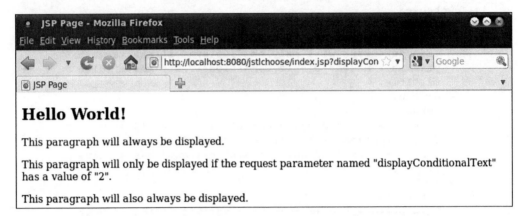

Just like the JSTL `<c:if>` tag, the JSTL `<c:when>` tag has access to all JSTL implicit objects.

In our examples we have been using the equality logical operator (`==`) to compare two objects. This operator is equivalent to the `equals()` method in `java.lang.Object`. There are several other operators that can be used in JSTL expressions; the following table summarizes the most commonly used ones:

Operator type	Operators
Arithmetic	+, -, *, / (or `div`), % (or `mod`)
Logical	&& (or `and`), || (or `or`), ! (or `not`), `empty`
Relational	== (or `eq`), > (or `gt`), < (or `lt`), >= (or `ge`), <= (or `le`)

All of these operators should be intuitive to any moderately experienced Java programmer. Notice that many of the operators have both symbolic and textual versions. The reason for the textual versions is that they do not invalidate XML pages, allowing us to use JSTL in XHTML or any other XML markup.

Iterating through arrays or collections with the <c:forEach> tag

Many times it is necessary to repeatedly generate markup that is almost identical, a typical example is the need to generate table rows, the only difference between the markup for each row is the contents of each cell, other than that the markup is identical. In cases like this, it is useful to iterate through an array or collection of objects, generating the required markup in each iteration.

For cases like this, JSTL provides the <c:forEach> tag, just like tags previously discussed in this chapter, the <c:forEach> tag can be dragged from the NetBeans palette and dropped into our page.

After dropping the **JSTL For Each** item into the appropriate location in our page, we are prompted for additional information.

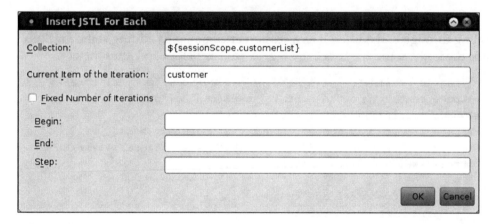

The value of the **Collection** text field must be a JSTL expression resolving to either a class implementing the `java.util.Collection` interface, or to an array. In our example, we are retrieving an `ArrayList` attached to the session scope with the name `customerList`.

The value of the **Current item of the Iteration** text field is the name we wish to use to refer to the current iteration item inside the body of the tag. In our example, we chose to name the current item `customer`.

Although we typically wish to iterate through the whole collection or array, the JSTL `<c:forEach>` tag allows us to specify the index of the element in the array or `Collection` to begin iterating from, where the first element has an index of 0. To do this, we need to check the **Fixed Number of Iterations** checkbox, and specify the index of the element we wish to start iterating from as the value of the **Begin** text field.

Similarly, if we wish to stop iterating at a specific element in the array or collection, we can specify the index of the element we wish to end iterating by entering its index as the value of the **End** text field.

If we don't wish to process every item in the array or collection we are iterating through, and instead we wish to process every other item, or every three items, and so on, we can specify this by entering a value for the **Step** text field. For example, if we wished to process every other item, we would enter a value of 2 for this field.

After filling out the fields of the **Insert JSTL Field** window as shown in the above screenshot, and clicking on **OK**, the following markup is added to our page:

```
<c:forEach var="customer" items="{sessionScope.customerList}">
</c:forEach>
```

We then modify the page, by adding a scriptlet to create the `ArrayList` we are iterating through and adding it as a session attribute, plus adding some markup inside the body of the `<c:forEach>` tag, as well as before and after the tag.

```
<%@taglib prefix="c" uri="http://java.sun.com/jsp/jstl/core"%>
<%@page contentType="text/html" pageEncoding="UTF-8"%>
<%@page import="java.util.ArrayList" %>
<%@page import="com.ensode.nbbook.CustomerBean" %>
<!DOCTYPE HTML PUBLIC "-//W3C//DTD HTML 4.01 Transitional//EN"
"http://www.w3.org/TR/html4/loose.dtd">
<%
  ArrayList<CustomerBean> customerList = new
      ArrayList<CustomerBean>();

  customerList.add(new CustomerBean("David", "Heffelfinger"));
  customerList.add(new CustomerBean("Jeff", "Wu"));
  customerList.add(new CustomerBean("Jacqueline", "Smith"));

  session.setAttribute("customerList", customerList);
%>
<html>
    <head>
```

```
        <meta http-equiv="Content-Type" content="text/html;
charset=UTF-8">
        <title>JSP Page</title>
    </head>
    <body>
        <h2>Hello World!</h2>
        <table border="1" cellpadding="1" cellspacing="0">
            <thead>
                <tr>
                    <th>First Name</th>
                    <th>Last Name</th>
                </tr>
            </thead>
            <tbody>
                <c:forEach var="customer"
                    items="${sessionScope.customerList}">
                    <tr>
                        <td>${customer.firstName}</td>
                        <td>${customer.lastName}</td>
                    </tr>
                </c:forEach>
            </tbody>
        </table>
    </body>
</html>
```

Notice at the top of the JSP, the `ArrayList` we attach to the session instances of a class called `CustomerBean`. This class is a simple JavaBean with two properties, `firstName` and `lastName`. In the body of the `<c:forEach>` tag, we access the getter methods for these properties by simply entering the name of the property after the name we gave for the current item in the list (customer). For example, to invoke the `getFirstName()` getter method in `CustomerBean`, we simply need to type `${customer.firstName}` inside the body of the `<c:forEach>` tag. This notation allows us to easily invoke getter methods in JavaBeans from JSTL expressions. The notation can be used with any expression that resolves to a JavaBean, it is not limited to the body of a `<c:forEach>` tag.

As we have seen before, the easiest way to deploy our web application and execute our file in the browser is to right-click anywhere in the file and select **Run File** from the resulting pop up menu.

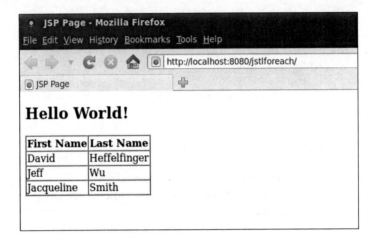

All table rows are generated by iterating through the collection. The values we see in each cell are the values of the firstName and lastName of each instance of CustomerBean in the ArrayList we iterated through.

SQL JSTL tags

JSTL includes an SQL tag library that allows us to quickly and easily write web applications that interact with a relational database. NetBeans supports the most commonly used tags in the SQL tag library, allowing us to use these tags by simply dragging them from its palette into our JSP pages.

All JSTL tags are supported in NetBeans, however, only a subset of them is available in the NetBeans palette to be dropped in our JSPs. For tags not included in the palette, we simply need to type the appropriate tag in the page markup. Code completion is available for all JSTL tags.

Although SQL JSTL tags allow us to quickly create web applications that interact with a database, they tend to create applications that are hard to maintain, since they mix database access with display logic. For this reason, these tags are suitable for prototyping and for "throwaway" applications.

In order to successfully use the SQL JSTL tags, we need to create a connection pool and data source in the application server we are using to deploy our application. NetBeans comes pre-configured with a sample database, and the integrated GlassFish application server included with NetBeans comes with a datasource to access this sample database out of the box. In this section we will be using the sample database and its corresponding datasource. In *Chapter 5* we will explain how to configure NetBeans and GlassFish to interact with a relational database that hasn't been pre-configured.

Before we can interact with a relational database through the JSTL SQL tags, we need to configure our application to have access to the data source providing access to the appropriate relational database. We can accomplish this by adding a resource reference in our application's web.xml deployment descriptor.

Since web.xml is optional in Java EE 6, NetBeans does not generate it by default. To add a web.xml deployment descriptor to our project, we simply need to right-click on the project node, select **New | Other**, then select **Standard Deployment Descriptor (web.xml)** file type from the **Web** category.

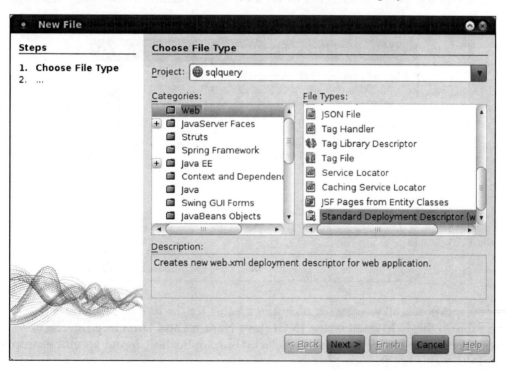

After clicking **Next>**, we can click on **OK** on the following window to generate the deployment descriptor.

Once we have our `web.xml`, we are ready to add our datasource reference. When creating our `web.xml`, NetBeans automatically opens it using the built-in `web.xml` editor.

We can add the resource reference by clicking on the **Add...** button under **Resource References**.

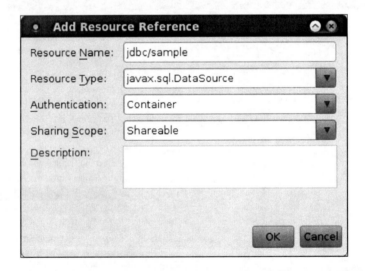

For our purposes, all we need to do is add a value for the **Resource Name** text field, the value of this field must be the **JNDI (Java Naming and Directory Interface)** name of the data source we wish to use with our application, in our specific example, this JNDI name is `jdbc/sample`.

After entering the resource name for our datasource, saving, then clicking on **OK**, we can see it listed in the **Resource References** section of our application's web.xml.

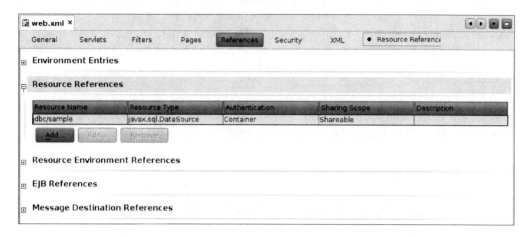

At this point we are ready to use the JSTL SQL library.

Retrieving database data with the <sql:query> tag

The first JSTL SQL tag that we will cover is the <sql:query> tag. This tag allows us to execute an SQL SELECT statement, and store it in an object implementing the javax.servlet.jsp.jstl.sql.Result interface. We can then iterate through this object with the standard JSTL <c:forEach> tag.

The javax.servlet.jsp.jstl.sql.Result interface defines a number of methods that we can call from a <c:forEach> tag in order to display database data on the page. These methods are outlined in the following table:

Method Name	Description
getColumnNames()	Returns an array of String objects containing the column names in the result set.
getRowCount()	Returns an int indicating the number of rows in the result set.
getRows()	Returns an array of java.util.SortedMap objects. Each element in the array represents a row in the result set. Keys in each SortedMap are String objects containing the column names, values are objects representing the value for the column in the current row.

Method Name	Description
getRowsByIndex()	Returns a bi-dimensional array of Objects representing the rows and columns of the result set.
isLimitedByMaxRows()	Returns a Boolean indicating if the maximum number of rows in the result set was limited by the maxRows attribute of the <sql:query> tag.

As we can see, all methods defined in the javax.servlet.jsp.jstl.sql.Result interface are getter methods that conform to the JavaBean specification, therefore these methods can be accessed as JavaBean properties from JSTL tags.

The easiest way to add an <sql:query> tag to one of our JSPs is to simply drag the **DB Query** item from the NetBeans palette into our page.

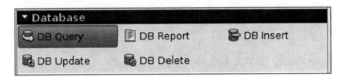

After dropping this item into our page, we are prompted for additional information.

The **Variable Name** field is the name that will be given to the variable that will hold the result set generated by our query. The **Scope** field is the scope where this variable will be stored, the variable can be stored on any valid scope (page, request, session, or application). The **Data Source** field is for the JNDI name of the data source we will be using to obtain a connection to the database, this data source must be added as a resource reference to our web application's `web.xml` deployment descriptor, as explained in the previous section.

After entering appropriate values for all fields and clicking on **OK**, the following markup is generated in our page:

```
<sql:query var="allRows" dataSource="jdbc/sample">
    SELECT name, city, state FROM customer
</sql:query>
```

The values of the `var` and `dataSource` attributes of the tag correspond to the values we entered in the **Variable Name** and **Data Source** fields in the **Insert DB Query** window. Since page scope is the default scope, we don't see an attribute defining the variable scope, had we picked a scope different from page, NetBeans would have added a scope attribute to the tag, containing the scope for the variable as its value (i.e. `scope="session"`).

We then need to add some logic to our page to traverse the result set, this is typically done through the `<c:forEach>` tag. After adding the required markup, the body of our page now looks like this:

```
<body>
    <h2>Hello World!</h2>
    <sql:query var="allRows" dataSource="jdbc/sample">
        SELECT name, city, state FROM customer
    </sql:query>
    <table border="1">
        <thead>
            <tr>
                <th>Name</th>
                <th>Location</th>
            </tr>
        </thead>
        <tbody>
            <c:forEach var="currentRow"
                items="${allRows.rows}">
                <tr>
                    <td>${currentRow.name}</td>
                    <td>${currentRow.city},
                        ${currentRow.state}
```

```
                        </td>
                    </tr>
                </c:forEach>
            </tbody>
        </table>
    </body>
```

Notice how we dynamically generate table rows with the `<c:forEach>` tag.

After deploying our application we can see the resulting page.

The technique illustrated in this example is very common. Frequently a `<sql:query>` tag is used, followed by a `<c:forEach>` tag used to generate a database table from the result set. Since the technique is so common, NetBeans provides an item in its palette to generate both the `<sql:query>` tag and the `<c:forEach>` tag, including the static markup for the table just before and after the `<c:forEach>` tag. To take advantage of this functionality, we simply drag the **DB Report** item from the NetBeans palette into our page.

After dropping the **DB Report** item into our page, we get a window that is very similar to the one we get when dropping the **DB Query** item. After entering values for the **Variable Name, Scope, Data Source**, and **Query Statement** fields, the following markup is generated in the location where we dropped the **DB Report** item.

```
<sql:query var="result" dataSource="jdbc/sample">
    SELECT name, city, state FROM customer
</sql:query>

<table border="1">
    <!-- column headers -->
    <tr>
        <c:forEach var="columnName"
            items="${result.columnNames}">
            <th><c:out value="${columnName}"/></th>
        </c:forEach>
    </tr>
    <!-- column data -->
    <c:forEach var="row" items="${result.rowsByIndex}">
        <tr>
            <c:forEach var="column" items="${row}">
                <td><c:out value="${column}"/></td>
            </c:forEach>
        </tr>
    </c:forEach>
</table>
```

Notice that the generated `<c:forEach>` tags dynamically generate the table header by invoking the `getColumNames()` method of the `javax.servlet.jsp.jstl.sql.Result` interface as a JavaBean property. Similarly, the bi-dimensional array returned by the `getRowsByIndex()` method is used to traverse the result set and display its contents on the page.

Modifying database data with the <sql:update> tag

The JSTL `<sql:update>` tag allows us to modify database data either through SQL INSERT, UPDATE, or DELETE statements. Just like other JSTL tags we have discussed so far, the easiest way to use this tag with NetBeans is to drag the appropriate item from the NetBeans palette into our page.

Inserting database data

To execute an `INSERT` statement, we can drag the **DB Insert** item from the NetBeans palette into our page.

After dropping the **DB Insert** item into our page, we are prompted for additional information.

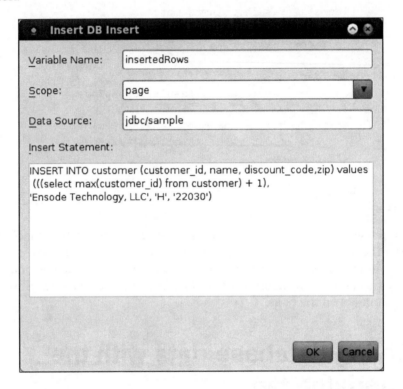

The value of the **Variable Name** field is a variable of type `java.lang.Integer` that will hold the number of rows that were inserted into the database after the `INSERT` statement was executed.

The **Scope** field must contain the scope where the value of the **Variable Name** field will be stored.

The **Data Source** field must contain the JNDI name of the data source used to obtain a database connection. This data source must be added as a Resource Reference to our application's web.xml deployment descriptor as explained earlier in this chapter.

Finally, the value of the **Insert Statement** field allows us to specify the SQL INSERT statement to be executed.

After entering the appropriate data for all fields in the **Insert DB Insert** window, the following markup is generated in our page:

```
<sql:update var="insertedRows" dataSource="jdbc/sample">
    INSERT INTO customer (customer_id, name,
    discount_code,zip) values
    (((select max(customer_id) from customer) + 1),
    'Ensode Technology, LLC', 'H', '22030')
</sql:update>
```

The attributes and the body of the generated <sql:update> tag get populated from the data we entered in the **Insert DB Insert** window.

We can add a **DB Report** item from the NetBeans palette, so that we can see the value we inserted into the database. After doing so, the body of our page looks like this:

```
<body>
    <h2>Hello World!</h2>
    <sql:update var="insertedRows" dataSource="jdbc/sample">
        INSERT INTO customer (customer_id, name,
        discount_code, zip) values
        (((select max(customer_id) from customer) + 1),
        'Ensode Technology, LLC', 'H', '22030')
    </sql:update>

    <sql:query var="result" dataSource="jdbc/sample">
        SELECT customer_id, name, discount_code, zip FROM
        customer where name like ?
        <sql:param value="Ensode%" />
    </sql:query>

    <table border="1">
        <!-- column headers -->
        <tr>
            <c:forEach var="columnName" items="${result.columnNames}">
                <th><c:out value="${columnName}"/></th>
            </c:forEach>
        </tr>
```

```
    <!-- column data -->
    <c:forEach var="row" items="${result.rowsByIndex}">
        <tr>
            <c:forEach var="column" items="${row}">
                <td><c:out value="${column}"/></td>
            </c:forEach>
        </tr>
    </c:forEach>
    </table>
</body>
```

Notice that inside the body of the <sql:query> tag we added an <sql:param> tag, this tag is used to dynamically substitute items in the WHERE clause of the SQL SELECT statement in the tag, similar to the way the java.sql.PreparedStatement interface works. In the query, question marks are used to indicate parameters that need to be substituted with <sql:param> tags. Should our query have multiple parameters (for example, when the values of two or more columns are used in its WHERE clause), we can use a question mark for each parameter in the query. The body of the <sql:query> tag must have a <sql:param> tag for each question mark in the query, the first <sql:param> will contain the value for the first question mark, the second one will contain the value for the second question mark, and so forth. The value attribute of the <sql:param> tag can contain a String literal or a JSTL expression.

By deploying our application and pointing the browser to our page (or simply right-clicking on the page and selecting **Run File**), we can see the **<sql:update>** tag in action.

Every time we reload our page, a new row is added to the database, and the table on the page is updated accordingly.

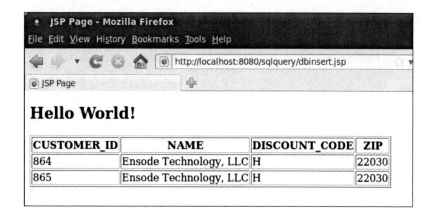

Updating database data

As we mentioned earlier, the `<sql:update>` tag can be used for executing both SQL INSERT and UPDATE statements in the database. The easiest way to use this tag to execute an SQL UPDATE statement is to drag the **DB Update** item from the NetBeans palette into our page.

In addition to being used to insert rows into a database table, the `<sql:update>` tag can be used to modify existing rows in the database table. The main difference is that an SQL UPDATE statement is used in its body, as opposed to an SQL INSERT statement.

Like most JSTL SQL tags discussed so far, the easiest way to create an `<sql:update>` statement that updates existing rows in a database table is to drag the **DB Update** item from the NetBeans palette into our page.

After doing so, we are prompted for the usual additional information.

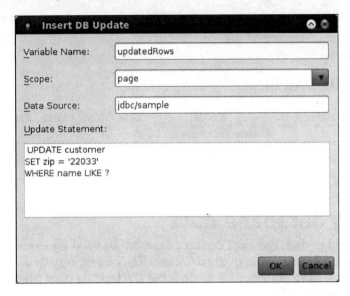

Here we see the same fields we saw when we were using this tag to insert a row into a database table. In this case the **Variable Name** field indicates the number of rows that were updated by the UPDATE statement. When clicking on the **OK** button, the following markup is generated in the location where we dropped the **DB Update** palette item:

```
<sql:update var="updatedRows" dataSource="jdbc/sample">
    UPDATE customer
    SET zip = '22033'
    WHERE name LIKE ?
</sql:update>
```

Since we have a parameter in our query, we need to add a `<sql:param>` tag inside our `<sql:update>` tag:

```
<sql:update var="updatedRows" dataSource="jdbc/sample">
    UPDATE customer
    SET zip = '22033'
    WHERE name LIKE ?
    <sql:param value="Ensode%"/>
</sql:update>
```

Just as we did in our last page, we can add a **DB Report** item from the NetBeans palette so that we can visually inspect the effect of the `<sql:update>` tag. After doing so, the body of our page looks like this:

```
<body>
    <h2>Hello World!</h2>
    <sql:update var="updatedRows" dataSource="jdbc/sample">
        UPDATE customer
        SET zip = '22033'
        WHERE name LIKE ?
        <sql:param value="Ensode%"/>
    </sql:update>

    <sql:query var="result" dataSource="jdbc/sample">
        SELECT customer_id, name, discount_code, zip
        FROM customer where name like ?
        <sql:param value="Ensode%" />
    </sql:query>

    <table border="1">
        <!-- column headers -->
        <tr>
            <c:forEach var="columnName"
                items="${result.columnNames}">
                <th><c:out value="${columnName}"/></th>
            </c:forEach>
        </tr>
        <!-- column data -->
        <c:forEach var="row" items="${result.rowsByIndex}">
            <tr>
                <c:forEach var="column" items="${row}">
                    <td><c:out value="${column}"/></td>
                </c:forEach>
            </tr>
        </c:forEach>
    </table>
</body>
```

After deploying our application and opening our page in the browser, we can see the results of our SQL UPDATE statement.

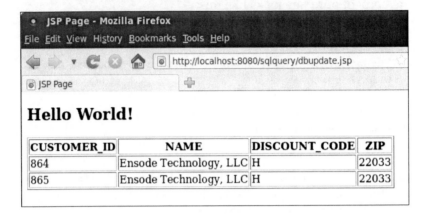

As we can see, the zip codes for all rows we inserted earlier were modified by our SQL UPDATE statement.

Deleting database data

The <sql:update> tag can be used to delete data from the database. This can be done by placing an SQL DELETE statement inside its body. With NetBeans, we can simply drag the **DB Delete** item from the NetBeans palette into our page.

After doing so, we are asked for the usual additional information.

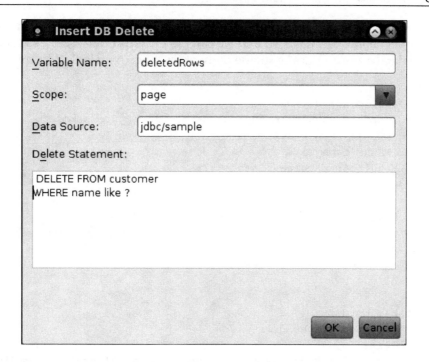

In this case the **Variable Name** field will hold the number of rows that were deleted, the **Scope** and **Data Source** fields hold the scope for the **Variable Name** field and the JNDI name for the data source to be used to connect to the database, respectively. The **Delete Statement** field contains the SQL DELETE statement we will use to delete data from the database, notice in our example, we used a question mark as a placeholder for an <sql:param> tag.

After clicking on the **OK** button, the following markup is generated in our page:

```
<sql:update var="deletedRows" dataSource="jdbc/sample">
    DELETE FROM customer
    WHERE name LIKE ?
</sql:update>
```

In order to substitute the question mark with the appropriate value, we need to add an <sql:param> tag inside the <sql:update> tag.

```
<sql:update var="deletedRows" dataSource="jdbc/sample">
    DELETE FROM customer
    WHERE name like ?
    <sql:param value="Ensode%"/>
</sql:update>
```

Just as we did in previous examples, we will drag the **DB Report** item from the NetBeans palette into our page, so that we can see the effect the DELETE statement had in the database. After doing so, the body of our page now looks like this:

```
<body>
    <h2>Hello World!</h2>
    <sql:update var="deletedRows" dataSource="jdbc/sample">
        DELETE FROM customer
        WHERE name like ?
        <sql:param value="Ensode%"/>
    </sql:update>

    <sql:query var="result" dataSource="jdbc/sample">
        SELECT customer_id, name, discount_code, zip FROM customer
where name like ?
        <sql:param value="Ensode%" />
    </sql:query>

    <table border="1">
        <!-- column headers -->
        <tr>
            <c:forEach var="columnName" items="${result.columnNames}">
                <th><c:out value="${columnName}"/></th>
            </c:forEach>
        </tr>
        <!-- column data -->
        <c:forEach var="row" items="${result.rowsByIndex}">
            <tr>
                <c:forEach var="column" items="${row}">
                    <td><c:out value="${column}"/></td>
                </c:forEach>
            </tr>
        </c:forEach>
    </table>
</body>
```

After executing our page by right-clicking on it and selecting **Run File** from the pop up menu, we can see the results of our DELETE statement.

Since we deleted all rows matching the criteria in the WHERE clause of the
<sql:query> tag generated by the **DB Report** item we dragged into our page,
all we see in the rendered page is a table containing only column headers.

Closing remarks about JSTL

We covered all the JSTL tags supported by NetBeans through the drag and drop
functionality. Additional JSTL tags exist, however they aren't used very frequently,
and therefore are not included in the NetBeans palette. NetBeans certainly supports
code completion for these tags. For more information about JSTL, see the JSTL site at
http://www.oracle.com/technetwork/java/index-jsp-135995.html.

Custom JSP tags

Sometimes we need to add very similar snippets of HTML to our pages. For
example, we might have a calendar component used to input all dates in our system,
or we might have a specific format for all address input fields in our application.

Although we can certainly copy and paste the code throughout all JSP pages that
we need in our application, this approach is not very desirable, since, if we need to
make a change to the common code, we need to go through all the pages and make
individual modifications. When using JSPs, we can create custom JSP tags. These JSP
tags allow us to create the HTML code we need in one place, then we simply use the
tag in any page that requires it. NetBeans has great support for helping us develop
custom JSP tags.

Creating a JSP tag is not much different to creating a JSP. To create a JSP tag, a
tag file is created, it needs to be placed under the WEB-INF/tags folder in our
application, or in any subdirectory of this directory.

To create a custom JSP tag file in NetBeans, we need to go to **File | New File...**, select the **Web** category, and the **Tag File** file type.

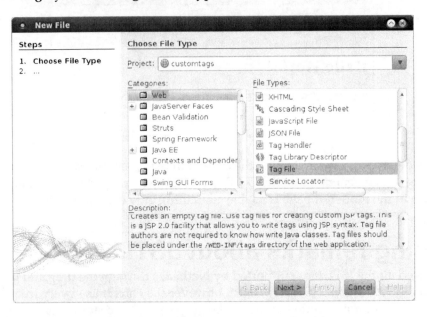

After clicking **Next>**, we are presented with additional choices.

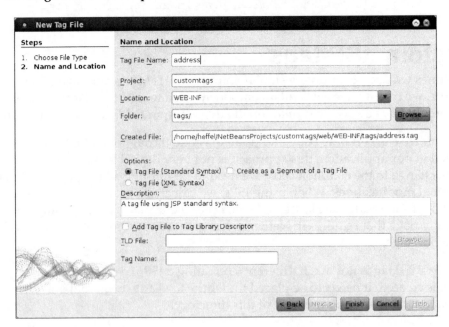

Entering the tag file name into the first field will result in the value of the **Created File** field to be filled automatically, default values for all other fields are sensible and in most cases there is no need to modify them.

At this point, NetBeans creates an initial tag file that we can use as a starting point.

```
<%@tag description="put the tag description here"
pageEncoding="UTF-8"%>

<%-- The list of normal or fragment attributes can be specified here:
--%>
<%@attribute name="message"%>

<%-- any content can be specified here e.g.: --%>
<h2>${message}</h2>
```

Tag files can contain one or more `tag` directives. The `tag` directive is similar to the `page` directive in a JSP. The generated `tag` directive contains two attributes, a `description` attribute used to describe the purpose of the tag, and a `pageEncoding` attribute used to set the page encoding of the tag.

The `attribute` directive allows us to specify what attributes may be sent from the JSP using our tag.

Using the above markup as a starting point, we will now create a tag file that will generate an HTML table containing a series of input fields for entering an address:

```
<%@tag description="Address Input Field" pageEncoding="UTF-8"%>
<jsp:useBean id="addressBean" scope="session"
             class="com.ensode.netbeansbook.AddressBean"/>
<%@ taglib prefix="c" uri="http://java.sun.com/jsp/jstl/c<%-- The list
of normal or fragment attributes can be specified here: --%>
<%@attribute name="addressType" required="true" %>

<table cellpadding="0" cellspacing="0" border="0">
  <tr>
      <td>Line 1: </td>
    <td>
      <input type="text" size="20"
        name="${addressType}_line1"
        id="${addressType}_line1"
        value="${addressBean.line1}"/>
    </td>
  </tr>
  <tr>
    <td>Line 2: </td>
    <td>
```

```
      <input type="text" size="20"
       name="${addressType}_line2"
       id="${addressType}_line2"
       value="${addressBean.line2}"/>
    </td>
  </tr>
  <tr>
    <td>City: </td>
    <td>
      <input type="text" size="20"
        name="${addressType}_city"
        id="${addressType}_city"
        value="${addressBean.city}"/>
    </td>
  </tr>
  <tr>
    <td>State: </td>
    <td>
      <select name="${addressType}_state"
       id="${addressType}.state">
       <option value=""></option>
       <option value="AL"
         <c:if test="${addressBean.state == 'AL'}">
           selected</c:if>>Alabama
       </option>
       <option value="AK"
         <c:if test="${addressBean.state == 'AK'}">
           selected</c:if>>Alaska
       </option>
       <option value="AZ"
         <c:if test="${addressBean.state == 'AZ'}">
           selected</c:if>>Arizona
       </option>
       <option value="AR"
         <c:if test="${addressBean.state == 'AR'}">
           selected</c:if>>Arkansas</option>
       <option value="CA"
         <c:if test="${addressBean.state == 'CA'}">
           selected</c:if>>California
       </option>
      </select>
    </td>
  </tr>
  <tr>
```

```
    <td>Zip: </td>
    <td><input type="text"
        name="${addressType}_zip"
        id="${addressType}.zip"
        value="${addressBean.zip}" />
    </td>
  </tr>
</table>
```

Notice that a tag file is not much different from a JSP, it can use JSTL and other tag libraries, it has access to the same implicit objects that a JSP has access to. In our example we use the `<jsp:useBean>` tag to access a JavaBean of type `net.ensode.netBeansbook.AddressBean`, this is a simple JavaBean containing a default argument constructor and a few properties.

 Since the `AddressBean` is so simple, its code is not shown, however it is available as part of this book's code download.

Our tag file also uses the JSTL core tag library to implement some conditional logic.

As we mentioned earlier, a tag file can contain one or more attributes. Our tag file contains a single simple attribute, named `addressType`, this attribute is a `String` we use to append to the names of all input fields in the tag file. The reason we do this is to allow a single JSP to use multiple instances of our tag, allowing fields generated by each tag in the page to have a unique name. Tags can be optional or required, to make a tag required the `required` attribute of the attribute directive is used, setting its value to `true`, since not passing the `addressType` attribute to our tag would potentially generate duplicate input field names and IDs in a single page, we made this attribute required in our custom address tag.

Notice the comment generated by NetBeans states that normal or fragment attributes can be defined. Fragment attributes allow the page using our tag to send snippets of HTML code to our tag, fragment attributes are defined

```
<%@attribute name="myattribute" fragment="true"%>
```

Setting the `fragment` attribute to `true` indicates that this attribute is a fragment attribute.

To render the fragment attribute in our tag, the `<jsp:invoke>` standard action:

```
<jsp:invoke fragment="myattribute"/>
```

The JSP using our tag file would need to send the fragment via the `<jsp:fragment>` action.

```
<prefix:tagname>
  <jsp:attribute name="myattribute">
    <!-- Any HTML or JSP markup can be put here -->
  </jsp:attribute>
</prefix:tagname>
```

The rest of our example generates an HTML table with input fields and tables (for simplicity and brevity, only US addresses are supported, and only a small subset of US states are used as drop down options).

A JSP invoking our tag would need to include our tag library via the `taglib` directive:

```
<%@ taglib prefix="ct" tagdir="/WEB-INF/tags/" %>
```

Our custom tag library would consist of all custom tags placed in the `WEB-INF/tags` directory in our web application. For our custom tags, we used the `tagdir` attribute of the `taglib` directive to indicate the location of our tags.

All of our tags must be either directly under `WEB-INF/tags` or in a subdirectory of `WEB-INF/tags`. A custom tag library consists of all custom tags under a single directory.

Our tag can then be invoked by placing the following markup in the JSP file:

```
<ct:address addressType="home"/>
```

The following JSP illustrates how to use our custom tag.

```
<%@page contentType="text/html" pageEncoding="UTF-8"%>
<!DOCTYPE HTML PUBLIC "-//W3C//DTD HTML 4.01 Transitional//EN"
    "http://www.w3.org/TR/html4/loose.dtd">

<%@ taglib prefix="ct" tagdir="/WEB-INF/tags/" %>
<%@ page import="com.ensode.netbeansbook.AddressBean" %>
<!DOCTYPE HTML PUBLIC "-//W3C//DTD HTML 4.01 Transitional//EN"
    "http://www.w3.org/TR/html4/loose.dtd">
<%
            AddressBean addressBean = new AddressBean();

            addressBean.setAddressType("home");
            addressBean.setLine1("123 Tennis Ct");
            addressBean.setCity("Phoenix");
            addressBean.setState("AZ");
            addressBean.setZip("85001");
```

```
                session.setAttribute("addressBean", addressBean);
%>
<html>
    <head>
        <meta http-equiv="Content-Type" content="text/html;
charset=UTF-8">
        <title>JSP Page</title>
    </head>
    <body>
        <form>
            <ct:address addressType="home"/>
            <table cellpadding="0" cellspacing="0" border="0">
                <tr>
                    <td style="width:65px;"></td>
                    <td>
                        <input type="submit" value="Submit"/>
                    </td>
                </tr>
            </table>
        </form>
    </body>
</html>
```

In the above JSP, we create an instance of our Address bean and set values for some of its properties. We then set this bean as a session attribute, so that our custom tag can pick it up from as before `<jsp:useBean>` tag. In the JSP markup, we have a JSP form using our custom tag, plus an additional submit button.

We run our project, and can see how our custom tag renders on the browser.

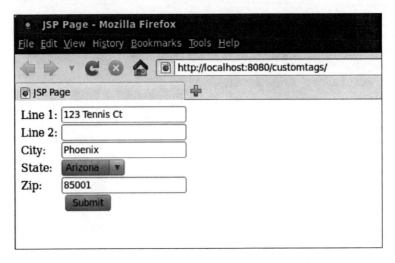

All of the form input fields were generated by our custom tag.

Custom JSP tags can contain a body (our example tag does not have one), in which case the JSP markup invoking our tag would look like the following example:

```
<prefix:sometag>
    <b>Hello there!</b>
</prefix:sometag>
```

If our tag contains `<jsp:attribute>` actions, we need to place its body between `<jsp:body>` and `</jsp:body>` tags.

Any HTML or JSP markup can be placed in the body of our tag. Our tag renders its body by placing a `<jsp:doBody>` action in the location where we wish to render its body.

Summary

In this chapter we covered how to use NetBeans graphical tools to add JSTL tags to our JSP pages. We saw how JSTL can enhance JSP functionality while at the same time making our JSPs more readable by minimizing the use of scriptlets.

We also saw how to develop our own custom JSP tags to encapsulate JSP markup and functionality, and how NetBeans can generate an initial tag file, that we can use as a starting point to develop our own custom tags.

4
Developing Web Applications using JavaServer Faces 2.0

In the previous two chapters we covered how to develop web applications in Java using Servlets and JSPs. Although a lot of legacy applications have been written using these APIs, most modern Java web applications are written using some kind of web application framework. The standard framework for building web applications is **Java Server Faces (JSF)**. In this chapter we will see how using JSF can simplify web application development.

The following topics will be covered in this chapter:

- Creating a JSF project with NetBeans
- Laying out JSF tags by taking advantage of the JSF `<h:panelGrid>` tag
- Using static and dynamic navigation to define navigation between pages
- Using the NetBeans **New JSF Managed Bean** wizard to create a JSF managed bean
- Implementing custom JSF validators
- How to easily generate JSF 2.0 templates via NetBeans wizards
- How to easily create JSF 2.0 composite components with NetBeans

Introduction to JavaServer faces

Before JSF existed, most Java web applications were typically developed using non-standard web application frameworks such as Apache Struts, Tapestry, Spring Web MVC, or many others. These frameworks are built on top of the Servlet and JSP standards, and automate a lot of functionality that needs to be manually coded when using these APIs directly.

Having a wide variety of web application frameworks available (at the time of writing, Wikipedia lists 31 Java web application frameworks, and this list is far from exhaustive!), often resulted in "analysis paralysis", that is, developers often spend an inordinate amount of time evaluating frameworks for their applications.

The introduction of JSF to the Java EE specification resulted in having a standard web application framework available in any Java EE compliant application server.

> We don't mean to imply that other web application frameworks are obsolete or that they shouldn't be used at all. However, a lot of organizations consider JSF the "safe" choice since it is part of the standard and should be well supported for the foreseeable future. Additionally, NetBeans offers excellent JSF support, making JSF a very attractive choice.

Strictly speaking, JSF is not a web application framework per se, but a component framework. In theory, JSF can be used to write applications that are not web-based, however, in practice JSF is almost always used for this purpose.

In addition to being the standard Java EE component framework, one benefit of JSF is that it provides good support for tools vendors, allowing tools such as NetBeans to take advantage of the JSF component model with drag and drop support for components.

Developing our first JSF application

From an application developer's point of view, a JSF application consists of a series of XHTML pages containing custom JSF tags, one or more **JSF managed beans**, and an optional configuration file named `faces-config.xml`.

> `faces-config.xml` used to be required in JSF 1.x, however, in JSF 2.0, some conventions were introduced that reduce the need for configuration. Additonally, a lot of JSF configuration can be specified using annotations, reducing, and in some cases, eliminating the need for this XML configuration file.

Creating a new JSF project

To create a new JSF project, we need to go to **File | New Project**, select the **Java Web** project category, and **Web Application** as the project type.

After clicking **Next>**, we need to enter a project name, and optionally change other information for our project, although NetBeans provides sensible defaults.

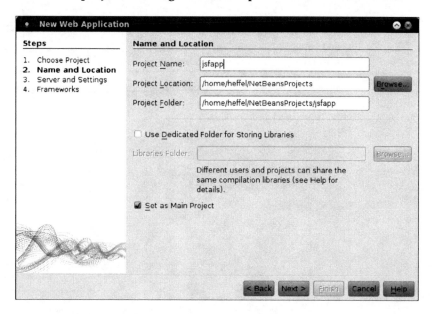

On the next page in the wizard, we can select the server, Java EE version, and context path of our application. In our example we will simply pick the default values.

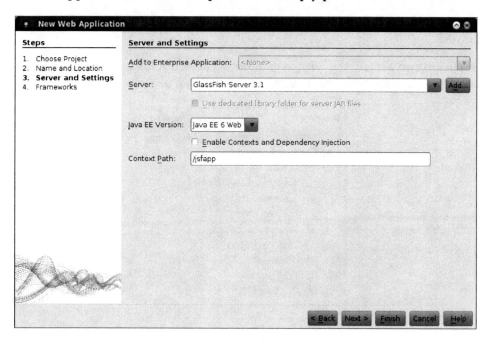

On the next page of the new project wizard, we can select what frameworks our web application will use.

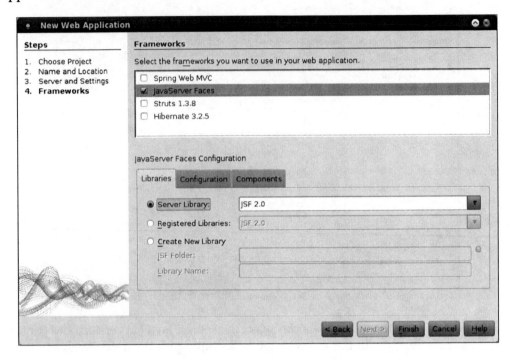

Unsurprisingly, for JSF applications we need to select the JavaServer Faces framework.

When clicking on **Finish**, the wizard generates a skeleton JSF project for us, consisting of a single facelet file called index.xhtml, a web.xml configuration file.

`web.xml` is the standard, optional configuration file needed for Java web applications, this file became optional in version 3.0 of the Servlet API, which was introduced with Java EE 6. In many cases, `web.xml` is not needed anymore, since most of the configuration options can now be specified via annotations. For JSF applications, however, it is a good idea to add one, since it allows us to specify the **JSF project stage**.

```xml
<?xml version="1.0" encoding="UTF-8"?>
<web-app version="3.0" xmlns="http://java.sun.com/xml/ns/javaee"
xmlns:xsi="http://www.w3.org/2001/XMLSchema-instance"
xsi:schemaLocation="http://java.sun.com/xml/ns/javaee
http://java.sun.com/xml/ns/javaee/web-app_3_0.xsd">
    <context-param>
        <param-name>javax.faces.PROJECT_STAGE</param-name>
        <param-value>Development</param-value>
    </context-param>
    <servlet>
        <servlet-name>Faces Servlet</servlet-name>
        <servlet-class>javax.faces.webapp.FacesServlet</servlet-class>
        <load-on-startup>1</load-on-startup>
    </servlet>
    <servlet-mapping>
        <servlet-name>Faces Servlet</servlet-name>
        <url-pattern>/faces/*</url-pattern>
    </servlet-mapping>
    <session-config>
        <session-timeout>
            30
        </session-timeout>
    </session-config>
    <welcome-file-list>
        <welcome-file>faces/index.xhtml</welcome-file>
    </welcome-file-list>
```

As we can see, NetBeans automatically sets the JSF project stage to `Development`, setting the project stage to development configures JSF to provide additional debugging help not present in other stages. For example, one common problem when developing a page is that while a page is being developed, validation for one or more of the fields on the page fails, but the developer has not added an `<h:message>` or `<h:messages>` tag to the page (more on this later). When this happens and the form is submitted, the page seems to do nothing, or page navigation doesn't seem to be working. When setting the project stage to Development, these validation errors will automatically be added to the page, without the developer having to explicitly add one of these tags to the page (we should, of course, add the tags before releasing our code to production, since our users will not see the automatically generated validation errors).

The following are the valid values for the `javax.faces.PROJECT_STAGE` context parameter for the faces servlet:

- Development
- Production
- SystemTest
- UnitTest

As we previously mentioned, the `Development` project stage adds additional debugging information to ease development. The `Production` project stage focuses on performance. The other two valid values for the project stage (`SystemTest` and `UnitTest`), allow us to implement our own custom behavior for these two phases. The `javax.faces.application.Application` class has a `getProjectStage()` method that allows us to obtain the current project stage. Based on the value of this method, we can implement the code that will only be executed in the appropriate stage. The following code snippet illustrates this:

```java
public void someMethod() {
        FacesContext facesContext = FacesContext.getCurrentInstance();
        Application application = facesContext.getApplication();
        ProjectStage projectStage = application.getProjectStage();

        if (projectStage.equals(ProjectStage.Development)) {
            //do development stuff
        } else if (projectStage.equals(ProjectStage.Production)) {
            //do production stuff
        } else if (projectStage.equals(ProjectStage.SystemTest)) {
            // do system test stuff
        } else if (projectStage.equals(ProjectStage.UnitTest)) {
            //do unit test stuff
        }
}
```

As illustrated in the snippet above, we can implement the code to be executed in any valid project stage, based on the return value of the `getProjectStage()` method of the `Application` class.

When creating a Java Web project using JSF, a facelet is automatically generated.

The generated facelet file looks like this:

```xml
<?xml version='1.0' encoding='UTF-8' ?>
<!DOCTYPE html PUBLIC "-//W3C//DTD XHTML 1.0 Transitional//EN"
    "http://www.w3.org/TR/xhtml1/DTD/xhtml1-transitional.dtd">
<html xmlns="http://www.w3.org/1999/xhtml"
```

```
    xmlns:h="http://java.sun.com/jsf/html">
<h:head>
    <title>Facelet Title</title>
</h:head>
<h:body>
    Hello from Facelets
</h:body>
</html>
```

As we can see, a facelet is nothing but an XHTML file using some facelets-specific XML name spaces. In the automatically generated page above, the following namespace definition allows us to use the "h" (for HTML) JSF component library:

```
xmlns:h="http://java.sun.com/jsf/html"
```

The above namespace declaration allows us to use JSF specific tags such as `<h:head>` and `<h:body>` which are a drop in replacement for the standard HTML/XHTML `<head>` and `<body>` tags, respectively.

The application generated by the new project wizard is a simple, but complete JSF web application. We can see it in action by right-clicking on our project in the project window and selecting **Run**. At this point the application server is started (if it wasn't already running), the application is deployed and the default system browser opens, displaying our application's default page.

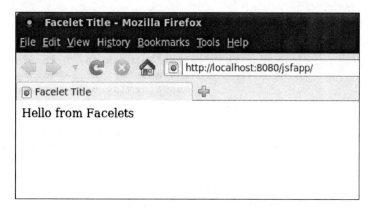

Modifying our page to capture user data

The generated application, of course, is nothing but a starting point for us to create a new application. We will now modify the generated `index.xhtml` file to collect some data from the user.

The first thing we need to do is add an `<h:form>` tag to our page. The `<h:form>` tag is equivalent to the `<form>` tag in standard HTML pages. After typing the first few characters of the `<h:form>` tag into the page, and hitting *Ctrl+Space*, we can take advantage of NetBeans' excellent code completion.

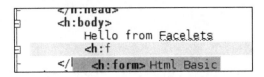

After adding the `<h:form>` tag and a number of additional JSF tags, our page now looks like this:

```xml
<?xml version='1.0' encoding='UTF-8' ?>
<!DOCTYPE html PUBLIC "-//W3C//DTD XHTML 1.0 Transitional//EN"
    "http://www.w3.org/TR/xhtml1/DTD/xhtml1-transitional.dtd">
<html xmlns="http://www.w3.org/1999/xhtml"
     xmlns:h="http://java.sun.com/jsf/html"
     xmlns:f="http://java.sun.com/jsf/core">
    <h:head>
        <title>Registration</title>
        <h:outputStylesheet library="css" name="styles.css"/>
    </h:head>
    <h:body>
        <h3>Registration Page</h3>
        <h:form>
            <h:panelGrid columns="3"
                    columnClasses="rightalign,leftalign,leftalign">
                <h:outputLabel value="Salutation: " for="salutation"/>
                <h:selectOneMenu id="salutation" label="Salutation"
                        value="#{registrationBean.salutation}" >
                    <f:selectItem itemLabel="" itemValue=""/>
                    <f:selectItem itemLabel="Mr." itemValue="MR"/>
                    <f:selectItem itemLabel="Mrs." itemValue="MRS"/>
                    <f:selectItem itemLabel="Miss" itemValue="MISS"/>
                    <f:selectItem itemLabel="Ms" itemValue="MS"/>
                    <f:selectItem itemLabel="Dr." itemValue="DR"/>
                </h:selectOneMenu>
                <h:message for="salutation"/>
                <h:outputLabel value="First Name:" for="firstName"/>
                <h:inputText id="firstName" label="First Name"
                        required="true"
                        value="#{registrationBean.firstName}" />
                <h:message for="firstName" />
                <h:outputLabel value="Last Name:" for="lastName"/>
                <h:inputText id="lastName" label="Last Name"
                        required="true"
                        value="#{registrationBean.lastName}" />
```

```
                    <h:message for="lastName" />
                    <h:outputLabel for="age" value="Age:"/>
                    <h:inputText id="age" label="Age" size="2"
                                 value="#{registrationBean.age}"/>
                    <h:message for="age"/>
                    <h:outputLabel value="Email Address:" for="email"/>
                    <h:inputText id="email" label="Email Address"
                                 required="true"
                                 value="#{registrationBean.email}">
                    </h:inputText>
                    <h:message for="email" />
                    <h:panelGroup/>
                    <h:commandButton id="register" value="Register"
                                     action="confirmation" />
                </h:panelGrid>
            </h:form>
        </h:body>
    </html>
```

The following screenshot illustrates how our page will be rendered at runtime:

All JSF input fields must be inside an `<h:form>` tag. The `<h:panelGrid>` helps us to easily lay out JSF tags on our page. It can be thought of as a grid where other JSF tags will be placed. The `columns` attribute of the `<h:panelGrid>` tag indicates how many columns the grid will have, each JSF component inside the `<h:panelGrid>` component will be placed in an individual cell of the grid. When the number of components matching the value of the `columns` attribute (three in our example) has been placed inside `<h:panelGrid>`, a new row is automatically started.

The following table illustrates how tags will be laid out inside an `<h:panelGrid>` tag:

First Tag	Second Tag	Third Tag
Fourth Tag	Fifth Tag	Sixth Tag
Seventh Tag	Eighth Tag	Ninth Tag

Each row in our `<h:panelGrid>` consists of an `<h:outputLabel>` tag, an input field, and an `<h:message>` tag.

The `columnClasses` attribute of `<h:panelGrid>` allows us to assign CSS styles to each column inside the panel grid, its `value` attribute must consist of a comma separated list of CSS styles (defined in a CSS stylesheet). The first style will be applied to the first column, the second style will be applied to the second column, the third style will be applied to the third column, so on and so forth. Had our panel grid had more than three columns, then the fourth column would have been styled using the first style in the `columnClasses` attribute, the fifth column would have been styled using the second style in the `columnClasses` attribute, so on and so forth.

If we wish to style rows in an `<h:panelGrid>`, we can do so with its `rowClasses` attribute, which works the same way that the `columnClasses` works for columns.

Notice the `<h:outputStylesheet>` tag inside `<h:head>` near the top of the page, this is a new tag that was introduced in JSF 2.0. One new feature that JSF 2.0 brings to the table is standard resource directories. Resources such as CSS stylesheets, JavaScript files, images, and so on, can be placed under a top level directory named `resources`, and JSF tags will have access to those resources automatically. In our NetBeans project, we need to place the `resources` directory under the **Web Pages** folder.

We then need to create a subdirectory to hold our CSS stylesheet (by convention, this directory should be named `css`), then we place our CSS stylesheet(s) on this subdirectory.

The CSS stylesheet for our example is very simple, therefore it is not shown. However, it is part of the code download for this chapter.

The value of the library attribute in `<h:outputStylesheet>` must match the directory where our CSS file is located, and the value of its `name` attribute must match the CSS file name.

In addition to CSS files, we should place any JavaScript files in a subdirectory called `javascript` under the `resources` directory. The file can then be accessed by the `<h:outputScript>` tag using `"javascript"` as the value of its library attribute and the file name as the value of its `name` attribute.

Similarly, images should be placed in a directory called `images` under the `resources` directory. These images can then be accessed by the JSF `<h:graphicImage>` tag, where the value of its library attribute would be `"images"` and the value of its `name` attribute would be the corresponding file name.

Now that we have discussed how to lay out elements on the page and how to access resources, let's focus our attention on the input and output elements on the page.

The `<h:outputLabel>` tag generates a label for an input field in the form, the value of its `for` attribute must match the value of the `id` attribute of the corresponding input field.

`<h:message>` generates an error message for an input field, the value of its `for` field must match the value of the `id` attribute for the corresponding input field.

The first row in our grid contains an `<h:selectOneMenu>`. This tag generates an HTML `<select>` tag on the rendered page.

Every JSF tag has an `id` attribute, the value for this attribute must be a string containing a unique identifier for the tag. If we don't specify a value for this attribute, one will be generated automatically. It is a good idea to explicitly state the ID of every component, since this ID is used in runtime error messages. Affected components are a lot easier to identify if we explicitly set their IDs.

When using `<h:label>` tags to generate labels for input fields, or when using `<h:message>` tags to generate validation errors, we need to explicitly set the value of the `id` tag, since we need to specify it as the value of the `for` attribute of the corresponding `<h:label>` and `<h:message>` tags.

Every JSF input tag has a `label` attribute. This attribute is used to generate validation error messages on the rendered page. If we don't specify a value for the `label` attribute, then the field will be identified in the error message by its ID.

Each JSF input field has a `value` attribute, in the case of `<h:selectOneMenu>`, this attribute indicates which of the options in the rendered `<select>` tag will be selected. The value of this attribute must match the value of the `itemValue` attribute of one of the nested `<f:selectItem>` tags. The value of this attribute is usually a **value binding expression**, that means that the value is read at runtime from a JSF managed bean. In our example, the value binding expression `#{registrationBean.salutation}` is used. What will happen is at runtime JSF will look for a managed bean named `registrationBean`, and look for an attribute named `salutation` on this bean, the getter method for this attribute will be invoked, and its return value will be used to determine the selected value of the rendered HTML `<select>` tag.

Nested inside the `<h:selectOneMenu>` there are a number of `<f:selectItem>` tags. These tags generate HTML `<option>` tags inside the HTML `<select>` tag generated by `<h:selectOneMenu>`. The value of the `itemLabel` attribute is the value that the user will see while the value of the `itemValue` attribute will be the value that will be sent to the server when the form is submitted.

All other rows in our grid contain `<h:inputText>` tags, this tag generates an HTML `input` field of type `text`, which accept a single line of typed text as input. We explicitly set the `id` attribute of all of our `<h:inputText>` fields, this allows us to refer to them from the corresponding `<h:outputLabel>` and `<h:message>` fields. We also set the `label` attribute for all of our `<h:inputText>` tags, this results in more user-friendly error messages.

Some of our `<h:inputText>` fields require a value, these fields have their `required` attribute set to `true`, each JSF input field has a `required` attribute, if we need to require the user to enter a value for this attribute, then we need to set this attribute to `true`. This attribute is optional, if we don't explicitly set a value for it, then it defaults to `false`.

In the last row of our grid, we added an empty `<h:panelGroup>` tag. The purpose of this tag is to allow adding several tags into a single cell of an `<h:panelGrid>`. Any tags placed inside this tag are placed inside the same cell of the grid where `<h:panelGrid>` is placed. In this particular case, all we want to do is to have an "empty" cell in the grid so that the next tag, `<h:commandButton>`, is aligned with the input fields in the rendered page.

`<h:commandButton>` is used to submit a form to the server. The value of its `value` attribute is used to generate the text of the rendered button. The value of its `action` attribute is used to determine what page to display after the button is pressed.

In our example, we are using **static navigation**. When using JSF static navigation, the value of the `action` attribute of a command button is hard-coded in the markup.

When using static navigation, the value of the action attribute of `<h:commandButton>` corresponds to the name of the page we want to navigate to, minus its `.xhtml` extension. In our example, when the user clicks on the button, we want to navigate to a file named `confirmation.xhtml`, therefore we used a value of `"confirmation"` for its `action` attribute.

An alternative to static navigation is **dynamic navigation**. When using dynamic navigation, the value of the `action` attribute of the command button is a value binding expression resolving to a method returning a `String` in a managed bean. The method may then return different values based on certain conditions. Navigation would then proceed to a different page depending on the value of the method.

As long as it returns a `String`, the managed bean method executed when using dynamic navigation can contain any logic inside it, and is frequently used to save data in a managed bean into a database.

When using dynamic navigation, the return value of the method executed when clicking the button must match the name of the page we want to navigate to (again, minus the file extension).

In earlier versions of JSF, it was necessary to specify navigation rules in `faces-config.xml`, with the introduction of the conventions introduced in the previous paragraphs, this is no longer necessary.

Creating our managed bean

JSF managed beans are standard JavaBeans that are used to hold user-entered data in JSF applications.

In order to create a new managed bean, we need to go to **File | New File...**, select **JavaServer Faces** from the category list, and **JSF Managed Bean** from the file type list.

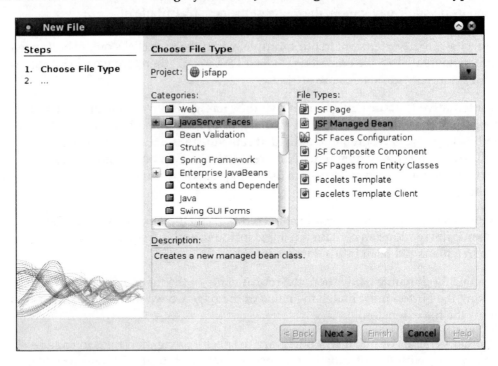

On the next screen in the wizard, we need to enter a name for our managed bean, as well as a package:

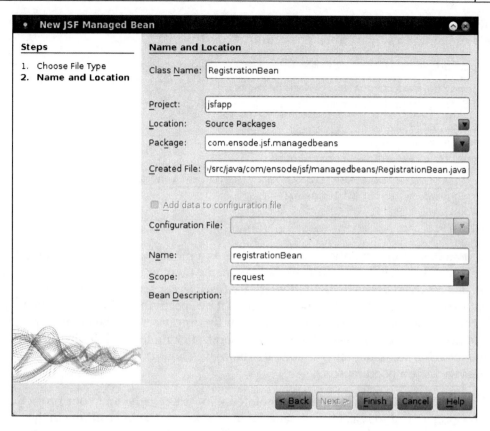

Most default values are sensible and in most cases can be accepted. The only one we should change if necessary is the **Scope** field.

Managed beans can have different scopes. A scope of request means that the bean is only available in a single HTTP request. Managed beans can also have session scope, in which case they are available in a single user's HTTP session. A scope of application means that the bean is accessible to all users in the application, across user sessions. Managed beans can also have a scope of none, which means that the managed bean is not stored at any scope, but is created on demand as needed. Additionally, managed beans can have a scope of view, in which case the bean is available until the user navigates to another page. View scoped managed beans are available across Ajax requests.

We should select the appropriate scope for our managed bean, in our particular example, the default request scope will meet our needs.

After finishing the wizard, a boilerplate version of our managed bean is created in the specified package.

The generated managed bean source simply consists of the annotated managed bean class containing a single public no argument constructor.

```
package com.ensode.jsf.managedbeans;

import javax.faces.bean.ManagedBean;
import javax.faces.bean.RequestScoped;

@ManagedBean
@RequestScoped
public class RegistrationBean {

    /** Creates a new instance of RegistrationBean */
    public RegistrationBean() {
    }
}
```

The @ManagedBean annotation marks the class as a JSF managed bean. By default, the managed bean name defaults to the class name (RegistrationBean, in our case) with its first character switched to lower case (registrationBean, in our case). If we want to override the default name, we can do it by specifying a different name in the NetBeans **New JSF Managed Bean** wizard, or by simply setting the name attribute of @ManagedBean to the desired value. In general, sticking to the defaults allows for more readable and maintainable code therefore we shouldn't deviate from them unless we have a good reason.

With the addition of any Java class annotated with @ManagedBean in our project, we no longer need to register FacesServlet in web.xml as the JSF runtime in the application server will automatically register the servlet.

The @RequestScoped annotation designates that our managed bean will have a scope of request. Had we selected a different scope when creating the managed bean with the NetBeans wizard, it would have been annotated with the appropriate annotation corresponding to the selected scope. Session scoped managed beans are annotated with the @SessionScoped annotation. Application scoped managed beans are annotated with the @ApplicationScoped annotation. Managed beans with a scope of "none", are annotated with the @NoneScoped annotation. View scoped managed beans are annotated with the @ViewScoped annotation.

At this point, we need to modify our managed bean by adding properties that will hold the user-entered values.

Automatic Generation of Getter and Setter Methods

Netbeans can automatically generate getter and setter methods for our properties. We simply need to click the keyboard shortcut for "insert code", which defaults to *Alt+Insert* in Windows and Linux, then select **Getters and Setters**.

```java
package com.ensode.jsf.managedbeans;

import javax.faces.bean.ManagedBean;
import javax.faces.bean.RequestScoped;

@ManagedBean
@RequestScoped
public class RegistrationBean {

    /** Creates a new instance of RegistrationBean */
    public RegistrationBean() {
    }
    private String salutation;
    private String firstName;
    private String lastName;
    private Integer age;
    private String email;

    //getters and setters omitted for brevity
}
```

Notice that the names of all of the bean's properties (instance variables) match the names we used in the page's value binding expressions. These names must match so that JSF knows how to map the bean's properties to the value binding expressions.

Implementing the confirmation page

Once our user fills out the data on the input page and submits the form, we want to show a confirmation page displaying the values that the user entered. Since we used value binding expressions on every input field on the input page, the corresponding fields on the managed bean will be populated with user-entered data. Therefore all we need to do in our confirmation page is display the data on the managed bean via a series of <h:outputText> JSF tags.

We can create the confirmation page via the **New JSF File** wizard.

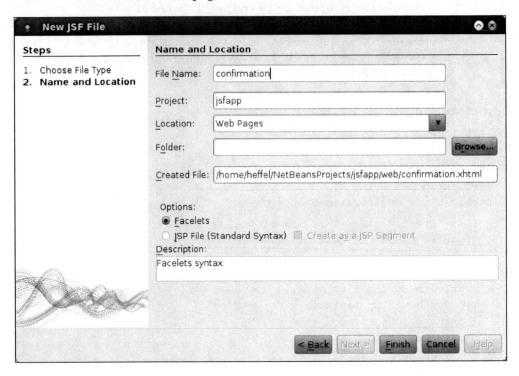

We need to make sure the name of the new file matches the value of the action attribute in the command button of the input page (`confirmation.xhtml`) so that static navigation works properly.

After modifying the generated page to meet the requirements, it should look like this:

```
<?xml version='1.0' encoding='UTF-8' ?>
<!DOCTYPE html PUBLIC "-//W3C//DTD XHTML 1.0 Transitional//EN"
    "http://www.w3.org/TR/xhtml1/DTD/xhtml1-transitional.dtd">
<html xmlns="http://www.w3.org/1999/xhtml"
    xmlns:h="http://java.sun.com/jsf/html">
    <h:head>
        <title>Confirmation Page</title>
        <h:outputStylesheet library="css" name="styles.css"/>
    </h:head>
    <h:body>
        <h2>Confirmation Page</h2>
        <h:panelGrid columns="2"
                    columnClasses="rightalign-bold,normal">
```

```
            <h:outputText value="Salutation: "/>
            <h:outputText
                value="#{registrationBean.salutation}" />
            <h:outputText value="First Name:"/>
            <h:outputText value="#{registrationBean.firstName}" />
            <h:outputText value="Last Name:"/>
            <h:outputText value="#{registrationBean.lastName}" />
            <h:outputText value="Age:"/>
            <h:outputText value="#{registrationBean.age}"/>
            <h:outputText value="Email Address:"/>
            <h:outputText value="#{registrationBean.email}" />
        </h:panelGrid>
    </h:body>
</html>
```

As we can see, our confirmation page is very simple. It consists of a series of `<h:outputText>` tags containing labels and value binding expressions bound to our managed bean's properties. The JSF `<h:outputText>` tag simply displays the value of the expression of its value attribute on the rendered page.

Executing our application

We are now ready to execute our JSF application. The easiest way to do so is to right-click on our project and click on **Run** in the resulting pop up menu

At this point GlassFish (or whatever application server we are using for our project) will start automatically, if it hadn't been started already, the default browser will open and it will automatically be directed to our page's URL.

After entering some data on the page, it should look something like the following screenshot:

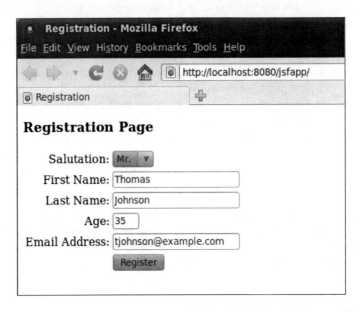

When we click on the **Register** button, our `RegistrationBean` managed bean is populated with the values we entered into the page. Each property in the field will be populated according to the value binding expression in each input field.

At this point JSF navigation "kicks in", and we are taken to the confirmation page.

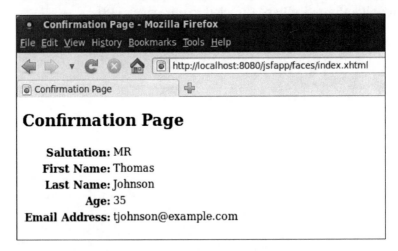

The values displayed in the confirmation page are taken from our managed bean, confirming that the bean's properties were populated correctly.

JSF validation

Earlier in this chapter we discussed how the `required` attribute for JSF input fields allows us to easily make input fields mandatory.

If a user attempts to submit a form with one or more required fields missing, an error message is automatically generated.

The error message is generated by the `<h:message>` tag corresponding to the invalid field. The string "First Name" in the error message corresponds to the value of the `label` attribute for the field, had we omitted the label attribute, the value of the field's `id` attribute would have been shown instead. As we can see, the `required` attribute makes it very easy to implement mandatory field functionality in our application.

Recall that the age field is bound to a property of type Integer in our managed bean. If a user enters a value that is not a valid integer into this field, a validation error is automatically generated.

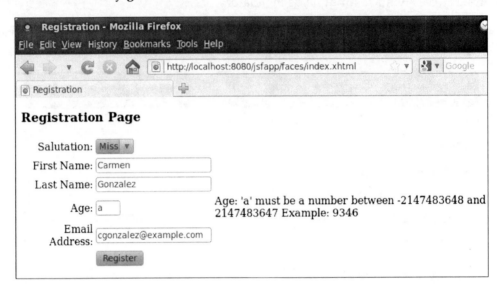

Of course, a negative age wouldn't make much sense. However, our application validates that user input is a valid Integer with essentially no effort on our part.

The email address input field of our page is bound to a property of type String in our managed bean. As such, there is no built in validation to make sure that the user enters a valid email address. In cases like this, we need to write our own custom JSF validator.

Custom JSF validators must implement the javax.faces.validator.Validator interface. This interface contains a single method named validate(), this method takes three parameters, an instance of javax.faces.context.FacesContext, an instance of javax.faces.component.UIComponent containing the JSF component we are validating, and an instance of java.lang.Object containing the user-entered value for the component. The following example illustrates a typical custom validator:

```
package com.ensode.jsf.validators;

import java.util.regex.Matcher;
import java.util.regex.Pattern;
import javax.faces.application.FacesMessage;
import javax.faces.component.UIComponent;
import javax.faces.component.html.HtmlInputText;
import javax.faces.context.FacesContext;
```

```
import javax.faces.validator.Validator;
import javax.faces.validator.ValidatorException;

@FacesValidator("emailValidator")
public class EmailValidator implements Validator {
    public void validate(FacesContext facesContext,
            UIComponent uIComponent, Object value) t
ValidatorException {
        Pattern pattern = Pattern.compile("\\w+@\\w+\\.\\w+");
        Matcher matcher = pattern.matcher(
            (CharSequence) value);
        HtmlInputText htmlInputText =
            (HtmlInputText) uIComponent;
        String label;

        if (htmlInputText.getLabel() == null ||
            htmlInputText.getLabel().trim().equals("")) {
            label = htmlInputText.getId();
        } else {
            label = htmlInputText.getLabel();
        }

        if (!matcher.matches()) {
            FacesMessage facesMessage =
                new FacesMessage(label +
                ": not a valid email address");

            throw new ValidatorException(facesMessage);
        }
    }
}
```

In our example, the `validate()` method does a regular expression match against the value of the JSF component we are validating. If the value matches the expression, validation succeeds, otherwise, validation fails and an instance of `javax.faces.validator.ValidatorException` is thrown.

 The primary purpose of our custom validator is to illustrate how to write custom JSF validations, and not to create a foolproof email address validator. There may be a valid email address that doesn't validate using our validator.

The constructor of `ValidatorException` takes an instance of `javax.faces.application.FacesMessage` as a parameter. This object is used to display the error message on the page when validation fails. The message to display is passed as a `String` to the constructor of `FacesMessage`. In our example, if the `label` attribute of the component is not `null` nor empty, we use it as part of the error message, otherwise we use the value of the component's `id` attribute. This behavior follows the pattern established by standard JSF validators.

Our validator needs to be annotated with the `@FacesValidator` annotation. The value of its `value` attribute is the ID that will be used to reference our validator in our JSF pages.

Once we are done implementing our validator, we are ready to use it in our pages.

In our particular case, we need to modify the email field to use our custom validator.

```
<h:inputText id="email" label="Email Address"
        required="true" value="#{registrationBean.email}">
    <f:validator validatorId="emailValidator"/>
</h:inputText>
```

All we need to do is nest a `<f:validator>` tag inside the input field we wish to have validated using our custom validator. The value of the `validatorId` attribute of `<f:validator>` must match the value of the value attribute in the `@FacesValidator` annotation in our validator.

At this point we are ready to test our custom validator.

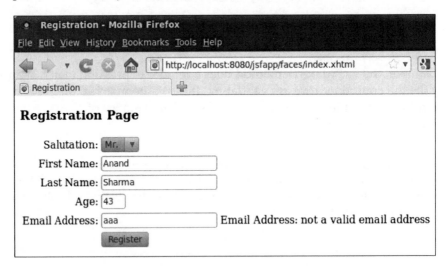

When entering an invalid email address into the email address input field and submitting the form, our custom validator logic was executed and the `String` we passed as a parameter to `FacesMessage` in our `validator()` method is shown as the error text by the `<h:message>` tag for the field.

Facelets templating

One advantage that Facelets has over JSP is its templating mechanism. Templates allow us to specify page layout in one place, then we can have template clients that use the layout defined in the template. Since most web applications have consistent layout across pages, using templates makes our applications much more maintainable, since changes to the layout need to be made in a single place. If at one point we need to change the layout for our pages (add a footer, or move a column from the left side of the page to the right side of the page, for example), we only need to change the template, and the change is reflected in all template clients.

NetBeans provides very good support for facelets templating. It provides several templates "out of the box", using common web page layouts.

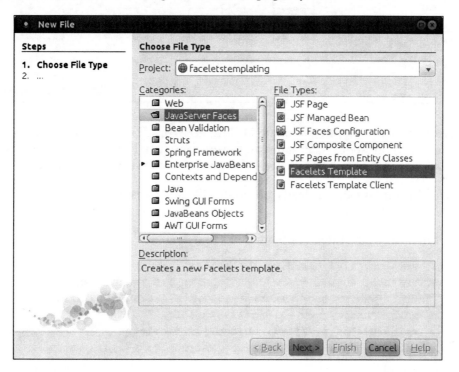

We can then select from one of several predefined templates to use as a base for our template or simply to use it "out of the box".

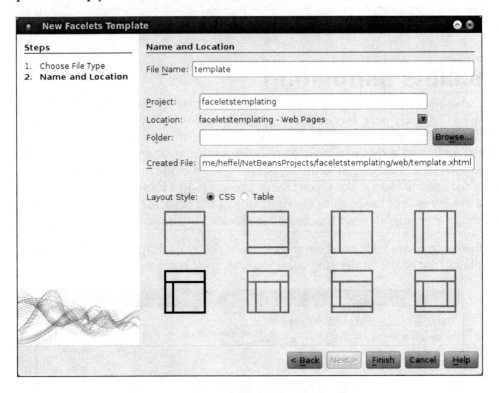

NetBeans gives us the option of using HTML tables or CSS for layout. For most modern web applications, CSS is the preferred approach. For our example we will pick a layout containing a header area, a single left column, and a main area.

After clicking on **Finish**, NetBeans automatically generates our template, along with the necessary CSS files.

The automatically generated template looks like this:

```
<?xml version='1.0' encoding='UTF-8' ?>
<!DOCTYPE html PUBLIC "-//W3C//DTD XHTML 1.0 Transitional//EN"
    "http://www.w3.org/TR/xhtml1/DTD/xhtml1-transitional.dtd">
<html xmlns="http://www.w3.org/1999/xhtml"
      xmlns:ui="http://java.sun.com/jsf/facelets"
      xmlns:h="http://java.sun.com/jsf/html">

    <h:head>
        <meta http-equiv="Content-Type" content="text/html;
charset=UTF-8" />
```

```
        <link href="./resources/css/default.css" rel="stylesheet"
type="text/css" />
        <link href="./resources/css/cssLayout.css" rel="stylesheet"
type="text/css" />
        <title>Facelets Template</title>
    </h:head>
    <h:body>
        <div id="top" class="top">
            <ui:insert name="top">Top</ui:insert>
        </div>
        <div>
            <div id="left">
                <ui:insert name="left">Left</ui:insert>
            </div>
            <div id="content" class="left_content">
                <ui:insert name="content">Content</ui:insert>
            </div>
        </div>
    </h:body>
</html>
```

As we can see, the template doesn't look much different from a regular Facelets file.

Adding a Facelets template to our project

We can add a Facelets template to our project simply by clicking on **File | New File**, then selecting the **JavaServer Faces** category and the **Facelets Template** file type.

Notice that the template uses the following namespace: xmlns:ui="http://java. sun.com/jsf/facelets". This namespace allows us to use the <ui:insert> tag, the contents of this tag will be replaced by the content in a corresponding <ui:define> tag in template clients.

Using the template

To use our template, we simply need to create a Facelets template client, which can be done by clicking on **File | New File**, selecting the **JavaServer Faces** category and the **Facelets Template Client** file type.

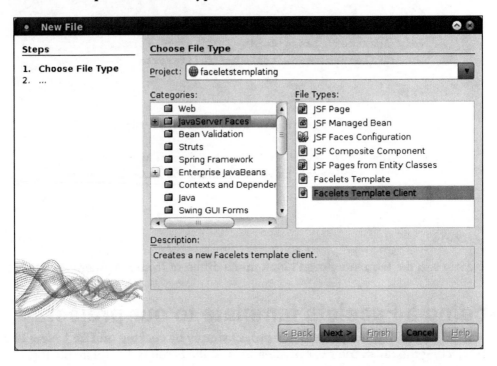

After clicking on **Next >**, we need to enter a file name (or accept the default), and select the template that we will use for our template client.

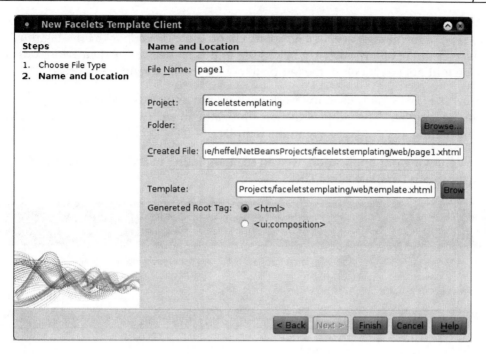

After clicking on **Finish**, our template client is created.

```
<?xml version='1.0' encoding='UTF-8' ?>
<!DOCTYPE html PUBLIC "-//W3C//DTD XHTML 1.0 Transitional//EN"
"http://www.w3.org/TR/xhtml1/DTD/xhtml1-transitional.dtd">
<html xmlns="http://www.w3.org/1999/xhtml"
      xmlns:ui="http://java.sun.com/jsf/facelets">

    <body>
        <ui:composition template="./template.xhtml">
            <ui:define name="top">
                top
            </ui:define>
            <ui:define name="left">
                left
            </ui:define>
            <ui:define name="content">
                content
            </ui:define>
        </ui:composition>

    </body>
</html>
```

As we can see, the template client also uses the `xmlns:ui="http://java.sun.com/jsf/facelets"` namespace. In a template client, the `<ui:composition>` tag must be the parent tag of any other tag belonging to this namespace. Any markup outside this tag will not be rendered; the template markup will be rendered instead.

The `<ui:define>` tag is used to insert markup into a corresponding `<ui:insert>` tag in the template. The value of the `name` attribute in `<ui:define>` must match the corresponding `<ui:insert>` tag in the template.

After deploying our application, we can see templating in action by pointing the browser to our template client URL.

Notice that NetBeans generated a template that allows us to create a fairly elegant page with very little effort on our part. Of course, we should replace the markup in the `<ui:define>` tags to suit our needs.

Here is a modified version of our template, adding markup to be rendered in the corresponding places in the template:

```xml
<?xml version='1.0' encoding='UTF-8' ?>
<!DOCTYPE html PUBLIC "-//W3C//DTD XHTML 1.0 Transitional//EN"
"http://www.w3.org/TR/xhtml1/DTD/xhtml1-transitional.dtd">
<html xmlns="http://www.w3.org/1999/xhtml"
      xmlns:ui="http://java.sun.com/jsf/facelets"
      xmlns:h="http://java.sun.com/jsf/html">
    <body>
        <ui:composition template="./template.xhtml">
            <ui:define name="top">
                <h2>Welcome to our Site</h2>
            </ui:define>
            <ui:define name="left">
                <h3>Links</h3>
```

```
    <ul>
        <li>
            <h:outputLink value="http://www.packtpub.com">
                <h:outputText value="Packt Publishing"/>
            </h:outputLink>
        </li>
        <li>
            <h:outputLink value="http://www.ensode.net">
                <h:outputText value="Ensode.net"/>
            </h:outputLink>
        </li>
        <li>
            <h:outputLink value="http://www.ensode.com">
                <h:outputText value="Ensode Technology,
                LLC"/>
            </h:outputLink>
        </li>

        <li>
            <h:outputLink value="http://www.netbeans.org">
                <h:outputText value="NetBeans.org"/>
            </h:outputLink>
        </li>
        <li>
            <h:outputLink value="http://www.glassfish.
            org">
                <h:outputText value="GlassFish.org"/>
            </h:outputLink>
        </li>
        <li>
            <h:outputLink
                value="http://www.oracle.com/technetwork/
                java/javaee/overview/index.html">
                <h:outputText value="Java EE 6"/>
            </h:outputLink>
        </li>
        <li><h:outputLink value="http://www.oracle.com/
        technetwork/java/index.html">
                <h:outputText value="Java"/>
            </h:outputLink></li>
    </ul>
</ui:define>
<ui:define name="content">                    <p>
        In this main area we would put our main text,
        images, forms, etc. In this example we will simply
        use the typical filler text that web designers
        love to use.
    </p>
    <p>
```

```
                        Lorem ipsum dolor sit amet, consectetur
        adipiscing elit. Nunc venenatis, diam nec tempor dapibus, lacus erat
        vehicula mauris, id lacinia nisi arcu vitae purus. Nam vestibulum
        nisi non lacus luctus vel ornare nibh pharetra. Aenean non lorem
        lectus, eu tempus lectus. Cras mattis nibh a mi pharetra ultricies.
        In consectetur, tellus sit amet pretium facilisis, enim ipsum
        consectetur magna, a mattis ligula massa vel mi. Maecenas id arcu a
        erat pellentesque vestibulum at vitae nulla. Nullam eleifend sodales
        tincidunt. Donec viverra libero non erat porta sit amet convallis enim
        commodo. Cras eu libero elit, ac aliquam ligula. Quisque a elit nec
        ligula dapibus porta sit amet a nulla. Nulla vitae molestie ligula.
        Aliquam interdum, velit at tincidunt ultrices, sapien mauris sodales
        mi, vel rutrum turpis neque id ligula. Donec dictum condimentum arcu
        ut convallis. Maecenas blandit, ante eget tempor sollicitudin, ligula
        eros venenatis justo, sed ullamcorper dui leo id nunc. Suspendisse
        potenti. Ut vel mauris sem. Duis lacinia eros laoreet diam cursus nec
        hendrerit tellus pellentesque.
                    </p>
                </ui:define>
            </ui:composition>
        </body>
    </html>
```

After making the above changes, our template client now renders as follows:

As we can see, creating Facelets templates and template clients with NetBeans is a breeze.

Composite components

A very nice JSF 2.0 feature is the ability to easily write custom JSF components. With JSF 2, creating a custom component involves little more than creating the markup for it, with no Java code or configuration needed. Since custom components are typically composed of other JSF components, they are referred to as **composite components**.

We can generate a composite component by clicking on **File | New**, selecting the **JavaServer Faces** category and the **JSF Composite Component** file type.

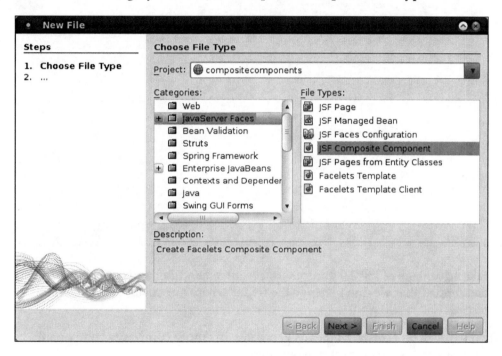

After clicking on **Next >**, we can specify the file name, project, and folder for our custom component.

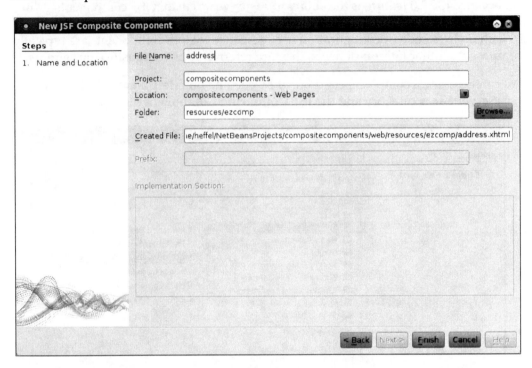

To take advantage of JSF 2.0's automatic resource handling and conventions, it is recommended that we don't change the folder where our custom component will be placed.

When we click on **Finish**, NetBeans generates an empty composite component that we can use as a base to create our own.

```
<?xml version='1.0' encoding='UTF-8' ?>
<!DOCTYPE html PUBLIC "-//W3C//DTD XHTML 1.0 Transitional//EN"
    "http://www.w3.org/TR/xhtml1/DTD/xhtml1-transitional.dtd">
<html xmlns="http://www.w3.org/1999/xhtml"
    xmlns:cc="http://java.sun.com/jsf/composite">

    <!-- INTERFACE -->
    <cc:interface>
    </cc:interface>
    <!-- IMPLEMENTATION -->
    <cc:implementation>
    </cc:implementation>
</html>
```

Every JSF 2.0 composite component contains two sections, an interface and an implementation.

The interface section must be enclosed inside a `<cc:interface>` tag. In the interface, we define any attributes that our component will have.

The implementation section contains the markup that will be rendered when we use our composite component.

In our example, we will develop a simple component which we can use to enter the addresses. That way, if we have to enter several addresses in an application, we can encapsulate the logic and/or display in our component. If later we need to change the address entry (to support international addresses, for example), we only need to change our component and all address entry forms in our application will be updated automatically.

After "filling in the blanks", our composite component now looks like this:

```
<?xml version='1.0' encoding='UTF-8' ?>
<!DOCTYPE html PUBLIC "-//W3C//DTD XHTML 1.0 Transitional//EN"
    "http://www.w3.org/TR/xhtml1/DTD/xhtml1-transitional.dtd">
<html xmlns="http://www.w3.org/1999/xhtml"
    xmlns:cc="http://java.sun.com/jsf/composite"
    xmlns:h="http://java.sun.com/jsf/html"
    xmlns:f="http://java.sun.com/jsf/core">

  <!-- INTERFACE -->
  <cc:interface>
      <cc:attribute name="addrType"/>
      <cc:attribute name="managedBean" required="true"/>
  </cc:interface>

  <!-- IMPLEMENTATION -->
  <cc:implementation>
      <h:panelGrid columns="2">
          <f:facet name="header">
              <h:outputText value="#{cc.attrs.addrType} Address"/>
          </f:facet>
          <h:outputLabel for="line1" value="Line 1"/>
          <h:inputText id="line1" value="#{cc.attrs.managedBean.
          line1}"/>
          <h:outputLabel for="line2" value="Line 2"/>
          <h:inputText id="line2" value="#{cc.attrs.managedBean.
          line2}"/>
          <h:outputLabel for="city" value="City"/>
          <h:inputText id="city" value="#{cc.attrs.managedBean.
          city}"/>
```

```
                    <h:outputLabel for="state" value="state"/>
                    <h:inputText id="state" value="#{cc.attrs.managedBean.
                    state}" size="2" maxlength="2"/>
                    <h:outputLabel for="zip" value="Zip"/>
                    <h:inputText id="zip" value="#{cc.attrs.managedBean.zip}"
                    size="5" maxlength="5"/>
                </h:panelGrid>
            </cc:implementation>
        </html>
```

We specify attributes for our component via the <cc:attribute> tag. This tag has a name attribute used to specify the attribute name, and an optional required attribute that we can use to specify if the attribute is required.

The body of the <cc:implementation> tag looks almost like plain old JSF markup, with one exception, by convention, we can access the tag's attributes by using the #{cc.attrs.ATTRIBUTE_NAME} expression to access the attributes we defined in the component's interface section. Notice that the managedBean attribute of our component must resolve to a JSF managed bean. Pages using our component must use a JSF expression resolving to a managed bean as the value of this attribute. We can access the attributes of this managed bean by simply using the familiar .property notation we have used before, the only difference here is that instead of using a managed bean name in the expression, we must use the attribute name as defined in the interface section.

Now we have a simple but complete composite component, using it in our pages is very simple.

```
<?xml version='1.0' encoding='UTF-8' ?>
<!DOCTYPE html PUBLIC "-//W3C//DTD XHTML 1.0 Transitional//EN"
"http://www.w3.org/TR/xhtml1/DTD/xhtml1-transitional.dtd">
<html xmlns="http://www.w3.org/1999/xhtml"
      xmlns:h="http://java.sun.com/jsf/html"
      xmlns:ezcomp="http://java.sun.com/jsf/composite/ezcomp">
    <h:head>
        <title>Address Entry</title>
    </h:head>
    <h:body>
        <h:form>
            <h:panelGrid columns="1">
                <ezcomp:address managedBean="#{addressBean}"
                                            addrType="Home"/>
                <h:commandButton value="Submit" action="confirmation"
                            style="display: block; margin: 0
                            auto;"/>
```

```
            </h:panelGrid>
        </h:form>
    </h:body>
</html>
```

By convention, the namespace for our custom components will always be
`xmlns:ezcomp="http://java.sun.com/jsf/composite/ezcomp"`. This is why it is
important not to override the default folder where our component will be placed, as
doing so breaks this convention. NetBeans provides code completion for our custom
composite components, just like it does for standard components.

In our application, we created a simple managed bean named addressBean. It is a
simple managed bean with a few properties and corresponding getters and setters,
therefore it is not shown (it is part of this chapter's code download). We use this
bean as the value of the `managedBean` attribute of our component. We also used an
`addressType` of "Home", this value will be rendered as a header for our address
input component.

After deploying and running our application, we can see our component in action:

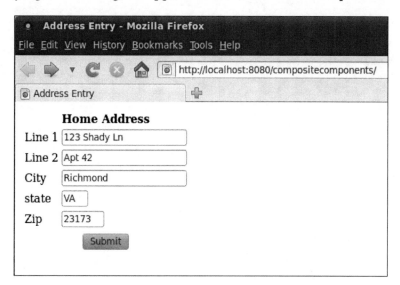

As we can see, creating JSF 2.0 composite components with NetBeans is a breeze.

Summary

In this chapter we saw how NetBeans can help us easily create new JSF projects by automatically adding all required libraries.

We saw how we can quickly create JSF pages by taking advantage of NetBeans' code completion.

Additionally, we saw how we can significantly save time and effort by allowing NetBeans to generate JSF 2.0 templates, including generating the necessary CSS to easily create fairly elegant pages.

Finally, we saw how NetBeans can help us develop JSF 2.0 custom components.

5

Elegant Web Applications with PrimeFaces

One of the advantages of JSF is that it is very easy to develop custom components. As such, several open source component libraries have been developed. One of these component libraries is PrimeFaces. PrimeFaces allows us to develop elegant web applications with little effort. As of version 7.0, PrimeFaces is bundled with NetBeans.

Our first PrimeFaces project

To use PrimeFaces in our project, we simply need to create a Java Web application project as usual. When we pick the JavaServer Faces Framework, we need to click on the **Components** tab and select **PrimeFaces 2.2.1** as our component suite.

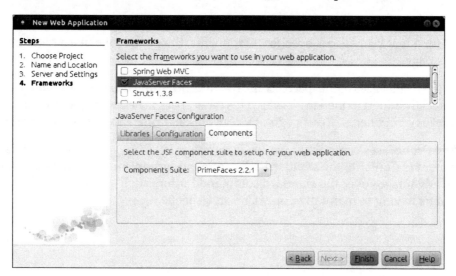

When our project is created, NetBeans will add the required libraries to our project, PrimeFaces tags will autocomplete in our project's JSF pages.

When selecting PrimeFaces as our JSF component suite, NetBeans creates a sample page using PrimeFaces components when our project is created. The markup for the file looks like this:

```
<?xml version='1.0' encoding='UTF-8' ?>
<!DOCTYPE html PUBLIC "-//W3C//DTD XHTML 1.0 Transitional//EN"
"http://www.w3.org/TR/xhtml1/DTD/xhtml1-transitional.dtd">
<html xmlns="http://www.w3.org/1999/xhtml"
      xmlns:p="http://primefaces.prime.com.tr/ui"
      xmlns:h="http://java.sun.com/jsf/html">
    <h:head>
        <title>Facelet Title</title>
    </h:head>
    <h:body>
        <h:form>
            <p:commandButton value="Hello from PrimeFaces"
                                onclick="dlg1.show();" type="button"
                                />
            <p:dialog header="PrimeFaces Dialog" widgetVar="dlg1"
                width="500">
                For more information visit <a href="http://primefaces.
                org">
                    http://primefaces.org</a>.
            </p:dialog>
        </h:form>
    </h:body>
</html>
```

Except for a few PrimeFaces-specific components, the page looks like a regular Facelets page.

Notice the PrimeFaces namespace, xmlns:p="http://primefaces.prime.com.tr/ui" is automatically added to the <html> tag. This namespace is necessary in order to use PrimeFaces components in our pages. By convention, PrimeFaces tags use a prefix of p.

The first PrimeFaces component we see in our page is <p:commandButton>, this component is similar to the standard JSF command button component, but provides certain advantages over the standard command button, such as rendering nicely without us having to manually apply CSS stylesheets.

The other PrimeFaces component we see in our page is `<p:dialog>`, this component renders as a popup that can overlay other components on the page. The value of its `widgetVar` attribute can be used to access the component from other components on the page. The Dialog component provides a client-side JavaScript API for this purpose. The most commonly used functions of this client API are `show()` and `hide()`, used to display or hide the dialog on the page. We can see the client API in action as the value of the onclick attribute of the commandButton we discussed earlier.

When we run our application, we can see the automatically generated page in action.

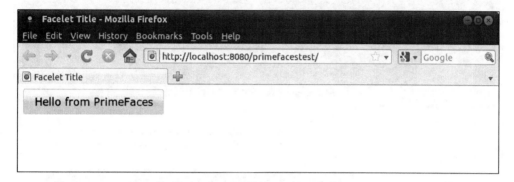

When we click on the button, the dialog is displayed.

Clicking on the link inside the dialog takes us to the PrimeFaces web site.

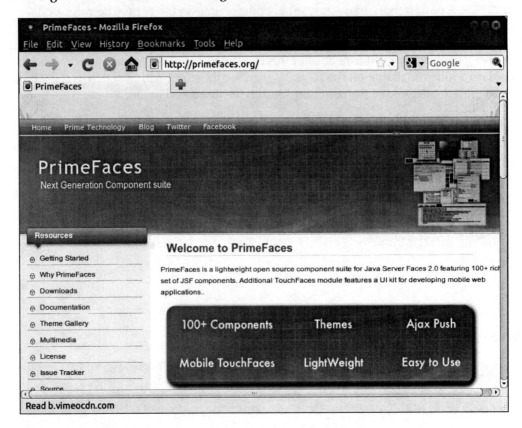

As we can see, PrimeFaces allows us to create elegant web applications with very little effort on our part. Next, we will see how to take advantage of several PrimeFaces components to greatly ease and simplify the work we need to do to create our web applications.

Using PrimeFaces components in our JSF applications

In this section, we will discuss how to use some simple PrimeFaces components to save us work when developing our JSF applications. The following page is a simple customer data entry page:

```
<?xml version='1.0' encoding='UTF-8' ?>
<!DOCTYPE html PUBLIC "-//W3C//DTD XHTML 1.0 Transitional//EN"
"http://www.w3.org/TR/xhtml1/DTD/xhtml1-transitional.dtd">
```

```
<html xmlns="http://www.w3.org/1999/xhtml"
    xmlns:p="http://primefaces.prime.com.tr/ui"
    xmlns:h="http://java.sun.com/jsf/html"
    xmlns:ui="http://java.sun.com/jsf/facelets">
  <ui:composition template="./template.xhtml">
    <ui:define name="top">
        <h2>Customer Information Data Entry</h2>
    </ui:define>

    <ui:define name="content">
        <h:form>
          <p:messages/>
            <p:panel header="Enter Customer Information">
              <h:panelGrid columns="2">
                  <h:outputLabel for="firstName" value="First
                  Name"
                                 styleClass="requiredLbl"/>
                  <h:inputText id="firstName" label="First Name"
                              value="#{customer.firstName}"
                              required="true"/>
                  <h:outputLabel for="middleName" value="Middle
                  Name"
                                 styleClass="optionalLbl"/>
                  <h:inputText id="middleName" label="Middle
                  Name"
                              value="#{customer.middleName}"/>
                  <h:outputLabel for="lastName" value="Last
                  Name"
                                 styleClass="requiredLbl"/>
                  <h:inputText id="lastName" label="Last Name"
                              value="#{customer.lastName}"
                              required="true"/>
                  <h:outputLabel for="birthDate" value="Date of
                  Birth"
                                 styleClass="optionalLbl"/>
                <p:calendar id="birthDate"
                            value="#{customer.birthDate}"
                            showOn="button"
                            inputStyle="width:100px;"
                            navigator="true"/>
                  <h:panelGroup/>
                <p:commandButton
                      value="Submit"
                      action="#{customerController.
                      saveCustomer}"
```

```
                          ajax="false"/>
                    </h:panelGrid>
                </p:panel>
            </h:form>
        </ui:define>
    </ui:composition>
</html>
```

> In our example, we took advantage of NetBean's Facelet Template generation, that way we can get some very nice CSS styles for "free", refer to the previous chapter for details on NetBeans' Facelets Template capabilities.

When we run our project, the above markup is rendered on the browser as shown in the following screenshot:

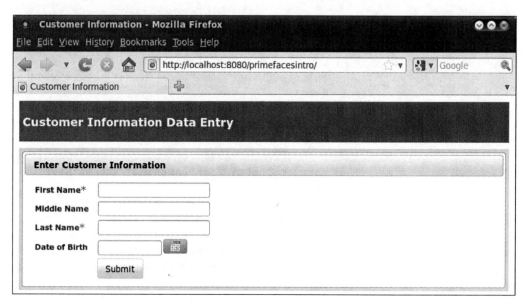

The first new PrimeFaces component we used on our page was the `<p:messages>` component. This component can be used as a drop-in replacement for the standard JSF `<h:messages>` component. The advantage of `<p:messages>` over `<h:messages>` is that with `<p:messages>`, error messages are nicely formatted by default.

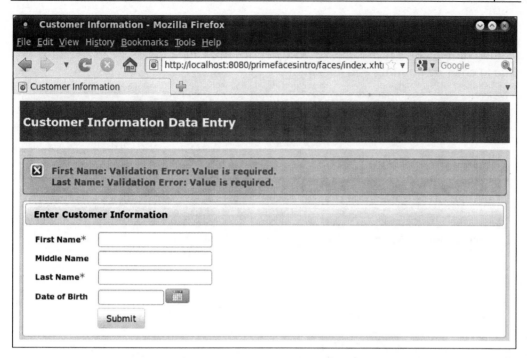

Similar to <p:messages>, PrimeFaces has a <p:message> component that can be used as a drop-in replacement for the standard JSF <h:message> component (not shown in the example). Just like <h:message>, <p:message> should be used when we wish to show validation errors next to the field whose value did not validate, as opposed to showing the message at the top of the page.

The other new PrimeFaces component we see in this example is <p:calendar>. This calendar can be used for date input fields. When the user clicks on the icon generated by this component, a nice calendar widget pops up, where the user can select the date to enter by pointing and clicking.

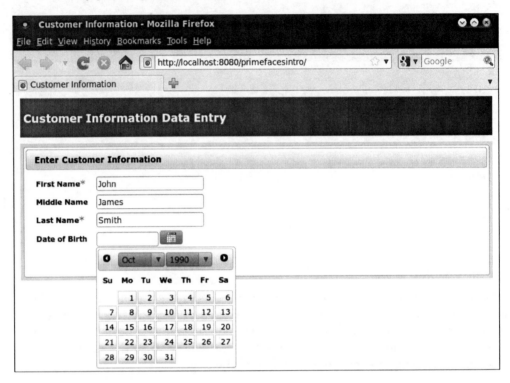

The PrimeFaces calendar component is very customizable. By default, it renders as a text field, and when the user clicks on this text field, the calendar widget pops up. In our example, we set the showOn attribute to button, this has the effect of rendering a calendar icon next to the text field, which gives a visual indication that this is a special field, and also allows users to enter dates manually if they prefer to do so.

By default, the month and year dropdowns are not rendered, this makes it cumbersome to enter dates that are far in the future or in the past (default day is always the present date). To get around this, we can set the navigator property to true like we did in our example.

Additionally, we can control the appearance of the text input field generated by using the inputStyle or inputStyleClass attributes of <p:calendar>. The inputStyle attribute value must be a valid inline CSS, where the value of the inputStyleClass attribute must be the name of a CSS class defined in one of our CSS stylesheets.

The last new PrimeFaces component we used in our page is `<p:commandButton>`, by default, this component renders a button that triggers AJAX requests to update parts of our page without doing a full page request. This component can also be used as a drop-in replacement for the standard JSF `<h:commandButton>` component. To do this, we need to set its `ajax` property to `false`, which is what we did in our example. The advantage of using `<p:commandButton>` as a drop-in replacement for `<h:commandButton>` is that `<p:commandButton>` is nicely rendered by default, without the need for us to create custom CSS styles for our buttons.

When clicking on the button in our example, the user is directed to a confirmation page.

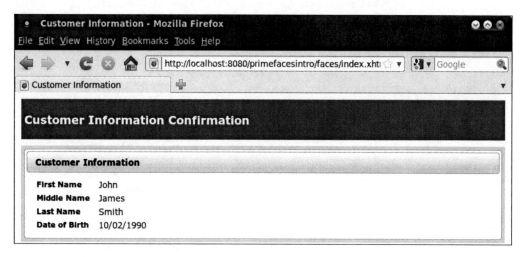

We didn't use any new PrimeFaces components in the confirmation page, therefore we won't be discussing it. Its markup can be found in this chapter's download (`confirmation.xhtml`).

Tabbed views

Frequently, HTML forms have several fields that would typically result in very long forms. It is common to divide a form into two or more tabs, that way the page looks less overwhelming to the user. Normally, creating a page with tabs requires some HTML and JavaScript tricks, however, PrimeFaces includes a `<p:tabView>` component we can use to easily generate tabs, the following example illustrates how to use this component:

```
<?xml version='1.0' encoding='UTF-8' ?>
<!DOCTYPE html PUBLIC "-//W3C//DTD XHTML 1.0 Transitional//EN"
"http://www.w3.org/TR/xhtml1/DTD/xhtml1-transitional.dtd">
```

```
<html xmlns="http://www.w3.org/1999/xhtml"
      xmlns:p="http://primefaces.prime.com.tr/ui"
      xmlns:h="http://java.sun.com/jsf/html"
      xmlns:ui="http://java.sun.com/jsf/facelets"
      xmlns:f="http://java.sun.com/jsf/core">
  <ui:composition template="./template.xhtml">
      <ui:define name="top">
          <h2>Customer Information Data Entry</h2>
      </ui:define>
      <ui:define name="content">
          <h:form>
              <p:messages/>
              <h:panelGrid columns="1" style="width: 100%">
                  <p:tabView>
                      <p:tab title="Personal Information">
                          <h:panelGrid columns="2">
                              <h:outputLabel for="firstName"
                              value="First Name"

                              styleClass="requiredLbl"/>
                              <h:inputText id="firstName"
                              label="First Name"
                                          value="#{customer.
                                          firstName}"
                                          required="true"/>
                              <h:outputLabel for="middleName"
                              value="Middle Name"

                              styleClass="optionalLbl"/>
                              <h:inputText id="middleName"
                              label="Middle Name"
                                          value="#{customer.
                                          middleName}"/>
                              <h:outputLabel for="lastName"
                              value="Last Name"

                              styleClass="requiredLbl"/>
                              <h:inputText id="lastName" label="Last
                              Name"
                                          value="#{customer.
                                          lastName}"
                                          required="true"/>
                              <h:outputLabel for="birthDate"
                                          value="Date of Birth"

                                          styleClass="optionalLbl"/>
                              <p:calendar id="birthDate"
                                          value="#{customer.
                                          birthDate}"
                                          showOn="button"
```

```
                                    inputStyle="width:100px;"
                                    navigator="true"/>
                </h:panelGrid>
        </p:tab>
        <p:tab title="Address">
                <h:panelGrid columns="2">
                        <h:outputLabel for="line1" value="Line
                        1"

                        styleClass="requiredLbl"/>
                        <h:inputText id="line1"
                                        value="#{customer.
                                        addrLine1}"
                                        required="true"/>
                        <h:outputLabel for="line2" value="Line
                        2"

                        styleClass="optionalLbl"/>
                        <h:inputText id="line2"
                                        value="#{customer.
                                        addrLine2}"/>
                        <h:outputLabel for="city" value="City"

                        styleClass="requiredLbl"/>
                        <h:inputText id="city"
                                        value="#{customer.
                                        addrCity}"
                                        required="true"/>
                        <h:outputLabel for="state"
                        value="State"

                        styleClass="requiredLbl"/>
                        <h:selectOneMenu id="state"
                        required="true"
                            value="#{customer.addrState}">
                            <f:selectItem itemValue=""
                            itemLabel=""/>
                            <f:selectItem itemValue="AL"

                            itemLabel="Alabama"/>
                            <f:selectItem itemValue="AK"
                                        itemLabel="Alaska"/>
                            <f:selectItem itemValue="AZ"

                            itemLabel="Arizona"/>
                            <f:selectItem itemValue="AR"

                            itemLabel="Arkansas"/>
                            <!-- other states omitted for
```

```
brevity -->
                                </h:selectOneMenu>
                                <h:outputLabel for="zip" value="Zip"

                                styleClass="requiredLbl"/>
                                <h:inputText id="zip"
                                            value="#{customer.
                                            addrZip}"
                                            required="true"/>
                            </h:panelGrid>
                        </p:tab>
                          <p:tab title="Phone Numbers">
                            <h:panelGrid columns="2">
                                <h:outputLabel for="homePhone"
                                value="Home"/>
                                <p:inputMask id="homePhone"
                                            mask="(999)-999-9999"
                                            value="#{customer.
                                            homePhone}"
                                            size="12"
                                            styleClass="optionalLbl"/>
                                <h:outputLabel for="mobilePhone"
value="Mobile"/>

                                <p:inputMask id="mobilePhone"
                                            mask="(999)-999-9999"
                                            value="#{customer.
                                            mobilePhone}"
                                            size="12"
                                            styleClass="optionalLbl"/>
                                <h:outputLabel for="workPhone"
                                value="Work"/>
                                <p:inputMask id="workPhone"
                                            mask="(999)-999-9999"
                                            value="#{customer.
                                            workPhone}"
                                            size="12"
                                            styleClass="optionalLbl"/>
                            </h:panelGrid>
                        </p:tab>
                    </p:tabView>
                    <p:commandButton
                        value="Submit"
                        action="#{customerController.saveCustomer}"
                        ajax="false"/>
                </h:panelGrid>
            </h:form>
        </ui:define>
    </ui:composition>
</html>
```

As we can see in the above example, the root component for a tabbed interface is
<p:tabView>; nested inside this component there must be one or more <p:tab>
components. Each <p:tab> contains the input fields that will be in the corresponding
tab. <p:tab> has a title attribute that will be rendered as the title for the tab.

When we execute our project we can see the tab component in action.

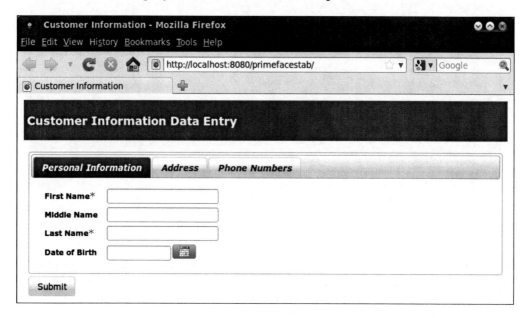

By clicking on each tab we can see the corresponding components.

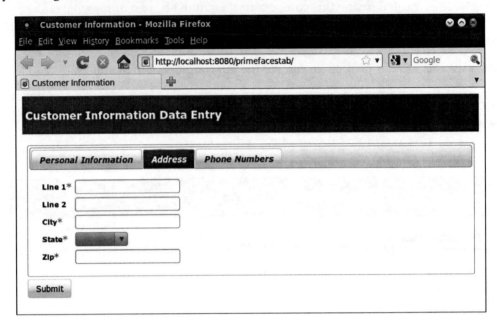

Alert readers may have noticed that we used a new PrimeFaces component in the third tab. `<p:inputMask>` allows us to prevent users from entering badly formatted data. In our example, we used it for every telephone number input field. The following screenshot shows `<p:inputMask>` in action:

As we can see in the screenshot, as soon as the user clicks on an inputMask component, the expected format is automatically displayed. All the user needs to do is "fill in the blanks" to have the input correctly formatted. In our case, we are expecting a phone number in the format (xxx)xxx-xxxx, where x is an integer value. When we define our mask, the number **9** represents any numeric value, the letter **a** represents any alphabetic character, and the asterisk (*) represents an alphanumeric character.

For our formatting, we gave the `mask` an attribute of `<p:inputMask>` the value of `(999)-999-9999`, which resulted in the desired mask.

As we can see, using `<p:inputMask>` allows us to enforce correctly formatted data without having to rely on JSF validation.

Back to our tab discussion, when the user clicks on the **submit** button at the bottom of the page, data in all tabs is submitted, and is treated as a single `<h:form>` submission, at this point, the JSF lifecycle "kicks in" as usual.

Wizard interfaces

In addition to using tabs, another common way of dividing long forms is by using wizards. Wizards are useful whenever we need the users to fill in input fields in a specific order. In our previous example, we had no way to force the user to enter address information before entering phone number information. This prevents us from validating that the phone numbers entered correspond to the geographical area in the address. To solve this problem we can use a wizard interface, which can be done easily with the PrimeFaces' `<p:wizard>` component. The following example illustrates how to use this component:

```
<?xml version='1.0' encoding='UTF-8' ?>
<!DOCTYPE html PUBLIC "-//W3C//DTD XHTML 1.0 Transitional//EN"
"http://www.w3.org/TR/xhtml1/DTD/xhtml1-transitional.dtd">
<html xmlns="http://www.w3.org/1999/xhtml"
      xmlns:p="http://primefaces.prime.com.tr/ui"
      xmlns:h="http://java.sun.com/jsf/html"
      xmlns:ui="http://java.sun.com/jsf/facelets"
      xmlns:f="http://java.sun.com/jsf/core">
   <ui:composition template="./template.xhtml">
      <ui:define name="top">
         <h2>Customer Information Data Entry</h2>
      </ui:define>

      <ui:define name="content">
         <h:form>
            <h:panelGrid columns="1" style="width: 100%">
```

```
<p:wizard>
    <p:tab title="Personal Information"
        id="personalInfo">
        <p:panel header="Personal Information">
            <p:messages/>
            <h:panelGrid columns="2">

                <h:outputLabel for="firstName"
                            value="First Name"

                        styleClass="requiredLbl"/>
                <h:inputText id="firstName"
                            label="First Name"
                            value="#{customer.
                            firstName}"
                            required="true"/>
                <h:outputLabel for="middleName"
                            value="Middle Name"

                        styleClass="optionalLbl"/>
                <h:inputText id="middleName"
                            label="Middle Name"
                            value="#{customer.
                            middleName}"
                            />
                <h:outputLabel for="lastName"
                            value="Last Name"

                        styleClass="requiredLbl"/>
                <h:inputText id="lastName"
                                label="Last Name"
                            value="#{customer.
                                    lastName}"
                            required="true"/>
                <h:outputLabel for="birthDate"
                            value="Date of
                                    Birth"

                        styleClass="optionalLbl"/>
                <p:calendar id="birthDate"
                            value="#{customer.
                            birthDate}"
                            showOn="button"

                        inputStyle="width:100px;"
```

```
                                                navigator="true"/>
                                </h:panelGrid>
                        </p:panel>
                </p:tab>

                <!-- Phone Number tab omitted for
brevity →

                <p:tab title="Confirmation" id="confirmation">
                        <p:messages/>
                        <h:panelGrid columns="2">
                                <h:outputText value="First Name"

                                        styleClass="optionalLbl"/>
                                <h:outputText id="firstNameTxt"
                                                value="#{customer.
                                                firstName}" />
                                <h:outputText value="Middle Name"

                                        styleClass="optionalLbl"/>
                                <h:outputText id="middleNameTxt"
                                                value="#{customer.
                                                middleName}"/>
                                <h:outputText  value="Last Name"

                                        styleClass="optionalLbl"/>
                                <h:outputText id="lastNameTxt"
                                                value="#{customer.
                                                lastName}" />
                                <h:outputText  value="Date of Birth"

                                        styleClass="optionalLbl"/>
                                <h:outputText id="birthDateTxt"
                                                value="#{customer.

                                                formattedBirthDate}" />
                                <h:outputText  value="Home Phone"

                                         styleClass="optionalLbl"/>
                                <h:outputText id="homePhoneTxt"
                                                value="#{customer.
                                                homePhone}" />
                                <h:outputText  value="Mobile Phone"

                                        styleClass="optionalLbl"/>
                                <h:outputText id="mobilePhoneTxt"
```

```
                                           value="#{customer.
                                           mobilePhone}" />
                          <h:outputText   value="Work Phone"

                          styleClass="optionalLbl"/>
                          <h:outputText id="workPhoneTxt"
                                        value="#{customer.
                                        workPhone}" />

                          <h:panelGroup/>
                          <h:inputHidden value="#{customer.
                          addrState}"/>
                          <p:commandButton id="submitButton"
                                           value="Submit"
                                           actionListener=

                          "#{customerController.saveCustomer}"
                                           ajax="false"/>
                      </h:panelGrid>
                  </p:tab>
              </p:wizard>
          </h:panelGrid>
        </h:form>
      </ui:define>
    </ui:composition>
  </html>
```

 Some of the wizard pages or "tabs" in the above example were omitted for brevity. Refer to the code download for this chapter for the complete listing.

As we can see, generating a wizard interface with PrimeFaces is easy. All we need to do is use the `<p:wizard>` component, then nest a `<p:tab>` component for each step in the wizard. Markup inside each `<p:tab>` component is standard JSF.

In the last tab, we added a `<p:commandButton>` component to submit the data to the server The value of the `actionListener` attribute of the `commandButton` is a method in our `CustomerController` managed bean.

```
package com.ensode.primefacesdemo.managedbeans;
import java.io.Serializable;
import javax.faces.bean.ManagedBean;
import javax.faces.bean.SessionScoped;
import javax.faces.event.ActionEvent;
import javax.faces.application.FacesMessage;
import javax.faces.context.FacesContext;
```

```
@ManagedBean
@SessionScoped
public class CustomerController implements Serializable {
    /** Creates a new instance of CustomerController */
    public CustomerController() {
    }
    public void saveCustomer(ActionEvent actionEvent) {
        //In a real application, we would save the data,
        //In this example we simply show a message.
        FacesMessage facesMessage = new FacesMessage(
          "Data Saved Successfully");
        facesMessage.setSeverity(FacesMessage.SEVERITY_INFO);
        FacesContext.getCurrentInstance().addMessage(null,
        facesMessage);
    }
}
```

As we can see, the `saveCustomer()` method simply adds a faces message that is displayed as a confirmation message in our page. In a real application, we of course would save the data to a database.

At this point we are ready to see the wizard component in action.

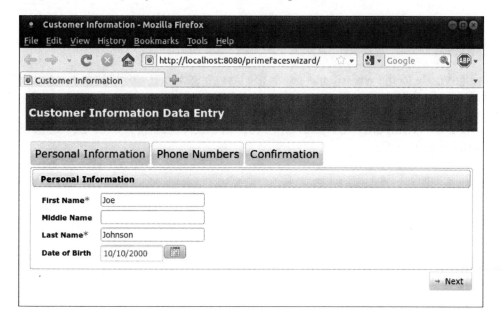

Notice that the wizard component automatically adds a **Next** button at the bottom right, clicking this button takes us to the next page in the wizard.

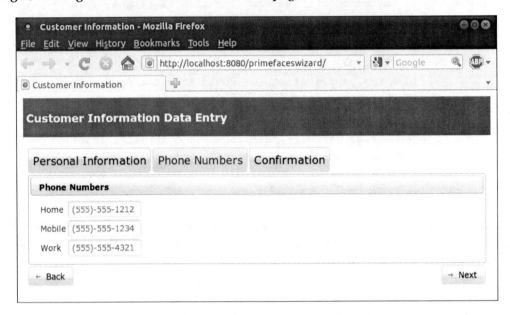

As expected, at this point the wizard component generates both a **Previous** and a **Next** button.

As we navigate to the wizard and reach the last page, when we click on the **Submit** button we see the confirmation message generated by the saveCustomer() method in our CustomerController managed bean. This message is rendered by the <p:messages> components, which takes care of nicely styling it without us having to explicitly use any CSS.

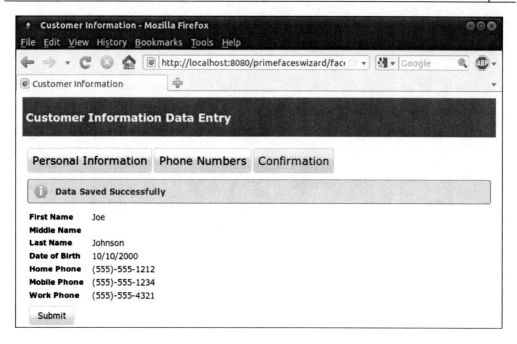

More information

In this chapter we only scratched the surface of the PrimeFaces' capabilities. A PrimeFaces component showcase, illustrating all PrimeFaces components can be found at `http://www.primefaces.org/showcase/ui/home.jsf`. For additional information on PrimeFaces, visit `http://www.primefaces.org`.

Summary

In this chapter we provided an introduction to the PrimeFaces JSF component library that has been included with NetBeans since version 7.0. We saw how PrimeFaces allows us to easily develop elegant looking, AJAX-enabled applications with little effort. Some of the major PrimeFaces components discussed include the Tab View component, which allows us to easily divide our pages into tabs. We also saw how to use the PrimeFaces wizard component, which allow us to easily create wizard like interfaces in our web applications.

6

Interacting with Databases through the Java Persistence API

The **Java Persistence API (JPA)** is an Object Relational Mapping API. Object Relational Mapping tools help us automate mapping Java objects to relational database tables. Earlier versions of J2EE used Entity Beans as the standard approach for Object Relational Mapping. Entity Beans attempted to keep the data in memory always synchronized with database data, a good idea in theory, however, in practice this feature resulted in poorly performing applications.

Several Object Relational Mapping APIs were developed to overcome the limitations of Entity Beans, such as Hibernate, iBatis, Cayenne, and Toplink among others.

With Java EE 5, Entity Beans were deprecated in favor of JPA. JPA took ideas from several object relational mapping tools and incorporated them into the standard. As we will see in this chapter NetBeans has several features that make development with JPA a breeze.

The following topics will be covered in this chapter:

- Creating our first JPA entity
- Interacting with JPA entities with EntityManager
- Generating forms in JSF pages from JPA entities
- Generating JPA entities from an existing database schema
- JPA named queries and JPQL
- Entity relationships
- Generating complete JSF applications from JPA entities

Creating our first JPA entity

JPA entities are Java classes whose fields are persisted to a database by the JPA API.
JPA entities are plain old Java objects (POJOs), as such, they don't need to extend any
specific parent class or implement any specific interface. A Java class is designated as
a JPA entity by decorating it with the `@Entity` annotation.

In order to create and test our first JPA entity, we will be creating a new web
application using the JavaServer Faces framework, in this example we will name
our application `jpaweb`, as with all of our examples, we will be using the bundled
GlassFish application server.

 Refer to Chapter 4 for instructions on creating a new JSF
project.

To create a new JPA Entity, from the new file dialog select the **Persistence** category
and **Entity Class** as the file type.

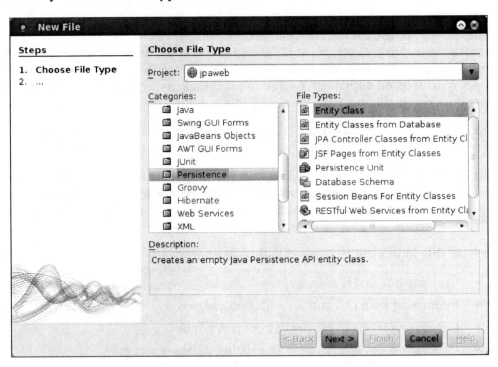

After doing so, NetBeans presents the **New Entity Class** wizard.

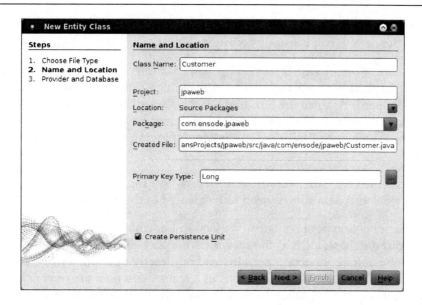

At this point, we should specify the values for the **Class Name** and **Package** fields
(`Customer` and `com.ensode.jpaweb` in our example).

Projects using JPA require a persistence unit. This persistence unit is defined in a
file called `persistence.xml`. When we create our first JPA entity for the project,
NetBeans detects that no `persistence.xml` exists and automatically checks the
checkbox labeled **Create Persistence Unit**. The next step in the wizard allows us to
enter the necessary information to create the persistence unit.

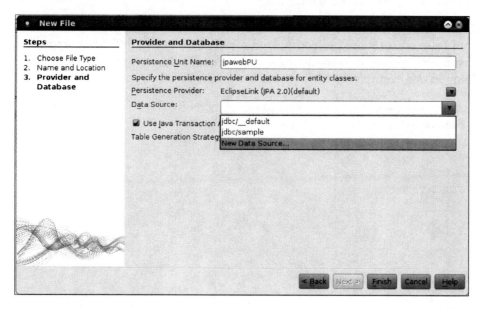

The **Create Persistence Unit** wizard will suggest a name for our persistence unit, in most cases the default can be safely accepted.

JPA is a specification for which several implementations exist. NetBeans supports several JPA implementations including EclipseLink, Toplink Essentials, Hibernate, KODO, and OpenJPA; since the bundled GlassFish application server includes EclipseLink as its default JPA implementation. It makes sense to take this default value for the **Persistence Provider** field when deploying our application to GlassFish.

Before we can interact with a database from any Java EE application, a database connection pool and data source need to be created in the application server.

A database connection pool contains connection information that allows us to connect to our database, such as the server name, port, and credentials. The advantage of using a connection pool instead of directly opening a JDBC connection to a database is that database connections in a connection pool are never closed, they are simply allocated to applications as they need them. This results in performance improvements since the operations of opening and closing database connections are expensive in terms of performance.

Data sources allow us to obtain a connection from a connection pool by obtaining an instance of `javax.sql.DataSource` via JNDI, then invoking its `getConnection()` method to obtain a database connection from a connection pool. When dealing with JPA, we don't need to directly obtain a reference to a data source, it is all done automatically by the JPA API, but we still need to indicate the data source to use in the application's Persistence Unit.

NetBeans comes with a few data sources and connection pools pre-configured, we could use one of these pre-configured resources for our application. However, NetBeans also allows us to create these resources "on the fly", which is what we will be doing in our example.

To create a new data source we need to select the **New Data Source...** item from the **Data Source** combo box.

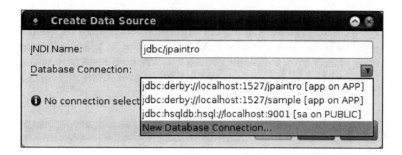

A data source needs to interact with a database connection pool. NetBeans comes preconfigured with a few connection pools out of the box, but just as with data sources, it allows us to create a new connection pool "on demand". In order to do this, we need to select the **New Database Connection...** item from the **Database Connection** combo box.

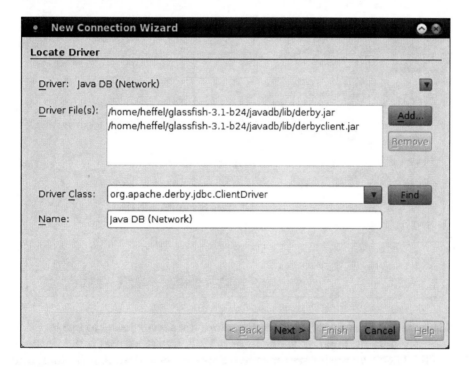

NetBeans includes JDBC drivers for a few **Relational Database Management Systems (RDBMS)** such as JavaDB, HSQLDB, MySQL, PostgreSQL and Oracle "out of the box". JavaDB is bundled with both GlassFish and NetBeans, therefore we picked JavaDB for our example, and this way we avoid having to install an external RDBMS.

For RDBMS systems that are not supported out-of-the-box, we need to obtain a JDBC driver and let NetBeans know of its location by selecting **New Driver** from the **Name** combo box. We then need to navigate to the location of a JAR file containing the JDBC driver. Consult your RDBMS documentation for details.

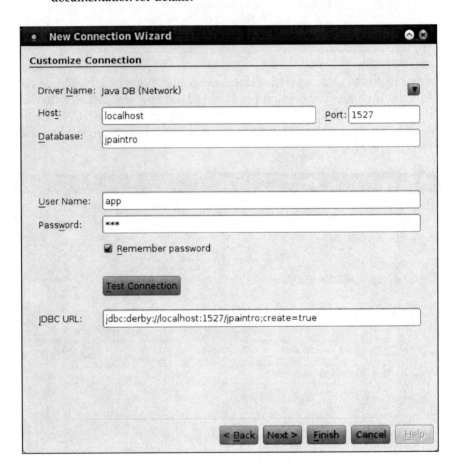

JavaDB is installed in our workstation, therefore the server name to use is `localhost`. By default, JavaDB listens to port 1527, therefore that is the port we specify in the URL. We wish to connect to a database called `jpaintro`, therefore we specify it as the database name. Since the `jpaintro` database does not exist yet, we pass the attribute `create=true` to JavaDB, this attribute is used to create the database if it doesn't exist yet. The user name and password we specify above will be automatically added to the newly created schema.

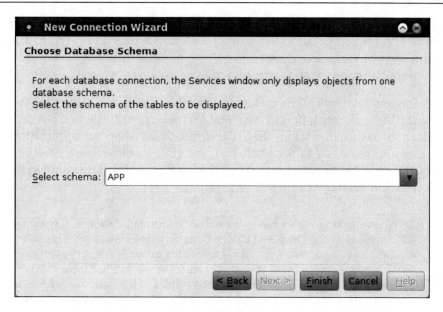

Every JavaDB database contains a schema named APP, since each user by default uses a schema named after his/her own login name. The easiest way to get going is to create a user named APP and select a password for this user.

Once we have created our new data source and connection pool, we can continue configuring our persistence unit.

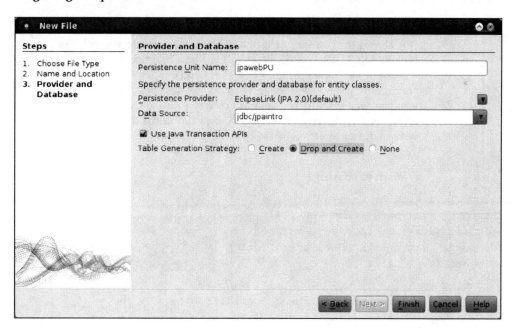

It is a good idea to leave the **Use Java Transaction APIs** checkbox checked. This will instruct our JPA implementation to use the **Java Transaction API (JTA)** to allow the application server to manage transactions. If we uncheck this box, we will need to manually write the code to manage transactions.

Most JPA implementations allow us to define a table generation strategy. We can instruct our JPA implementation to create tables for our entities when we deploy our application, to drop the tables then regenerate them when our application is deployed, or not create any tables at all. NetBeans allows us to specify the table generation strategy for our application by clicking the appropriate value in the **Table Generation Strategy** radio button group.

When working with a newly created development database, it is a good idea to select the **Drop and Create** table generation strategy. This will allow us to add, remove, and rename fields in our JPA entity at will without having to make the same changes in the database schema. When selecting this table generation strategy, tables in the database schema will be dropped and recreated every time we deploy our application, therefore any data previously persisted will be lost.

Once we have created our new data source, database connection, and persistence unit, we are ready to create our new JPA entity.

We can do so by simply clicking on the **Finish** button. At this point NetBeans generates the source for our JPA entity.

JPA allows the primary field of a JPA entity to map to any column type (VARCHAR, NUMBER, etc). It is a best practice to have a numeric surrogate primary key, that is, a primary key that serves only as an identifier and has no business meaning in the application. Selecting the default Primary Key Type of long will allow for a wide range of values to be available for the primary keys of our entities.

```
package com.ensode.jpaweb;

import java.io.Serializable;
import javax.persistence.Entity;
import javax.persistence.GeneratedValue;
import javax.persistence.GenerationType;
import javax.persistence.Id;

@Entity
public class Customer implements Serializable {
    private static final long serialVersionUID = 1L;
```

```
    @Id
    @GeneratedValue(strategy = GenerationType.AUTO)
    private Long id;

    public Long getId() {
        return id;
    }

    public void setId(Long id) {
        this.id = id;
    }

    //Other generated methods (equals(), hashCode(), toString())
  omitted for brevity
    }
```

As we can see, a JPA entity is a standard Java object, there is no need to extend any special class or implement any special interface. What differentiates a JPA entity from other Java objects are a few JPA-specific annotations.

The @Entity annotation is used to indicate that our class is a JPA entity. Any object we want to persist to a database via JPA must be annotated with this annotation.

The @Id annotation is used to indicate what field in our JPA entity is its primary key. The primary key is a unique identifier for our entity. No two entities may have the same value for their primary key field. This annotation can be placed just above the getter method for the primary key class, this is the strategy that the NetBeans wizard follows; it is also correct to specify the annotation right above the field declaration.

The @Entity and the @Id annotations are the bare minimum two annotations that a class needs in order to be considered a JPA entity. JPA allows primary keys to be automatically generated. In order to take advantage of this functionality, the @GeneratedValue annotation can be used, as we can see, the NetBeans generated JPA entity uses this annotation. This annotation is used to indicate the strategy to use to generate primary keys. All possible primary key generation strategies are listed in the following table:

Primary Key Generation Strategy	Description
GenerationType.AUTO	Indicates that the persistence provider will automatically select a primary key generation strategy. Used by default if no primary key generation strategy is specified.
GenerationType.IDENTITY	Indicates that an identity column in the database table the JPA entity maps to must be used to generate the primary key value.

Primary Key Generation Strategy	Description
GenerationType.SEQUENCE	Indicates that a database sequence should be used to generate the entity's primary key value.
GenerationType.TABLE	Indicates that a database table should be used to generate the entity's primary key value.

In most cases, the GenerationType.AUTO strategy works properly, therefore it is almost always used, for this reason the **New Entity Class** wizard uses this strategy.

 When using the sequence or table generation strategies, we might have to indicate the sequence or table used to generate the primary keys. These can be specified by using the @SequenceGenerator and @TableGenerator annotations, respectively. Consult the Java EE 6 JavaDoc at http://download.oracle.com/javaee/6/api/ for details.

Adding persistent fields to our entity

At this point, our JPA entity contains a single field, its primary key, admittedly not very useful. We need to add a few fields to be persisted to the database.

```
package com.ensode.jpaweb;

import java.io.Serializable;
import javax.persistence.Entity;
import javax.persistence.GeneratedValue;
import javax.persistence.GenerationType;
import javax.persistence.Id;

@Entity
public class Customer implements Serializable {
    private static final long serialVersionUID = 1L;
    @Id
    @GeneratedValue(strategy = GenerationType.AUTO)
    private Long id;
    private String firstName;
    private String lastName;

    public Long getId() {
        return id;
    }

    public void setId(Long id) {
        this.id = id;
    }

    public String getFirstName() {
```

```
        return firstName;
    }
    public void setFirstName(String firstName) {
        this.firstName = firstName;
    }
    public String getLastName() {
        return lastName;
    }
    public void setLastName(String lastName) {
        this.lastName = lastName;
    }
}
```

In this modified version of our JPA entity, we added two fields to be persisted to the database; firstName will be used to store the user's first name, lastName will be used to store the user's last name. JPA entities need to follow standard JavaBean coding conventions, this means that they must have a public constructor that takes no arguments (one is automatically generated by the Java compiler if we don't specify any other constructors), and all fields must be private, and accessed through **getter** and **setter** methods.

Automatically generating getters and setters

In NetBeans, getter and setter methods can be generated automatically, simply declare new fields as usual then use the "insert code" keyboard shortcut (default is *alt+insert*) then select **Getter and Setter** from the resulting pop up window, then click on the check box next to the class name to select all fields, then click on the **Generate** button.

Before we can use JPA persist our entity's fields into our database, we need to write some additional code.

Creating a DAO

It is a good idea to follow the **Data Access Object (DAO)** design pattern whenever we write code that interacts with a database. The DAO design patterns keep all database access functionality in DAO classes. This has the benefit of creating a clear separation of concerns, leaving other layers in our application, such as the user interface logic and the business logic, free of any persistence logic.

NetBeans can help us generate JPA controller classes from existing entities. These JPA controller classes follow the DAO design pattern. To generate a JPA controller class, we simply need to select the **Persistence** category and select the **JPA Controller Classes from Entity Classes** file type from the New File dialog.

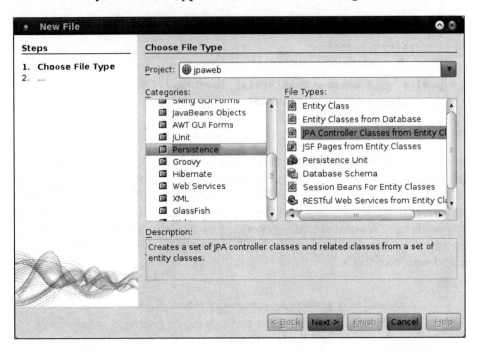

In the next step in the wizard, we need to select the entity classes we wish to generate JPA controller classes for.

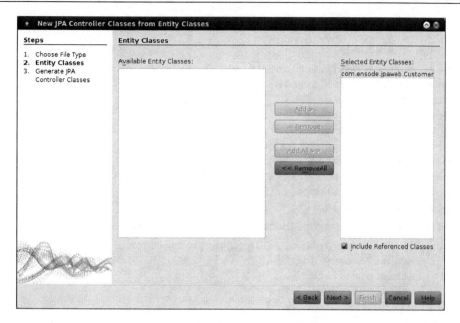

We then need to specify the project and package for our JPA controller classes.

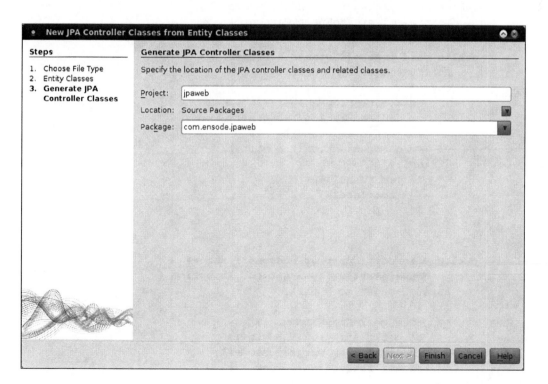

After clicking **Finish**, our JPA controller class is successfully generated.

```java
package com.ensode.jpaweb;

import com.ensode.jpaweb.exceptions.NonexistentEntityException;
import java.io.Serializable;
import java.util.List;
import javax.persistence.EntityManager;
import javax.persistence.EntityManagerFactory;
import javax.persistence.Query;
import javax.persistence.EntityNotFoundException;
import javax.persistence.criteria.CriteriaQuery;
import javax.persistence.criteria.Root;
import javax.transaction.UserTransaction;
public class CustomerJpaController implements Serializable {
    public CustomerJpaController(UserTransaction utx,
EntityManagerFactory emf) {
        this.utx = utx;
        this.emf = emf;
    }
    private UserTransaction utx = null;
    private EntityManagerFactory emf = null;

    public EntityManager getEntityManager() {
        return emf.createEntityManager();
    }
    public void create(Customer customer) {
        EntityManager em = null;
        try {
            em = getEntityManager();
            em.getTransaction().begin();
            em.persist(customer);
            em.getTransaction().commit();
        } finally {
            if (em != null) {
                em.close();
            }
        }
    }
    public void edit(Customer customer) throws
            NonexistentEntityException, Exception {
        EntityManager em = null;
        try {
            em = getEntityManager();
            em.getTransaction().begin();
            customer = em.merge(customer);
            em.getTransaction().commit();
```

```
    } catch (Exception ex) {
        String msg = ex.getLocalizedMessage();
        if (msg == null || msg.length() == 0) {
            Long id = customer.getId();
            if (findCustomer(id) == null) {
                throw new NonexistentEntityException(
                "The customer with id " + id +
                " no longer exists.");
            }
        }
        throw ex;
    } finally {
        if (em != null) {
            em.close();
        }
    }
}
public void destroy(Long id) throws NonexistentEntityException {
    EntityManager em = null;
    try {
        em = getEntityManager();
        em.getTransaction().begin();
        Customer customer;
        try {
            customer = em.getReference(Customer.class, id);
            customer.getId();
        } catch (EntityNotFoundException enfe) {
            throw new NonexistentEntityException("The customer
            with id " + id +
            " no longer exists.", enfe);
        }
        em.remove(customer);
        em.getTransaction().commit();
    } finally {
        if (em != null) {
            em.close();
        }
    }
}
public List<Customer> findCustomerEntities() {
    return findCustomerEntities(true, -1, -1);
}
public List<Customer> findCustomerEntities(int maxResults,
    int firstResult) {
    return findCustomerEntities(false, maxResults, firstResult);
}
```

```
        private List<Customer> findCustomerEntities(boolean all,
                int maxResults, int firstResult) {
            EntityManager em = getEntityManager();
            try {
                CriteriaQuery cq = em.getCriteriaBuilder().createQuery();
                cq.select(cq.from(Customer.class));
                Query q = em.createQuery(cq);
                if (!all) {
                    q.setMaxResults(maxResults);
                    q.setFirstResult(firstResult);
                }
                return q.getResultList();
            } finally {
                em.close();
            }
        }

        public Customer findCustomer(Long id) {
            EntityManager em = getEntityManager();
            try {
                return em.find(Customer.class, id);
            } finally {
                em.close();
            }
        }

        public int getCustomerCount() {
            EntityManager em = getEntityManager();
            try {
                CriteriaQuery cq = em.getCriteriaBuilder().createQuery();
                Root<Customer> rt = cq.from(Customer.class);
                cq.select(em.getCriteriaBuilder().count(rt));
                Query q = em.createQuery(cq);
                return ((Long) q.getSingleResult()).intValue();
            } finally {
                em.close();
            }
        }
    }
```

As we can see, NetBeans generates methods to create, read, update, and delete JPA entities.

The method to create a new entity is called `create()`, it takes an instance of our JPA entity as its sole argument. This method simply invokes the `persist()` method on `EntityManager`, that takes care of persisting the data on the JPA entity to the database.

For reading, several methods are generated, the `findCustomer()` method takes the primary key of the JPA entity we wish to retrieve as its sole parameter, then invokes the `find()` method on `EntityManager` to retrieve the data from the database and returns an instance of our JPA entity. Several overloaded versions of the `findCustomerEntities()` method are generated, these methods allow us to retrieve more than one JPA entity from the database. The version of this method that does all the "real work" is the one containing the following signature:

```
private List<Customer> findCustomerEntities(boolean all, int
maxResults, int firstResult)
```

The first parameter is a Boolean that we can use to indicate if we want to retrieve all values in the database. The second parameter allows us to specify the maximum number of results we wish to retrieve, and the last parameter allows us to indicate the first result we wish to retrieve. This method uses the Criteria API that was introduced in JPA 2.0 to build a query programmatically. If the value of the `all` parameter is false, then this method sets the maximum number of results and the first results by passing the appropriate parameters to the `setMaxResults()` and `setFirstResult()` method in the Query object.

The method to update existing entities is called `edit()`, it takes an instance of our JPA entity as its sole parameter. This method invokes the `merge()` method on `EntityManager`, which updates the data in the database with the data in the JPA entity it receives as a parameter.

The method to delete an entity is called `destroy()`, it takes the primary key of the object to delete as its sole parameter. It first checks to see if the object exists in the database, if it doesn't, this method throws an exception, otherwise, it deletes the corresponding row from the database by invoking the `remove()` method on `EntityManager`.

At this point we have all the code we need to persist our entity's properties in the database, all we need to do to perform CRUD operations involving our JPA entity is invoke methods on the generated JPA controller from our code.

Automated Generation of JPA Entities

In many projects, we will be working with an existing database schema created by a database administrator. NetBeans can generate JPA entities from an existing database schema, saving us a lot of potentially tedious work.

In this section, we will be using a custom database schema, in order to create the schema, we need to execute an SQL script that will create the schema and populate some of its tables. In order to do this, we need to go to the **Services** window, right-click on **JavaDB**, then select **Create Database....**

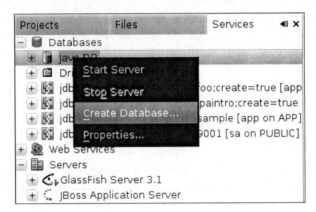

We then need to add the database information in the **Create Java DB Database** wizard.

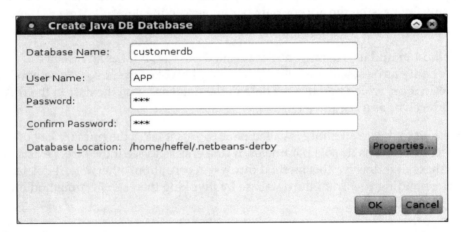

At this point, we can open the SQL script by going to **File | Open File...**, then navigating to its location on our disk and opening it.

> The file name of our script is `create_populate_tables.sql`, it is included as part of the source bundle for this chapter.

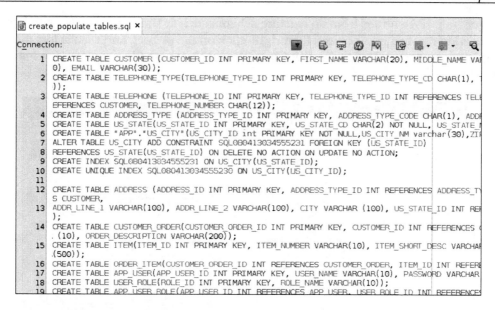

Once we have opened the SQL script, we need to select our newly created connection from the **Connection** combo box, then click on the following icon to execute it:

Our database will now have a number of tables.

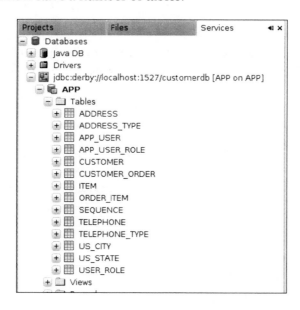

To generate JPA entities from an existing schema such as the one we just created, we need to create a new project, then right-click on the project, and then select the **Persistence** category and the **Entity Classes from Database** file type from the **New File** dialog.

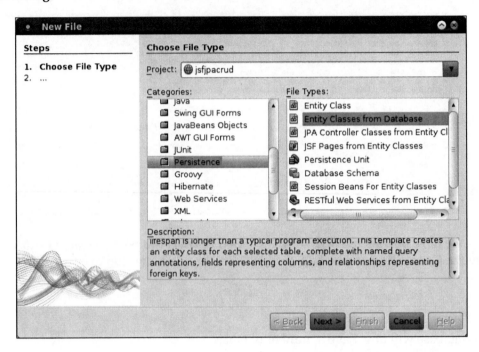

 NetBeans allows us to generate JPA entities from pretty much any kind of Java project, in our example we will be using a Web Application project.

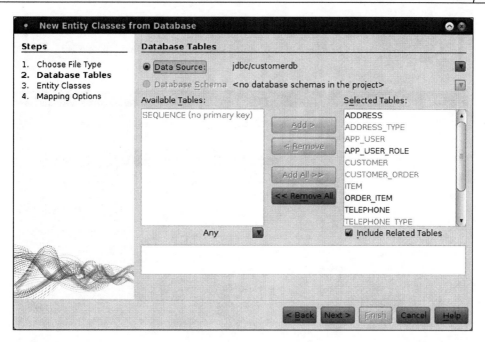

At this point we can either select an existing data source, or, as we did in the previous example, create one "on the fly". In our example we created a new one, then selected the database connection we created earlier in this section.

Once we have created or selected our data source, we need to select one or more tables to generate our JPA entities. If we wish to create JPA entities for all tables, we can simply click on the **Add All>>** button.

After clicking on **Next>**, NetBeans gives us the opportunity to change the names of the generated classes, although the defaults tend to be sensible. We should also specify a package for our classes, and it is a good idea to check the **Generate Named Query Annotations for Persistent Fields** checkbox. We can also optionally generate **JAXB (Java API for XML Binding)** annotations and create a persistence unit.

Named Queries are explained in detail in the next subsection.

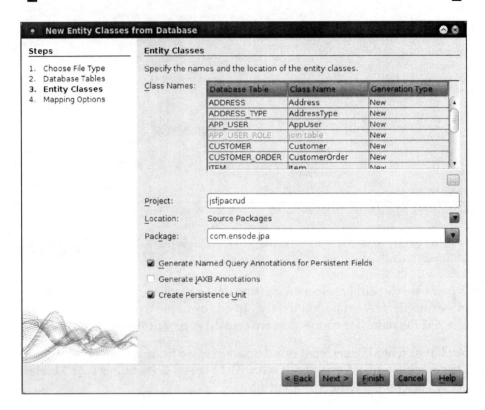

In the next screen in the wizard, we can select how associated entities will be fetched (eagerly or lazily), by default. The default behavior is selected, which is to fetch "one to one" and "many to one" relationships eagerly, and "one to many" and "many to many" relationships lazily.

Additionally, we can select what collection type to use for the "many" side of a "one to many" or "many to many" relationship. The default value is `java.util. Collection`, other valid values are `java.util.List` and `java.util.Set`.

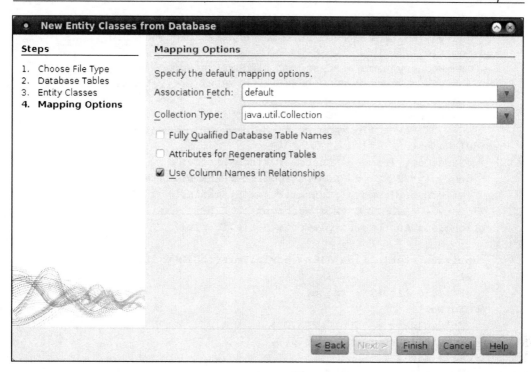

Checking the **Fully Qualified Database Table Names** checkbox results in adding the catalog and schema elements of the table being mapped to the @Table annotation for each generated entity.

Checking the **Attributes for Regenerating Tables** results in the generated @Column annotations having attributes such as length, which specifies the maximum length allowed in the column; nullable, which specifies if null values are allowed in the column; precision and scale, which specify the precision and scale of decimal values, respectively. Checking this attribute also adds the uniqueConstraints attribute to the generated @Table annotation to specify any unique constraints that apply to the table, if necessary. When clicking on **Finish**, NetBeans generates JPA entities for all tables in the database. Our database contained a table named CUSTOMER table, let's take a look at the generated Customer JPA entity.

```java
package com.ensode.jpa;

//imports removed for brevity
@Entity
@Table(name = "CUSTOMER")
@NamedQueries({
    @NamedQuery(name = "Customer.findAll",
    query = "SELECT c FROM Customer c"),
```

```
    @NamedQuery(name = "Customer.findByCustomerId",
    query = "SELECT c FROM Customer c WHERE c.customerId =
:customerId"),
    @NamedQuery(name = "Customer.findByFirstName",
    query = "SELECT c FROM Customer c WHERE c.firstName =
:firstName"),
    @NamedQuery(name = "Customer.findByMiddleName",
    query = "SELECT c FROM Customer c WHERE c.middleName =
:middleName"),
    @NamedQuery(name = "Customer.findByLastName",
    query = "SELECT c FROM Customer c WHERE c.lastName = :lastName"),
    @NamedQuery(name = "Customer.findByEmail",
    query = "SELECT c FROM Customer c WHERE c.email = :email")})
public class Customer implements Serializable {

    private static final long serialVersionUID = 1L;
    @Id
    @Basic(optional = false)
    @NotNull
    @Column(name = "CUSTOMER_ID")
    private Integer customerId;
    @Size(max = 20)
    @Column(name = "FIRST_NAME")
    private String firstName;
    @Size(max = 20)
    @Column(name = "MIDDLE_NAME")
    private String middleName;
    @Size(max = 20)
    @Column(name = "LAST_NAME")
    private String lastName;
    //@Pattern(regexp="[a-z0-9!#$%&'*+/=?^_`{|}~-]+(?:\\.
[a-z0-9!#$%&'*+/=?^_`{|}~-]+)*@(?:[a-z0-9](?:[a-z0-9-]*[a-z0-
9])?\\.)+[a-z0-9](?:[a-z0-9-]*[a-z0-9])?", message="Invalid email")//
if the field contains email address consider using this annotation to
enforce field validation
    @Size(max = 30)
    @Column(name = "EMAIL")
    private String email;
    @OneToMany(mappedBy = "customerId")
    private Collection<CustomerOrder> customerOrderCollection;
    @OneToMany(mappedBy = "customerId")
    private Collection<Address> addressCollection;
    @OneToMany(mappedBy = "customerId")
    private Collection<Telephone> telephoneCollection;

    //Constructors, getters, setters and other automatically generated
```

```
        //methods (equals,() hashCode() and toString() omitted for
    brevity.
    }
```

As we can see, NetBeans generates a class decorated with the `@Entity` annotation, that marks the class as a JPA entity. Notice that NetBeans automatically decorated one of the fields with the `@Id` annotation, based on the primary key constraint in the table used to generate the JPA entity. Notice that no primary key generation strategy is used, we either need to populate the primary key ourselves, or add the `@GeneratedValue` annotation manually.

Notice the `@Table` annotation, this is an optional annotation that indicates what table our JPA entity maps to. If the `@Table` annotation is not used, then our entity will map to a table having the same name as the entity class (case insensitive). In our particular example, the `@Table` annotation is redundant, but there are cases where it is useful. For example, some database schemas have tables named in plural (i.e. CUSTOMERS), but it makes sense to name our entities in singular (`Customer`). Additionally, the standard naming convention for database tables containing more than one word is to use underscores to separate words (i.e. CUSTOMER_ORDER) where in Java the standard is to use camel case (i.e. `CustomerOrder`), the `@Table` annotation allows us to follow established naming standards in both the relational database and the Java worlds.

Named Queries and JPQL

Next, we see the `@NamedQueries` annotation (this annotation is only generated if we click on the **Generate Named Query Annotations for Persistent Fields** checkbox of the **New Entity Classes from Database** wizard). This query contains a `value` attribute (the attribute name can be omitted from the code since it is the only attribute in this annotation). The value of this attribute is an array of `@NamedQuery` annotations, the `@NamedQuery` annotation has a `name` attribute, which is used to give it a logical name (by convention, the JPA entity name is used as part of the query name, as we can see in the generated code, the **New Entity Classes from Database** wizard follows this convention), and a `query` attribute, which is used to define a **Java Persistence Query Language (JPQL)** query to be executed by the named query. JPQL is a JPA-specific query language, its syntax is similar to SQL. The **New Entity Classes from Database** wizard generates a JPQL query for each field in our entity. When the query is executed, a `List` containing all instances of our entity that match the criteria in the query will be returned. The following code snippet illustrates this process.

```
    import java.util.List;
    import javax.persistence.EntityManager;
    import javax.persistence.Query;

    public class CustomerDAO {
```

```
public List findCustomerByLastName(String someLastName)
{
  //code to lookup EntityManager omitted for brevity
  Query query =
      em.createNamedQuery("Customer.findByLastName");
  query.setParameter("lastName", someLastName);
  List resultList = query.getResultList();
  return resultList;
  }
}
```

Here we see a DAO object containing a method that will return a list of `Customer` entities for customers whose last name equals the one provided in the method's parameter. In order to implement this, we need to obtain an instance of an object of type `javax.pesistence.Query`, as we can see in the above code snippet, this can be accomplished by invoking the `createNamedQuery()` method in `EntityManager`, passing the query name (as defined in the `@NamedQuery` annotation) as a parameter. Notice that the named queries generated by the NetBeans wizard contain strings preceded by a colon (:). These strings are **named parameters**, named parameters are "placeholders" we can use to substitute for appropriate values.

In our example, we set the `lastName` named parameter in JPQL query with the `someLastName` argument passed to our method.

Once we have populated all parameters in our query, we can obtain a `List` of all matching entities by invoking the `getResultList()` method in our `Query` object.

Going back to our generated JPA entity, notice that the wizard automatically placed the `@Id` annotation in the field mapping to the table's primary key. Additionally, each field is decorated with the `@Column` annotation, which allows us to follow standard naming conventions in both the relational database and Java worlds. In addition to allowing us to specify what column each field maps to, the `@Column` annotation has a `nullable` attribute that allows us to specify if the column accepts null values or not. As we can see, the wizard automatically sets `nullable` to `false` for the entity's primary key field.

Bean Validation

Bean validation, comes from Java Specification Request (JSR) 303, is a new addition to the Java EE specification. Bean validation is implemented as a set of annotations in the `javax.validation` package. The NetBeans JPA generation wizard takes full advantage of Bean Validation, adding Bean Validation annotations to any appropriate fields based on the column definitions of the tables we are using to generate our entities.

In our `Customer` entity, we see some Bean Validation annotations. The `customerId` field is decorated with the `@NotNull` annotation, which, as its name implies, prevents the field from accepting a null value.

Several fields in the `Customer` entity are decorated with the `@Size` annotation. This annotation specifies the maximum number of characters a bean's property may accept. Again the NetBeans wizard obtains this information from the tables used to generate our entity.

Another Bean Validation annotation we can use is the `@Pattern` annotation. This annotation is meant to make sure that the value of the decorated field matches a given regular expression.

Notice that right above the `email` property of the `Customer` annotation, the wizard added the `@Pattern` annotation and commented it out. The reason for this is that the wizard noticed that the name of the table column was `EMAIL`, and suspected (but couldn't verify), that this table is meant to store email addresses. Therefore the wizard added the annotation with a regular expression used to match email addresses, but since it couldn't be sure that this table is indeed meant to store email addresses, it commented out this line of code. This property is indeed meant to store email addresses, therefore we should uncomment this automatically generated line.

Entity Relationships

There are several annotations we can use in JPA entities to define relationships between them. In our `Customer` entity shown above, we can see that the wizard detected several one to many relationships in the `CUSTOMER` table, and automatically added the `@OneToMany` annotation to define these relationships in our entity. Notice that each field annotated with the `@OneToMany` annotation is of type `java.util.Collection`, the `Customer` is the "one" side of the relationship, since a customer can have many orders, many addresses (street, mail, etc), or many telephone numbers (home, work, cell, etc.). Notice that the wizard uses generics to specify the type of objects we can add to each collection. Objects in these collections are the JPA entities mapping to the corresponding tables in our database schema.

Notice that @OneToMany annotation has a mappedBy attribute, this attribute is necessary since each of these relationships is bi-directional (we can access all addresses for a customer, and for a given address, we can obtain what customer it belongs to). The value of this attribute must match the name of the field on the other side of the relationship. Let's take a look at the Address entity to illustrate the other side of the customer-address relationship.

```
package com.ensode.jpa;

//imports omitted for brevity

@Entity
@Table(name = "ADDRESS")
@NamedQueries({
    @NamedQuery(name = "Address.findAll",
    query = "SELECT a FROM Address a"),
    @NamedQuery(name = "Address.findByAddressId",
    query = "SELECT a FROM Address a WHERE a.addressId = :addressId"),
    @NamedQuery(name = "Address.findByAddrLine1",
    query = "SELECT a FROM Address a WHERE a.addrLine1 = :addrLine1"),
    @NamedQuery(name = "Address.findByAddrLine2",
    query = "SELECT a FROM Address a WHERE a.addrLine2 = :addrLine2"),
    @NamedQuery(name = "Address.findByCity",
    query = "SELECT a FROM Address a WHERE a.city = :city"),
    @NamedQuery(name = "Address.findByZip",
    query = "SELECT a FROM Address a WHERE a.zip = :zip")})
public class Address implements Serializable {

    private static final long serialVersionUID = 1L;
    @Id
    @Basic(optional = false)
    @NotNull
    @Column(name = "ADDRESS_ID")
    private Integer addressId;
    @Size(max = 100)
    @Column(name = "ADDR_LINE_1")
    private String addrLine1;
    @Size(max = 100)
    @Column(name = "ADDR_LINE_2")
    private String addrLine2;
    @Size(max = 100)
    @Column(name = "CITY")
    private String city;
    @Size(max = 5)
    @Column(name = "ZIP")
    private String zip;
```

```
@JoinColumn(name = "US_STATE_ID",
referencedColumnName = "US_STATE_ID")
@ManyToOne
private UsState usStateId;
@JoinColumn(name = "CUSTOMER_ID",
referencedColumnName = "CUSTOMER_ID")
@ManyToOne
private Customer customerId;
@JoinColumn(name = "ADDRESS_TYPE_ID",
referencedColumnName = "ADDRESS_TYPE_ID")
@ManyToOne
private AddressType addressTypeId;

//constructors, getters, setters, equals(), hashCode() and
toString()
//methods deleted for brevity.
}
```

Notice that the `Address` entity has a `customerId` field, this field is of type `Customer`, the entity we were just discussing.

 We admit that a more appropriate name for this field would have been customer, the **New Entity Classes** from Database names the field based on the column name in the database. This is one small disadvantage of using the wizard to generate JPA entities. Of course we are free to rename the field and the corresponding getter and setter methods, additionally; we would have to change the value of the `mappedBy` attribute of the `@OneToMany` annotation on the other side of the relationship.

Noticed that the field is decorated with a `@ManyToOne` annotation. This annotation marks the "many" side of the one to many relationship between `Customer` and `Address`. Notice that the field is also decorated with the `@JoinColumn` annotation. The `name` attribute of this annotation indicates the column in the database our entity maps to that defines the foreign key constraint between the `ADDRESS` and `CUSTOMER` tables. The `referencedColumnName` attribute of `@JoinColumn` is use to indicate the primary key column of the table on the "one" side of the relationship (`CUSTOMER`, in our case).

In addition to one-to-many and many-to-one relationships, JPA provides annotations to denote many-to-many, and one-to-one relationships. In our schema, we have many-to-many relationships between the `CUSTOMER_ORDER` and `ITEM` tables, since an order can have many items, and an item can belong to many orders.

The table to hold orders was named CUSTOMER_ORDER since the word "ORDER" is a reserved word in SQL.

Let's take a look at the CustomerOrder JPA entity to see how the many-to-many relationship is defined:

```java
package com.ensode.jpa;

//imports deleted for brevity
@Entity
@Table(name = "CUSTOMER_ORDER")
@NamedQueries({
    @NamedQuery(name = "CustomerOrder.findAll",
    query = "SELECT c FROM CustomerOrder c"),
    @NamedQuery(name = "CustomerOrder.findByCustomerOrderId",
    query = "SELECT c FROM CustomerOrder c WHERE "
    + "c.customerOrderId = :customerOrderId"),
    @NamedQuery(name = "CustomerOrder.findByOrderNumber",
    query = "SELECT c FROM CustomerOrder c WHERE "
    + "c.orderNumber = :orderNumber"),
    @NamedQuery(name = "CustomerOrder.findByOrderDescription",
    query = "SELECT c FROM CustomerOrder c WHERE "
    + "c.orderDescription = :orderDescription")})
public class CustomerOrder implements Serializable {
    private static final long serialVersionUID = 1L;
    @Id
    @Basic(optional = false)
    @NotNull
    @Column(name = "CUSTOMER_ORDER_ID")
    private Integer customerOrderId;
    @Size(max = 10)
    @Column(name = "ORDER_NUMBER")
    private String orderNumber;
    @Size(max = 200)
    @Column(name = "ORDER_DESCRIPTION")
    private String orderDescription;
    @JoinTable(name = "ORDER_ITEM", joinColumns = {
        @JoinColumn(name = "CUSTOMER_ORDER_ID",
        referencedColumnName = "CUSTOMER_ORDER_ID")},
    inverseJoinColumns = {
        @JoinColumn(name = "ITEM_ID",
        referencedColumnName = "ITEM_ID")})
    @ManyToMany
```

```
    private Collection<Item> itemCollection;
    @JoinColumn(name = "CUSTOMER_ID",
    referencedColumnName = "CUSTOMER_ID")
    @ManyToOne
    private Customer customerId;

    //constructors, getters, setters, equals(), hashCode(), toString()
    //omitted for brevity
}
```

Notice that the `CustomerOrder` entity has a property of type `java.util.Collection` named `itemCollection`. This property holds all items for the order. Notice that the field is decorated with the `@ManyToMany` annotation, this annotation is used to declare a many-to-many relationship between the `CustomerOrder` and `Item` JPA entities. Notice that the field is also annotated with the `@JoinTable` annotation, this annotation is necessary since a join table is necessary in a database schema whenever there is a many-to-many relationship between tables. Using a join table allows us to keep the data in the database normalized.

The `@JoinTable` annotation allows us to specify the table in the schema that is used to denote the many-to-many relationship in the schema. The value of the `name` attribute of `@JoinTable` must match the name of the join table in the schema. The value of the `joinColumns` attribute of `@JoinColumn` must be the foreign key relationship between the join table and the owning side of the relationship. We already discussed the `@JoinColumn` annotation when discussing one-to-many relationships. In this case, its `name` attribute must match the name of the column in the join table that has the foreign key relationship, and its `referencedColumnName` attribute must indicate the name of the primary key column on the owning side of the relationship. The value of the `inverseJoinColumns` attribute of `@JoinTable` has a similar role as its `joinColumns` attribute, except it indicates the corresponding columns for the non-owning side of the relationship.

The side of the many-to-many relationship containing the above annotations is said to be the **owning side** of the relationship. Let's look at how the many-to-many relationship is defined in the non-owning side of the relationship, which, in our case is the `Item` JPA entity.

```
package com.ensode.jpa;

//imports omitted for brevity

@Entity
@Table(name = "ITEM")
@NamedQueries({
    @NamedQuery(name = "Item.findAll",
    query = "SELECT i FROM Item i"),
    @NamedQuery(name = "Item.findByItemId",
```

```
        query = "SELECT i FROM Item i WHERE "
        + "i.itemId = :itemId"),
        @NamedQuery(name = "Item.findByItemNumber",
        query = "SELECT i FROM Item i WHERE "
        + "i.itemNumber = :itemNumber"),
        @NamedQuery(name = "Item.findByItemShortDesc",
        query = "SELECT i FROM Item i WHERE "
        + "i.itemShortDesc = :itemShortDesc"),
        @NamedQuery(name = "Item.findByItemLongDesc",
        query = "SELECT i FROM Item i WHERE "
        + "i.itemLongDesc = :itemLongDesc")})
    public class Item implements Serializable {
        private static final long serialVersionUID = 1L;
        @Id
        @Basic(optional = false)
        @NotNull
        @Column(name = "ITEM_ID")
        private Integer itemId;
        @Size(max = 10)
        @Column(name = "ITEM_NUMBER")
        private String itemNumber;
        @Size(max = 100)
        @Column(name = "ITEM_SHORT_DESC")
        private String itemShortDesc;
        @Size(max = 500)
        @Column(name = "ITEM_LONG_DESC")
        private String itemLongDesc;
        @ManyToMany(mappedBy = "itemCollection")
        private Collection<CustomerOrder> customerOrderCollection;

        //constructors, getters, setters, equals() and hashCode()
        //methods omitted for brevity.
    }
```

As we can see, the only thing we need to do on this side of the relationship is to create a `Collection` property, decorate it with the `@ManyToMany` annotation, and specify the property name in the other side of the relationship as the value of its `mappedBy` attribute.

In addition to one-to-many and many-to-many relationships, it is possible to create one-to-one relationships between JPA entities.

The annotation to use to indicate a one-to-one relationship between two JPA entities is @OneToOne. Our schema doesn't have any one-to-one relationship between tables, therefore this annotation was not added to any of the entities generated by the wizard.

 One-to-one relationships are not very popular in database schemas, all data in a single entity is typically kept in a single table, since nevertheless JPA supports one-to-one relationships in case it is needed.

The procedure to indicate a one-to-one relationship between two entities is similar to what we have already seen. The owning side of the relationship must have a field of the type of the JPA entity at the other side of the relationship, this field must be decorated with the @OneToOne and @JoinColumn annotations.

Suppose we had a schema in which a one-to-one relationship was defined between two tables named PERSON and BELLY_BUTTON, this is a one-to-one relationship since each person has one belly button and each belly button belongs to only one person (the reason the schema was modeled this way instead of having the columns relating to the BELLY_BUTTON table in the PERSON table escapes me, but bear with me, I'm having a hard time coming up with a good example!).

```
@Entity
public class Person implements Serializable {
  @JoinColumn(name="BELLY_BUTTON_ID")
  @OneToOne
  private BellyButton bellyButton;

  public BellyButton getBellyButton(){
    return bellyButton;
  }

  public void setBellyButton(BellyButton bellyButton){
    this.bellyButton = bellyButton;
  }
}
```

If the one-to-one relationship is **unidirectional** (we can only get the belly button from the person), this would be all we have to do. If the relationship is **bidirectional**, then we need to add the @OneToOne annotation on the other side of the relationship, and use its mappedBy attribute to indicate the other side of the relationship.

```
@Entity
@Table(name="BELLY_BUTTON")
public class BellyButton implements Serializable(
```

```
{
  @OneToOne (mappedBy="bellyButton")
  private Person person;

  public Person getPerson() {
    return person;
  }
  public void getPerson(Person person) {
    this.person=person;
  }
}
```

As we can see, the procedure to establish one-to-one relationships is very similar to the procedure that is used to establish one-to-many and many-to-many relationships.

Once we have generated JPA entities from a database, we need to write additional code containing business and presentation logic, alternatively, we can use NetBeans to generate code for these two layers.

Generating JSF applications from JPA entities

One very nice feature of NetBeans is that it allows us to generate JSF applications that will perform **Create, Read, Update, and Delete (CRUD)** operations from existing JPA entities. This feature, combined with the ability to create JPA entities from an existing database schema as described in the previous section, allows us to write web applications that interact with a database in record time.

To generate JSF pages from existing JPA entities, we need to right-click on the project, select **File | New File**, then select the **JavaServer Faces** category and the **JSF Pages from Entity Classes** file type.

 In order for us to be able to generate JSF pages from existing JPA entities, the current project must be a Web Application project.

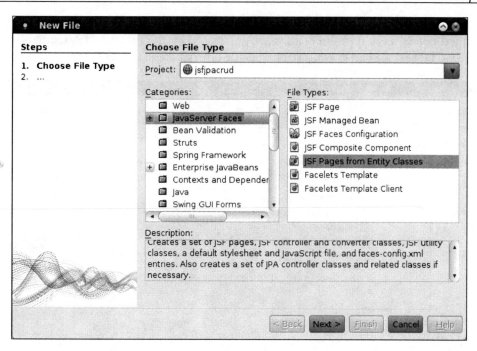

After clicking on **Next>**, we need to select one or more JPA entities. We would typically want to select all of them, they can easily be selected by clicking on the **Add All>>** button.

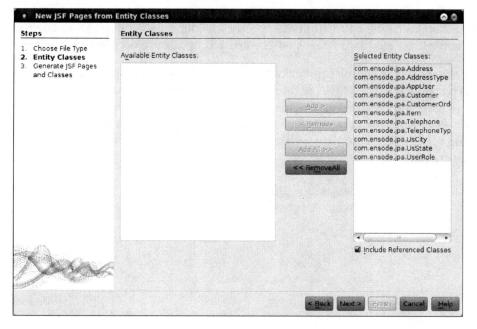

The next page in the wizard allows us to specify a package for newly created JSF managed beans. Two types of classes are generated by the wizard, **JPA Controllers** and **JSF Classes**, we can specify packages for both of these individually.

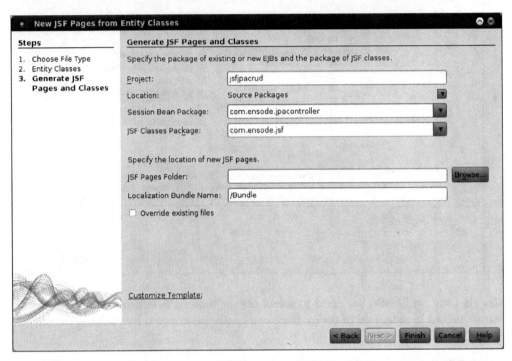

We are also given the opportunity to specify a folder for the JSF pages to be created, if we leave this field blank, pages will be created in our project's **Web Pages** folder.

The value of the **Session Bean Package** and **JSF Classes Package** text fields default to the package where our JPA entities reside. It is a good idea to modify this default since placing the JSF managed beans in a different package separates the data access layer classes from the user interface and controller layers of our application. After clicking on **Finish**, a complete web application that can perform CRUD operations will be created.

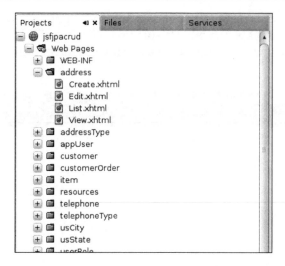

As we can see, NetBeans generates a folder for each of our entities under the **Web Pages** folder of our application. Each of the folders has a **Detail**, **Edit**, **List**, and **New** XHTML files. These files are JSF pages using Facelets as their view technology. The **Detail** page will display all properties for a JPA entity, the **Edit** page will allow users to update information for a specific entity, the **List** page will display all instances of a specific entity in the database, and the **New** page will provide functionality to create new entities.

The generated application is a standard JSF application. We can execute it by simply right-clicking on the project and selecting **Run**. At that point the usual things happen, the application server is started if it wasn't up already, the application is deployed, and a web browser window is opened displaying the welcome page for our application.

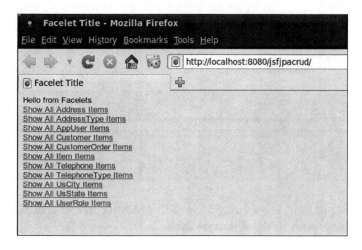

As we can see, the welcome page contains a link corresponding to each of our JPA entities. The links will display a table displaying all existing instances of our entity in the database. When we click on the **Show All Customer Items**, the following page is shown:

Since we haven't inserted any data to the database yet, the page displays the message **(No Customer Items Found)**. We can insert a customer into the database by clicking on the **Create New Customer** link.

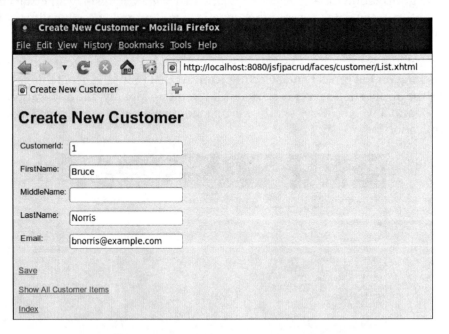

Notice how an input field is generated for each property in our entity, which in turn corresponds to a column in the database table.

As we can see, an input field was generated for the primary key field of our entity. This field is only generated if the JPA entity does not use a primary key generation strategy.

After entering some information on the page and clicking on the **Save** link, the data is saved, or the form is cleared and the message **Customer was successfully created.** is shown.

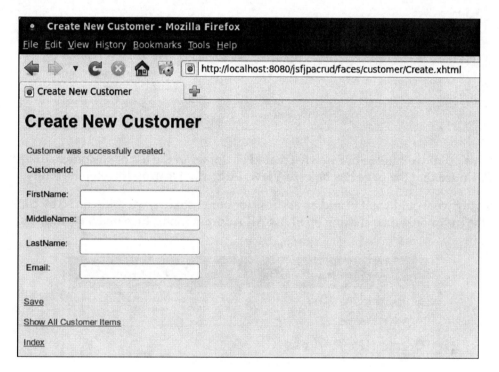

We can see our newly created customer by clicking on **Show All Customer Items**.

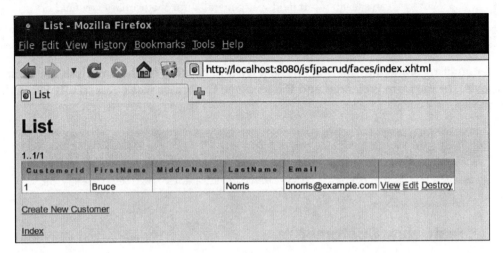

At this point we can see our newly created customer in the list of customers on this JSP. Notice that the page has links to **View**, **Edit**, and **Destroy** (delete) the entity.

Let's say we would want to add an address for our customer, we could do so by clicking on the **Index** link, then clicking on **Show All Address Items**, then on **New Address**.

The `Address` entity is at the "one" end of several one-to-many relationships, notice how a combo box is generated for each one of the entities at the "many" end. Since we wish to assign this address to the customer we just added, we attempt to select a customer from the **CustomerId** combo box.

 A better name could be used for the **CustomerId** field, the reason this is the label for the combo box is because it matches the property name on the `Address` JPA entity, which in turn could have a better name such as `customer`. Recall that all entities on this project were automatically generated from an existing database schema.

Clicking on the combo box reveals a cryptic, almost undecipherable (from the users' point of view anyway) label for our customer. The reason we see this label is because the labels generated for each item in the combo box come from the `toString()` method of the entities used to populate it. We can work around this issue by modifying the `toString()` method so that it returns a user-friendly `String` suitable to use as a label.

As we can see, the generated code from NetBeans wizards could certainly use some tweaking, such as modifying the `toString()` methods of each JPA entity so that it can be used as a label, modifying some of the property names on the entities so that they make more sense to us developers, modifying the labels on the generated JSF pages so that they are more user-friendly, and last but not least, the pages themselves are not very visually appealing. It would be a good idea to modify them so that they don't look so plain. Nevertheless, as we can see we can have a fully working application completely created by a few clicks of the mouse. This functionality certainly saves us a lot of time and effort (just don't tell your boss about it).

Summary

In this chapter, we saw the many ways in which NetBeans can help us speed up development of applications taking advantage of the Java Persistence API (JPA).

We saw how NetBeans can generate new JPA classes with all required annotations already in place.

Additionally, we covered how NetBeans can automatically generate code to persist a JPA entity to a database table.

We also covered how NetBeans can generate JPA entities from an existing database schema, including the automated generation of JPQL named queries and validation.

Finally, we saw how NetBeans can generate a complete JSF application from existing JPA entities.

7
Implementing the Business Tier with Session Beans

Most enterprise applications have a number of common requirements such as transactions, security, scalability, and so forth. **Enterprise JavaBeans (EJBs)** allow application developers to focus on implementing business logic, while not having to worry about implementing these requirements. There are two types of EJBs, Session Beans and Message-Driven Beans. In this chapter we will be discussing Session Beans, this type of EJB greatly simplify server side business logic implementation. In the next chapter we will discuss Message-Driven Beans, which allow us to easily implement messaging functionality in our applications.

 Previous versions of J2EE included Entity Beans as well, as of Java EE 5, Entity Beans have been deprecated in favor of the Java Persistence API.

The following topics will be covered in this chapter:

- Introduction to Session Beans
- Creating a Session Bean with NetBeans
- EJB transaction management
- Implementing aspect oriented programming with interceptors
- EJB timer service
- Generating Session Beans from JPA entities

Introducing Session Beans

Session Beans encapsulate business logic for enterprise applications. It is a good idea to use session beans when developing enterprise applications, since we as application developers can focus on developing business logic, and not worry worry about other enterprise application requirements such as scalability, security, transactions, so on.

 Even though we as application developers don't directly implement common enterprise application requirements such as transactions and security, we can configure these services via annotations.

There are two types of session beans **stateless session beans** and **stateful session beans**. The difference between the two of them is that stateful session beans maintain conversational state with their client between method invocations, whereas stateless session beans do not.

Creating a session bean in NetBeans

Session Beans can be created in three types of NetBeans projects, **Enterprise Application**, **EJB Module**, and **Web Application**. EJB Module projects can contain only EJBs, whereas Enterprise Application projects can contain EJBs along with their clients, which can be web applications or "standalone" Java applications. The ability to add EJBs to web applications is a new feature introduced in Java EE 6. Having this ability allows us to simplify packaging and deployment of web applications using EJBs. We can now package the web application code and the EJB code in a single WAR file, whereas with previous versions of Java EE and J2EE, we had to create an EAR (Enterprise Application) file.

When deploying enterprise applications to the GlassFish application server included with NetBeans, it is possible to deploy standalone clients as part of the application to the application server. These standalone clients are then available via Java Web Start (http://java.sun.com/products/javawebstart/); this feature also allows us to easily access EJBs from the client code by using the annotations. True standalone clients executing outside the application server require JNDI lookups to obtain a reference to the EJB.

To create an Enterprise Application project, go to **File | New Project**, select the **Enterprise** category, then **Enterprise Application**:

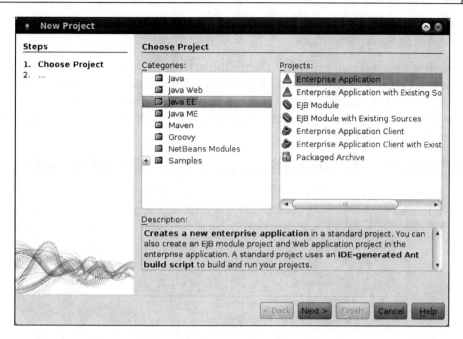

After clicking on **Next>**, we need to enter a project name.

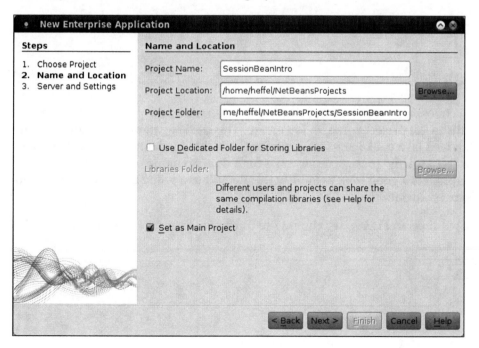

Usually the defaults for **Project Location** and **Project Folder** are sensible; therefore it makes sense to leave them alone.

In the next screen, we need to select the modules to be included in our enterprise application. **Create EJB Module** and **Create Web Application Module** are selected by default, in our example we will create an application client module and won't be creating a web application module, therefore we need to uncheck and check the corresponding checkboxes.

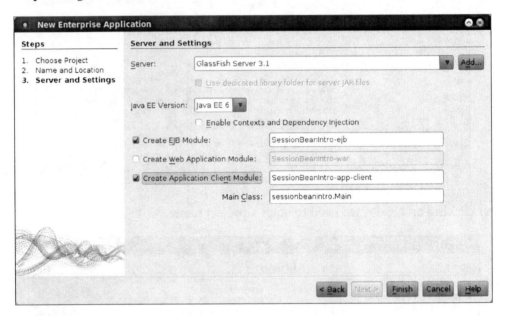

When choosing to create an application client module, the package of the main class defaults to the project name, in lowercase. This package name does not conform to standard Java package naming conventions, that by default start with a domain name "backwards" (`com.companyname` for a domain name of `companyname.com`). Therefore it is a good idea to modify this default to a value that does conform to the standard convention.

Once we click on **Finish**, we should see three new projects in our **Project** window.

In our example, **SessionBeanIntro** is our enterprise application project, **SessionBeanIntro-app-client** is our application client module, and **SessionBeanIntro-ejb** is our EJB module.

We are going to need a **Java Class Library** project down the line (more on that later), so we might as well create it now.

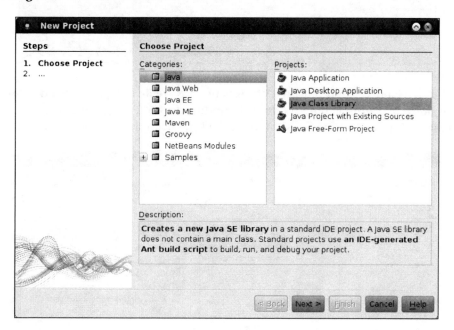

In the next step in the wizard, we simply name our project and click on **Finish**.

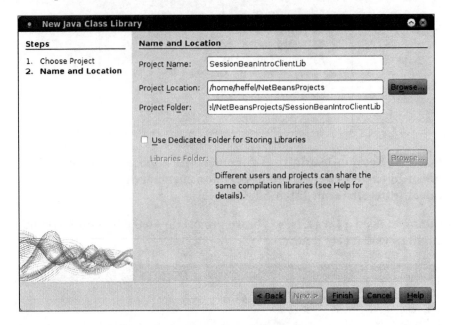

Now that we have created our projects, it is time to create our first session bean. We can do so by right-clicking on the EJB module and selecting the **Enterprise JavaBeans** category and the **Session Bean** file type from the New File wizard.

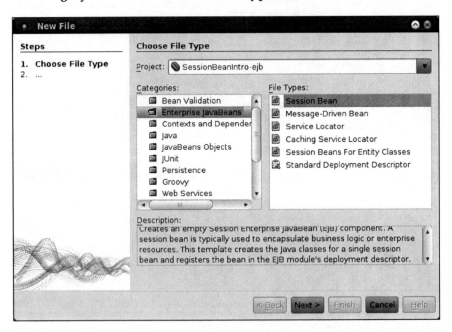

We now need to specify a number of options:

- It is a good idea to override the default name given to our session bean.
- We need to specify the package for our session bean.
- We need to specify the session bean type, stateless, stateful, or singleton:
  - ° Stateful session beans maintain conversational state with the client (which simply means that the values of any of their member variables are in a consistent state between method calls).
  - ° Stateless session beans don't maintain conversational state, for this reason they perform better than stateful session beans.
  - ° Singleton session beans are a new type of session bean introduced in Java EE 6. A single instance of each singleton session bean is created when our application is deployed. Singleton session beans are useful to cache frequently read database data.
- We need to specify if our session bean will have a remote interface, which is used for clients executing in a different JVM than our bean, a local interface, which is meant for clients running in the same JVM as our bean, or both a remote and a local interface.

A new feature of Java EE 6 is that local interfaces are optional. Therefore it isn't necessary to create any interface for our session beans if it will only be accessed by clients executing in the same JVM.

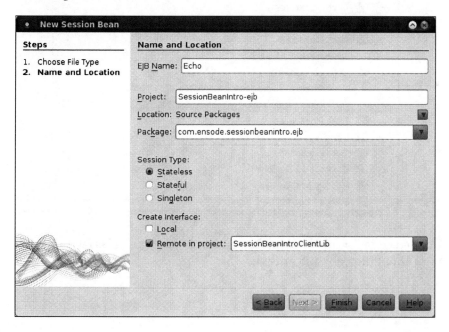

Our example bean does not need to maintain a conversational state with its clients, therefore we should make it a stateless session bean. Its only client will be executing in a different JVM, therefore we need to create a remote interface, and we don't need to create a local interface.

When creating a local interface, NetBeans requires us to specify a client library in which the remote interface will be added. This is the reason we had to create a java class library earlier. Our client library is selected by default.

After selecting all the appropriate options and clicking on **Finish**, our session bean is created in the EJB module project and the remote interface is created in the client library project.

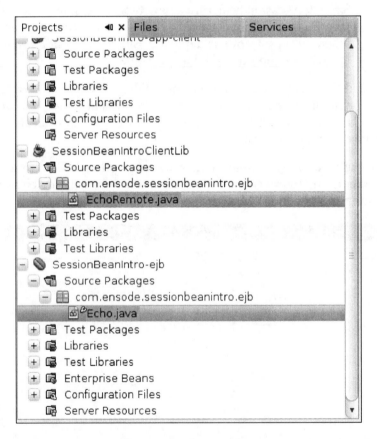

The generated code for our session bean is simply an empty class with the @ Stateless annotation already added.

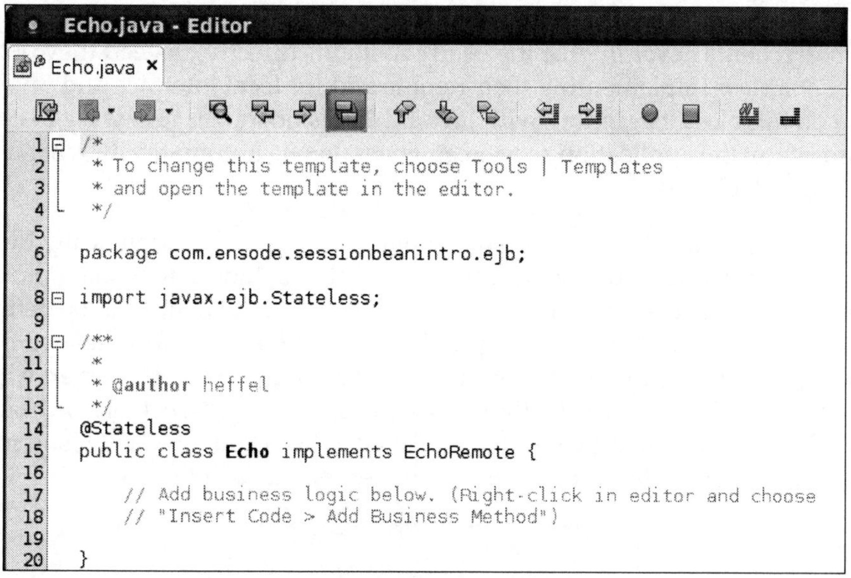

```
  ●   Echo.java - Editor

  Echo.java ×

  1  /*
  2    * To change this template, choose Tools | Templates
  3    * and open the template in the editor.
  4    */
  5
  6    package com.ensode.sessionbeanintro.ejb;
  7
  8    import javax.ejb.Stateless;
  9
 10   /**
 11    *
 12    * @author heffel
 13    */
 14   @Stateless
 15   public class Echo implements EchoRemote {
 16
 17        // Add business logic below. (Right-click in editor and choose
 18        // "Insert Code > Add Business Method")
 19
 20   }
```

Notice that our bean implements the remote interface, which at this point is an
empty interface with the @Remote annotation added. This annotation was added
because we chose to create a remote interface.

```
  ●   EchoRemote.java - Editor

  EchoRemote.java ×

  1  /*
  2    * To change this template, choose Tools | Templates
  3    * and open the template in the editor.
  4    */
  5
  6    package com.ensode.sessionbeanintro.ejb;
  7
  8    import javax.ejb.Remote;
  9
 10   /**
 11    *
 12    * @author heffel
 13    */
      @Remote
 15   public interface EchoRemote {
 16
 17   }
 18
```

The reason we need to have a remote and/or optional local interface is because session bean clients never invoke the bean's methods directly, instead they obtain a reference of a class implementing their remote and/or local interface and invoke the methods on this class. Beginning with Java EE 6, it is no longer necessary to create a local interface; the application server can generate one automatically when the application is deployed.

The remote and/or local interface implementation is created automatically by the EJB container when we deploy our bean. This implementation does some processing before invoking our session bean's method. Since the methods need to be defined both on the interface and our bean, typically we would need to add the method signature to both the bean and its remote and/or local interface. However, when working with session beans in NetBeans, we can simply right-click on the bean's source code and select **Insert Code | Add Business Method**, this will result in the method being added to both the bean and the remote/local interface.

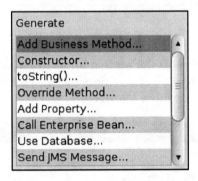

Doing this results in a window popping up, prompting us for the method name, return type, parameters, and the interface(s) where the method should be added (remote and/or local).

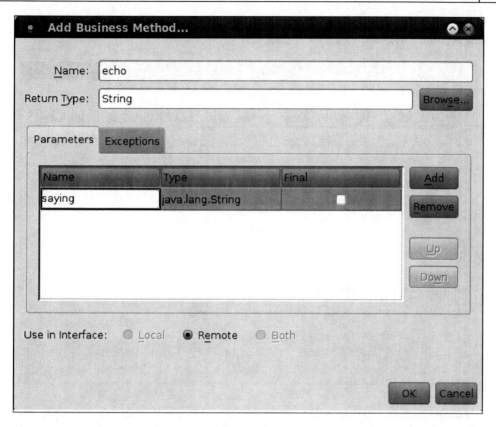

In our example we will add a method named echo that takes a String as a parameter and returns a String. Since our bean only has a remote interface, the radio buttons for **Local** and **Both** are grayed out.

After entering the appropriate information, the method is added both to the bean and its remote interface.

```
Echo.java - Editor

Echo.java ×

1   /*
2    * To change this template, choose Tools | Templates
3    * and open the template in the editor.
4    */
5   package com.ensode.sessionbeanintro.ejb;
6
7   import javax.ejb.Stateless;
8
9   /**
10   *
11   * @author heffel
12   */
13  @Stateless
14  public class Echo implements EchoRemote {
15      // Add business logic below. (Right-click in editor and choose
16      // "Insert Code > Add Business Method")
17
18      public String echo(String saying) {
19          return null;
20      }
21  }
```

The default implementation will simply return `null`. For this simple example we will simply modify it to return the string "echoing:" concatenated with the parameter that was passed.

```
    public String echo(String saying) {
        return "echoing: " + saying;
    }
```

At this point we have a simple, but complete stateless session bean.

Accessing the bean from a client

Now it is time to focus our attention to the client. For remote clients, the client project needs to use the Java Class Library project containing the remote interface.

Adding the class library project is very simple, we simply need to right-click on the **Libraries** node in the project and select **Add Project...**.

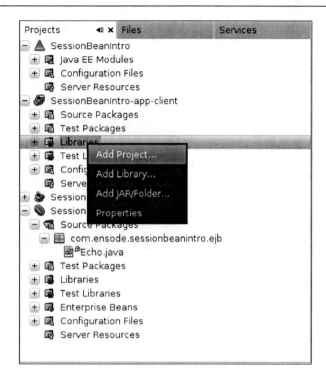

We then need to select the project we want to add as a library.

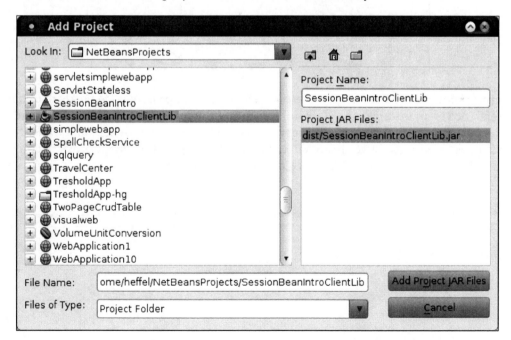

The Java Class Library project is now added to the Libraries node or our EJB client project.

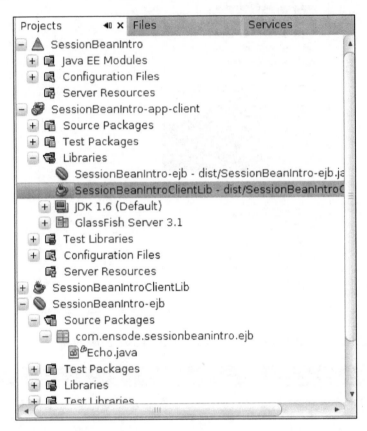

At this point, we are ready to invoke our EJB method. The client code needs to obtain a reference to an instance of a class implementing the remote interface for our bean. When using NetBeans, this is very easy, we simply need to right-click on the client code (`com.ensode.sessionbeanintro.Main` in the application client project in our example) and select **Insert Code... | Call Enterprise Bean**.

At this point we are shown a list of all open projects that have EJBs in them. We need to select the bean we wish to access from one of these projects.

If our bean had both a local and remote interface, we would have been given the choice to select the appropriate one. However, since it only has a remote interface, the option to select a local interface is disabled. In our particular example, even if we had the option of selecting a local interface, the correct option would have been to select the remote interface since our client will be executing in a different JVM from the server, and local interfaces are not accessible across JVMs.

At this point a member variable of type `EchoRemote` (our bean's remote interface) is added to the client, this variable is annotated with the `@EJB` annotation. This annotation is used to inject the instance of the remote interface at runtime.

In the previous versions of J2EE, it was necessary to perform a JNDI lookup to obtain a reference to the home interface of the bean, and then use the home interface to obtain a reference to the remote or local interface. As we can see, the procedure to obtain a reference to an EJB has been greatly simplified in Java EE.

```
Main.java

1  /*
2   * To change this template, choose Tools | Templates
3   * and open the template in the editor.
4   */
5
6  package com.ensodesessionbeanintro;
7
8  import com.ensode.sessionbeanintro.ejb.EchoRemote;
9  import javax.ejb.EJB;
10
11  /**
12   *
13   * @author heffel
14   */
15  public class Main {
16      @EJB
17      private static EchoRemote echo;
18
19      /**
20       * @param args the command line arguments
21       */
22      public static void main(String[] args) {
23          // TODO code application logic here
24
25      }
26
27  }
```

Now we simply need to add a call to the `echo()` method on the remote interface, and our client will be complete.

```
    public static void main(String[] args) {
        // TODO code application logic here
        JOptionPane.showMessageDialog(null,
            echo.echo("If you don't see this, it didn't work"));

    }
```

Executing the client

We can execute our client by simply right-clicking on the Enterprise Application Project and selecting **Run**. After a few seconds, we should see an information dialog displaying the output of the session bean's method.

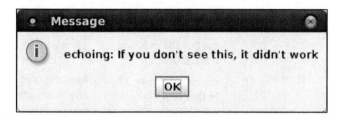

Clients deployed this way take advantage of Java Web Start technology. Java Web Start Applications run on the client workstation, however, they can be executed from an URL. The webstart URL for NetBeans enterprise application client modules defaults to the Enterprise project name, followed by the application client module name. In our example, the URL would be `http://localhost:8080/` `SessionBeanIntro/SessionBeanIntro-app-client`. We can verify this by pointing the browser to this URL. The application client will be executed after a brief wait.

Session bean transaction management

As previously mentioned, one of the advantages of Enterprise JavaBeans is that they automatically take care of transactions. However, there is still some configuration that we need to do in order to better control transaction management.

Transactions allow us to execute all the steps in a method or, if one of the steps fails (for instance, an exception is thrown), roll back the changes made in that method.

Primarily what we need to configure is our bean's behavior if one of its methods is called while a transaction is in progress. Should the bean's method become part of the existing transaction? Should the existing transaction be suspended, and a new transaction created just for the bean's method? We can configure this behavior via the `@TransactionAttribute` annotation.

The `@TransactionAttribute` annotation allows us to control how an EJB's methods will behave both when invoked while a transaction is in progress, and when invoked when no transaction is in progress. This annotation has a single `value` attribute that we can use to indicate how the bean's method will behave in both of these circumstances.

The following table summarizes the different values that we can assign to the `@TransactionAtttibute` annotation:

@TransactionAttribute value	Method invoked while a transaction is in progress	Method invoked while no transaction is in progress
`TransactionAttributeType.MANDATORY`	Method becomes part of the existing transaction.	`TransactionRequired Exception` is thrown.
`TransactionAttributeType.NEVER`	`RemoteException` is thrown.	Method is executed without any transaction support.
`TransactionAttributeType.NOT_SUPPORTED`	Client transaction is temporarily suspended, the method is executed without transaction support, and then the client transaction is resumed.	Method is executed without any transaction support.
`TransactionAttributeType.REQUIRED`	Method becomes part of the existing transaction.	A new transaction is created for the method.
`TransactionAttributeType.REQUIRES_NEW`	Client transaction is temporarily suspended, a new transaction is created for the method, and then the client transaction is resumed.	A new transaction is created for the method.
`TransactionAttributeType.SUPPORTS`	Method becomes part of the existing transaction.	Method is executed without any transaction support.

The `@TransactionAttribute` annotation can be used to decorate the class declaration of our Enterprise JavaBean, or it can be used to decorate a single method. If used to decorate the class declaration, then the declared transaction behavior will apply to all methods in the bean, where when used to decorate a single method, the declared behavior will affect only the decorated method. If a bean has an `@TransactionAttribute` annotation both at the class level and at the method level, the method level annotation takes precedence. If no transaction attribute is specified for a method, then `TransactionAttributeType.REQUIRED` attribute is used by default.

The following example illustrates how to use this annotation.

```
package com.ensode.sessionbeanintro.ejb;

import javax.ejb.Stateless;
import javax.ejb.TransactionAttribute;
import javax.ejb.TransactionAttributeType;

@Stateless
public class EchoBean implements EchoRemote {

    @TransactionAttribute(
        TransactionAttributeType.REQUIRES_NEW)
    public String echo(String saying) {
        return "echoing: " + saying;
    }

}
```

As we can see, we simply need to decorate the method to be configured with the @
`TransactionAttribute` annotation with the appropriate `TransactionAttributeType`
enumeration constant as a parameter to configure transactions for a single method.
As we mentioned before, if we wish for all of our methods to use the same transaction
strategy, we can place the `@TransactionAttribute` annotation at the class level.

Implementing aspect oriented programming with interceptors

Sometimes we wish to execute some logic just before and/or just after a method's
main logic executes. For example, we might want to measure the execution time of a
method to track down performance problems, or we might want to send a message
to a log every time we enter and leave a method, to make it easier to track down
bugs or exceptions.

The most common solution to these kind of problems is to add a little bit of code at
the beginning and end of every method, implementing the logic to profile or log in
each method. This approach has several problems: the logic needs to be implemented
several times, if we later wish to modify or remove the functionality; we need to
modify several methods.

Aspect Oriented Programming is a paradigm that solves the above problems by
providing a way to implement the logic to be executed just before and/or just after a
method's main logic in a separate class. EJB 3.0 introduced the ability to implement
aspect oriented programming via **interceptors**.

Implementing aspect oriented programming via interceptors consists of two steps: coding the interceptor class and decorating the EJBs to be intercepted with the `@Interceptors` annotation.

Implementing the interceptor class

An interceptor is a standard Java class, it must have a single method with the following signature:

```
@AroundInvoke
public Object methodName(InvocationContext invocationContext) throws
Exception
```

Notice that the method must be decorated with the `@AroundInvoke` annotation, which marks the method as an interceptor method. The `InvocationContext` parameter can be used to obtain information from the intercepted method, such as its name, parameters, the class that declares it, and more. It also has a `proceed()` method that is used to indicate when to execute the method logic.

The following table summarizes some of the most useful `InvocationContext` methods. Refer to the Java EE 6 JavaDoc (accessible within NetBeans by going to **Help | JavaDoc References | Java EE 6 - DRAFT**).

Method name	Description
getMethod()	Returns an instance of `java.lang.reflect.Method` that can be used to introspect the intercepted method.
getParameters()	Returns an array of Objects containing the parameters passed to the intercepted method.
getTarget()	Returns the object containing the method being invoked, return value is `java.lang.Object`.
proceed()	Invokes the method being intercepted.

The following example illustrates a simple interceptor class.

```
package com.ensode.sessionbeanintro.ejb;

import java.lang.reflect.Method;
import javax.interceptor.AroundInvoke;
import javax.interceptor.InvocationContext;

public class LoggingInterceptor {

    @AroundInvoke
    public Object logMethodCall(
            InvocationContext invocationContext)
            throws Exception {
```

```
Object interceptedObject =
    invocationContext.getTarget();
Method interceptedMethod =
    invocationContext.getMethod();

System.out.println("Entering " +
        interceptedObject.getClass().getName() + "." +
        interceptedMethod.getName() + "()");

Object o = invocationContext.proceed();

System.out.println("Leaving   " +
        interceptedObject.getClass().getName() + "." +
        interceptedMethod.getName() + "()");

    return o;
    }
}
```

The above example sends a message to the application server log just before and just after an intercepted method is executed. The purpose of implementing something like this would be to aid in debugging applications.

For simplicity, the above example simply uses `System.out.println` to output messages to the application server log. A real application more than likely would use a logging API such as the Java Logging API or Log4j.

The first thing we do in our interceptor method is to obtain a reference to the object and method being intercepted. We then output a message to the log indicating the class and method being invoked, this code is executed just before we let the intercepted method execute, which we do by invoking `invocationContext.proceed()`. We store the return value of this method in a variable, and then add some additional logic to be executed just after the method finishes. In our example, we simply send an additional line of text to the application server log. Finally our method returns the return value of `invocationContext.proceed()`.

Decorating the EJB with the @Interceptors annotation

In order for an EJB's method to be intercepted, it must be decorated with the `@Interceptors` annotation, this annotation has a single class array attribute. This attribute contains all the interceptors to be executed before and/or after the method call.

The @Interceptors annotation can be used at the method level, in which case it applies only to the method it decorates, or at the class level, in which it applies to every method in the bean.

The following example is a new version of our EchoBean session bean, slightly modified to have its echo() method intercepted by the LoggingInterceptor, that we wrote in the previous section.

```
package com.ensode.sessionbeanintro.ejb;

import javax.ejb.Stateless;
import javax.ejb.TransactionAttribute;
import javax.ejb.TransactionAttributeType;
import javax.interceptor.Interceptors;

@Stateless
public class Echo implements EchoRemote {
    // Add business logic below. (Right-click in editor and choose
    // "Insert Code > Add Business Method")

    @Interceptors({LoggingInterceptor.class})
    @TransactionAttribute(TransactionAttributeType.REQUIRES_NEW)
    public String echo(String saying) {
        return "echoing: " + saying;
    }
}
```

Notice that the only change we had to make to our session bean was to add the @ Interceptors annotation to its echo() method. In this particular case, the class array attribute has a single value, which is the LoggingInterceptor class we defined above. This has the effect of executing all the code in the interceptor's logMethodCall() method before the invocationContext.proceed() call just before the method is executed, and all the code after the invocationContext. proceed() call just after the method ends. In our example, we are using a single interceptor for our bean's method. If we need our method to be intercepted by more than one interceptor, we can do that by adding additional interceptor classes between the curly braces in the @Interceptors annotation, the list of interceptors between the curly braces must be separated by commas.

At this point we are ready to test our interceptor. In NetBeans, we can simply right-click on the project in the **Projects** window and select **Run**. After doing so, we should see the output of the interceptor's logMethodCall() in NetBean's GlassFish output window.

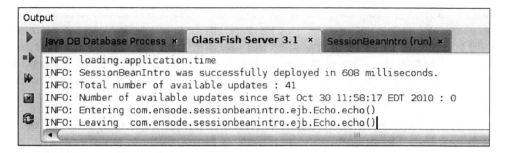

EJB timer service

Stateless session beans and Message-Driven Beans (another type of EJB discussed in the next chapter) can have a method that is executed automatically at regular intervals. This functionality is useful in case we want to execute some logic periodically (once a week, every day, every hour, and so on) without having to explicitly call any methods. This functionality is achieved by the **EJB Timer Service**.

In order to use the EJB timer service, we need to use the @Schedule annotation to specify when our method will be called. The following example illustrates how to use the EJB timer service:

```java
package com.ensode.ejbtimer.ejb;

import java.util.Date;
import javax.ejb.Stateless;
import javax.ejb.LocalBean;
import javax.ejb.Schedule;

@Stateless
@LocalBean
public class EJBTimerDemo {

    // Add business logic below. (Right-click in editor and choose
    // "Insert Code > Add Business Method")
    @Schedule(hour = "*", minute = "*", second = "*/30")
    public void logMessage() {
        System.out.println("logMessage() method invoked at: "
                + new Date(System.currentTimeMillis()));
    }
}
```

In this example, we decorated one of the methods in our EJB with the `@Schedule` annotation. We used a value of `"*"` for its `hour` attribute to specify that the method should be invoked every hour. We used the vale of `"*"` for the `minute` attribute as well to specify that the method should be invoked every minute. Finally, we used the value of `"*/30"` for its `second` attribute to specify that the method should be invoked every 30 seconds.

The `@Schedule` annotation uses a syntax similar to the cron utility commonly found in Unix and Unix-like operating systems such as Linux. Refer to `http://www.unixgeeks.org/security/newbie/unix/cron-1.html` for a good introduction to cron.

After deploying and executing our project in NetBeans, we should see the following output in the GlassFish output console:

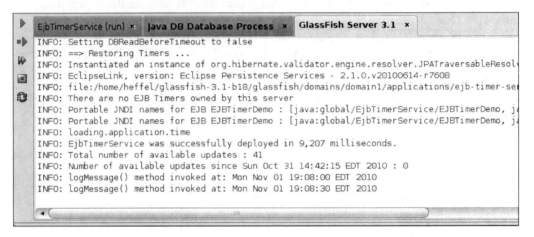

Generating session beans from JPA entities

One very nice NetBeans feature is that it allows generation of stateless session beans from existing JPA entities, the generated session beans act **as DAOs (Data Access Objects)**. This feature, combined with the ability to generate JPA entities from an existing database schema, allows us to completely generate the data access layers of our application without having to write a single line of Java code.

To take advantage of this functionality, we need to create an EJB project (**File | New Project**, select **Enterprise** from the **Categories** list, then select **EJB Module** from the **Projects** list), or use the EJB project from an **Enterprise Application** project, and add some JPA entities to it, either by manually coding them or by generating them from an existing schema as discussed in *Chapter 6*.

Once we have some JPA entities in the project, we need to go to **File | New**, select **Persistence** from the categories list, and **Session Beans For Entity Classes** from the **File Types** list.

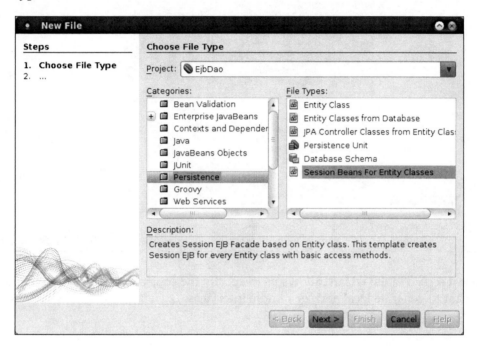

The next screen in the wizard allows us to select the existing JPA entity classes in the project we want to generate session beans. In most cases, they should be generated for all of them by simply clicking on the **Add All** button.

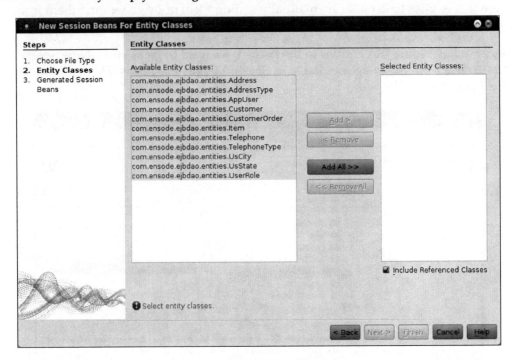

The last screen in the wizard allows us to specify the project, package, and whether we want to generate local and/or remote interfaces.

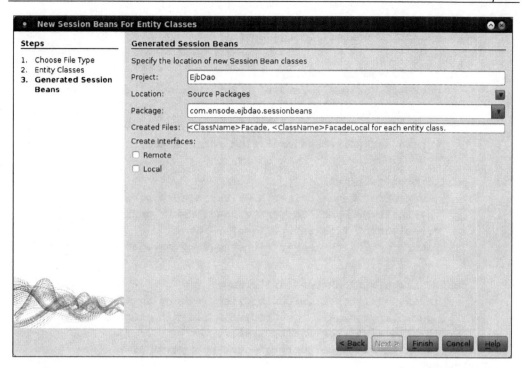

After clicking on **Finish**, the session beans are created and placed in the package we specified.

All of the generated session bean extends AbstractFacade, an abstract class that is also generated by the **Session Beans for Entity Classes** wizard. This abstract class contains a number of methods that allow us to perform **CRUD (Create, Read, Update, Delete)** operations on our entities.

```
package com.ensode.ejbdao.sessionbeans;

import java.util.List;
import javax.persistence.EntityManager;

public abstract class AbstractFacade<T> {

    private Class<T> entityClass;

    public AbstractFacade(Class<T> entityClass) {
        this.entityClass = entityClass;
    }

    protected abstract EntityManager getEntityManager();

    public void create(T entity) {
        getEntityManager().persist(entity);
    }
```

```
    public void edit(T entity) {
        getEntityManager().merge(entity);
    }

    public void remove(T entity) {
        getEntityManager().remove(getEntityManager().merge(entity));
    }

    public T find(Object id) {
        return getEntityManager().find(entityClass, id);
    }

    public List<T> findAll() {
        javax.persistence.criteria.CriteriaQuery cq =
         getEntityManager().getCriteriaBuilder().createQuery();
        cq.select(cq.from(entityClass));
        return getEntityManager().createQuery(cq).getResultList();
    }

    public List<T> findRange(int[] range) {
        javax.persistence.criteria.CriteriaQuery cq =
         getEntityManager().getCriteriaBuilder().createQuery();
        cq.select(cq.from(entityClass));
        javax.persistence.Query q = getEntityManager().
createQuery(cq);
        q.setMaxResults(range[1] - range[0]);
        q.setFirstResult(range[0]);
        return q.getResultList();
    }

    public int count() {
        javax.persistence.criteria.CriteriaQuery cq =
         getEntityManager().getCriteriaBuilder().createQuery();
        javax.persistence.criteria.Root<T> rt = cq.from(entityClass);
        cq.select(getEntityManager().getCriteriaBuilder().count(rt));
        javax.persistence.Query q = getEntityManager().
createQuery(cq);
        return ((Long) q.getSingleResult()).intValue();
    }
}
```

As we can see, `AbstractFacade` is not much more than a facade to `EntityManager`, wrapping its calls inside a session bean gives us all of its advantages, such as transaction management and distributed code. The generated `create()` method is used to create new entities, the `edit()` method updates an existing entity, the `remove()` method deletes an existing entity. The `find()` method finds an entity with the given primary key, and the `findAll()` method returns a `List` of all entities in the database. The `findRange()` method allows us to retrieve a subset of the entities in the database; it takes an array of int as its sole parameter. The first element in this array should have the index of the first result to retrieve, and the second element should have the index of the last element to retrieve. The `count()` method returns the number of entities in the database, it is similar to a `select count(*) from TABLE_NAME` in standard SQL.

Like we previously mentioned, all of the generated session beans extend `AbstractFacade`, let's look at one of these generated EJBs.

```
package com.ensode.ejbdao.sessionbeans;

import com.ensode.ejbdao.entities.Customer;
import javax.ejb.Stateless;
import javax.persistence.EntityManager;
import javax.persistence.PersistenceContext;

@Stateless
public class CustomerFacade extends AbstractFacade<Customer> {
    @PersistenceContext(unitName = "EjbDaoPU")
    private EntityManager em;

    protected EntityManager getEntityManager() {
        return em;
    }

    public CustomerFacade() {
        super(Customer.class);
    }

}
```

As we can see, the generated session beans are very simple. They simply include an instance variable of type `EntityManager` and take advantage of resource injection to initialize it. They also include a `getEntityManager()` method meant to be called by the parent class so that it has access to this session bean's `EntityManager` instance. Additionally, the session bean's constructor invokes the parent class constructor, which via generics initializes the `entityClass` instance variable on the parent class.

We are of course free to add additional methods to the generated session beans. For example, sometimes it is necessary to add a method to find all entities that meet specific criteria, such as finding all customers with the same last name.

One disadvantage of adding methods to the generated session beans is that if for any reason they need to be regenerated, we will lose our custom methods and they will need to be re-added. In order to avoid this situation, it is a good idea to extend the generated session beans and add additional methods in the child classes (as of Java EE 5, session beans can extend one another), this will prevent our methods from being "wiped out" if we ever need to regenerate our session beans.

Summary

In this chapter, we gave an introduction to session beans, and explained how NetBeans can help us speed up session bean development. We covered how Enterprise JavaBeans in general and session beans in particular, allow us to easily implement transaction strategies in our enterprise applications. We also covered how we can implement **Aspect Oriented Programming (AOP)** with session beans via interceptors. Additionally, we discussed how session beans can have one of their methods invoked periodically by the EJB container by taking advantage of the EJB Timer Service. Lastly, we covered how NetBeans can help speed up the implementation of the data access layer of our applications by generating session beans implementing the **Data Access Object (DAO)** design pattern automatically.

8

Contexts and Dependency Injection (CDI)

Contexts and Dependency Injection (CDI) is a new addition to the Java EE specification. CDI can be used to simplify integrating the different layers of a Java EE application. For example, CDI allows us to use a session bean as a managed bean, allowing us to take advantage of EJB features such as transactions directly in our managed beans.

In this chapter we will cover the following topics:

- Introduction to CDI
- Qualifiers
- Stereotypes
- Interceptor Binding Types

Introduction to CDI

All we need to do to take advantage of Contexts and Dependency Injection features in our Web Application projects is to click on the checkbox labeled **Enable Contexts and Dependency Injection** on the second page of the **New Web Application** wizard.

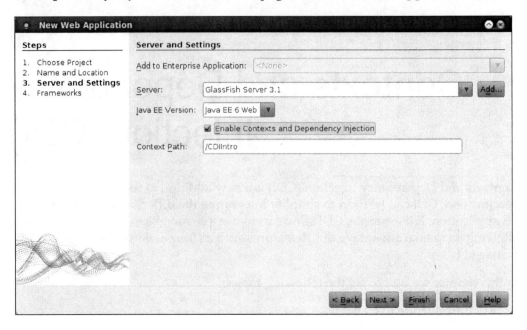

In most cases will want to use the JSF 2.0 framework as well, since typically CDI applications use JSF as their user interface component framework.

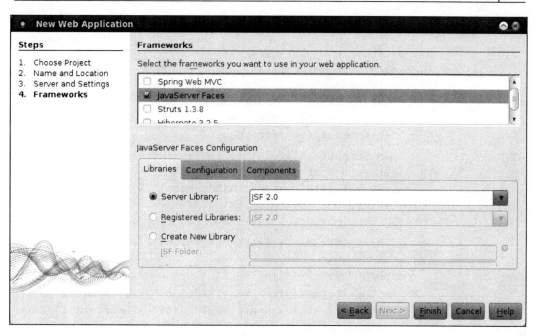

Clicking on the **Enable Contexts and Dependency Injection** checkbox has the effect of creating a file called `beans.xml` and placing it in the `WEB-INF` directory of our web application. The generated `beans.xml` file looks like this:

```
<?xml version="1.0" encoding="UTF-8"?>
<beans xmlns="http://java.sun.com/xml/ns/javaee"
       xmlns:xsi="http://www.w3.org/2001/XMLSchema-instance"
       xsi:schemaLocation="http://java.sun.com/xml/ns/javaee http://
java.sun.com/xml/ns/javaee/beans_1_0.xsd">
</beans>
```

When our application is deployed, the presence of this file indicates to the application server that our application is CDI-enabled.

Typically, just like standard JSF applications, CDI applications use Facelets as their view technology. The following example illustrates typical markup for a CDI page:

```
<?xml version='1.0' encoding='UTF-8' ?>
<!DOCTYPE html PUBLIC "-//W3C//DTD XHTML 1.0 Transitional//EN"
    "http://www.w3.org/TR/xhtml1/DTD/xhtml1-transitional.dtd">
<html xmlns="http://www.w3.org/1999/xhtml"
      xmlns:h="http://java.sun.com/jsf/html">
    <h:head>
        <title>Create New Customer</title>
    </h:head>
```

```
    <h:body>
        <h:form>
            <h3>Create New Customer</h3>
            <h:panelGrid columns="3">
                <h:outputLabel for="firstName" value="First Name"/>
                <h:inputText id="firstName"
                    value="#{customer.firstName}"/>
                <h:message for="firstName"/>

                <h:outputLabel for="middleName" value="Middle Name"/>
                <h:inputText id="middleName"
                    value="#{customer.middleName}"/>
                <h:message for="middleName"/>

                <h:outputLabel for="lastName" value="Last Name"/>
                <h:inputText id="lastName" value="#{customer.
lastName}"/>

                <h:message for="lastName"/>

                <h:outputLabel for="email" value="Email Address"/>
                <h:inputText id="email" value="#{customer.email}"/>
                <h:message for="email"/>
                <h:panelGroup/>
                <h:commandButton value="Submit"
                    action="#{controller.navigateToConfirmation}"/>
            </h:panelGrid>
        </h:form>
    </h:body>
</html>
```

As we can see, the above markup doesn't look any different than the markup used for a JSF application not using CDI. The above page renders as follows (shown after entering some data):

In our page markup, we have JSF components using Unified Expression Language expressions to bind themselves to managed bean properties and methods. In this case, however, the managed beans are not JSF managed beans but CDI managed beans. Let's take a look at the customer bean first.

```java
package com.ensode.model;

import java.io.Serializable;
import javax.enterprise.context.RequestScoped;
import javax.inject.Named;

@Named
@RequestScoped
public class Customer implements Serializable {

    private String firstName;
    private String middleName;
    private String lastName;
    private String email;

    public Customer() {
    }

    public String getFirstName() {
        return firstName;
    }

    public void setFirstName(String firstName) {
        this.firstName = firstName;
    }

    public String getMiddleName() {
        return middleName;
    }

    public void setMiddleName(String middleName) {
        this.middleName = middleName;
    }
```

```
        public String getLastName() {
            return lastName;
        }
        public void setLastName(String lastName) {
            this.lastName = lastName;
        }
        public String getEmail() {
            return email;
        }
        public void setEmail(String email) {
            this.email = email;
        }
    }
```

The `@Named` annotation marks this class as a CDI named bean. By default, the bean's name will be the class name with its first character switched to lowercase (In our example, the name of the bean is "customer", since the class name is Customer). We can override this behavior if we wish, simply by passing the desired name to the value attribute of the `@Named` annotation, as follows:

```
@Named(value="customerBean")
```

A CDI named bean's methods and properties are accessible via Facelets, just like a regular JSF managed bean.

 Facelets is the default view technology for JSF 2.0. Refer to *Chapter 4* for details.

Just like JSF-managed beans, CDI named beans can have one of the several scopes, the above named bean has a scope of request, as denoted by the `@RequestScoped` annotation.

Scope	Annotation	Description
Request	`@RequestScoped`	Request scoped beans are shared through the duration of a single request. A single request could refer to an HTTP request, an invocation to a method in an EJB, a web service invocation, or sending a JMS message to a message-driven bean.
Session	`@SessionScoped`	Session scoped beans across all requests in an HTTP session. Each user of an application gets their own instance of a session scoped bean.

Scope	Annotation	Description
Application	@ApplicationScoped	Application scoped beans live through the whole application lifetime. Beans in this scope are shared across user sessions.
Conversation	@ConversationScoped	The conversation scope can span multiple requests, but is typically shorter than the session scope.
Dependent	@Dependent	Dependent scoped beans are not shared, any time a dependent scoped bean is injected, a new instance is created.

As we can see, CDI has equivalent scopes to all JSF scopes. Additionally CDI adds two additional scopes. The first CDI-specific scope is the conversation scope, which allows us to have a scope that spans across multiple requests, but is shorter than the session scope. The second CDI-specific scope is the dependent scope, which is a pseudo scope. A CDI bean in the dependent scope is a dependent object of another object; beans in this scope are instantiated when the object they belong to is instantiated, and destroyed when the object they belong to is destroyed.

Our application has two CDI named beans. We already discussed the customer bean, the other CDI named bean in our application is the controller bean.

```java
package com.ensode.controller;
import com.ensode.model.Customer;
import javax.enterprise.context.RequestScoped;
import javax.inject.Inject;
import javax.inject.Named;
@Named
@RequestScoped
public class Controller {
    @Inject
    private Customer customer;
    public Customer getCustomer() {
        return customer;
    }
    public void setCustomer(Customer customer) {
        this.customer = customer;
    }
    public String navigateToConfirmation() {
        //In a real application, we would save new customer
        // data to database here.
        return "confirmation";
    }
}
```

In the above class, an instance of the `Customer` class is injected at runtime, this is accomplished via the `@Inject` annotation, this annotation allows us to easily use dependency injection in CDI applications.

The `navigateToConfirmation()` method in the above class is invoked when the user clicks on the Submit button on the page. `navigateToConfirmation()` works just like an equivalent method in a JSF managed bean would, that is, it returns a string, and based on the value of this string the application navigates to an appropriate page. Just like with JSF, by default the target page's name is the return value of this method plus an XHTML extension. For example, if no exceptions are thrown in the `navigateToConfirmation()` method, the user is directed to a page named `confirmation.xhtml`.

```xml
<?xml version='1.0' encoding='UTF-8' ?>
<!DOCTYPE html PUBLIC "-//W3C//DTD XHTML 1.0 Transitional//EN"
"http://www.w3.org/TR/xhtml1/DTD/xhtml1-transitional.dtd">
<html xmlns="http://www.w3.org/1999/xhtml"
      xmlns:h="http://java.sun.com/jsf/html">
    <h:head>
        <title>Success</title>
    </h:head>
    <h:body>
        New Customer created successfully.
        <h:panelGrid columns="2" border="1" cellspacing="0">
            <h:outputLabel for="firstName" value="First Name"/>
            <h:outputText id="firstName" value="#{customer.
            firstName}"/>

            <h:outputLabel for="middleName" value="Middle Name"/>
            <h:outputText id="middleName" value="#{customer.
            middleName}"/>

            <h:outputLabel for="lastName" value="Last Name"/>
            <h:outputText id="lastName" value="#{customer.lastName}"/>

            <h:outputLabel for="email" value="Email Address"/>
            <h:outputText id="email" value="#{customer.email}"/>

        </h:panelGrid>
    </h:body>
</html>
```

Again, there is nothing special we need to do to access the named bean's properties from the above markup, it works just as if the bean was a JSF-managed bean. The above page renders as follows:

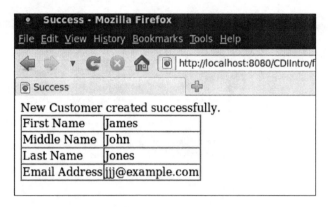

As we can see, CDI applications work just like JSF applications, however, CDI applications have several advantages over JSF. For example, like as we previously mentioned, CDI beans have additional scopes not found in JSF. Additionally, using CDI allows us to decouple our Java code from the JSF API. Also, like we mentioned previously, CDI allows us to use session beans as named beans.

Qualifiers

In some instances the type of the bean we wish to inject into our code may be an interface or a Java superclass, but we may be interested in injecting a subclass or a class implementing the interface. For cases like this, CDI provides qualifiers we can use to indicate the specific type we wish to inject into our code.

A CDI qualifier is an annotation that must be decorated with the `@Qualifier` annotation. This annotation can then be used to decorate the specific subclass or interface. In this section, we will develop a `Premium` qualifier for our customer bean, premium customers could get perks, such as discounts, not available to regular customers.

Creating a CDI qualifiers with NetBeans is very easy, all we need to do is go to **File | New**, select the **Contexts and Dependency Injection** category and the **Qualifier Type** file type.

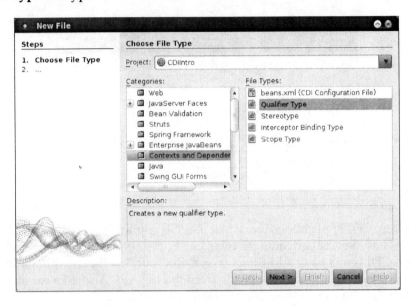

In the next step in the wizard, we need to enter a name and a package for our qualifier.

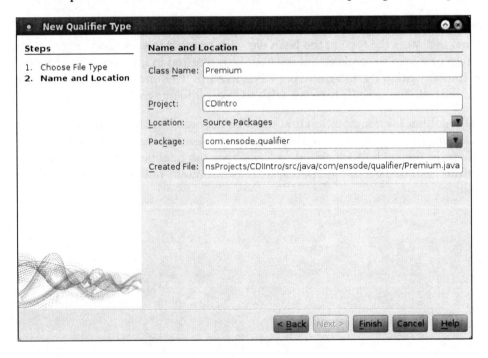

After these two simple steps, NetBeans generates the code for our qualifier.

```
package com.ensode.qualifier;

import static java.lang.annotation.ElementType.TYPE;
import static java.lang.annotation.ElementType.FIELD;
import static java.lang.annotation.ElementType.PARAMETER;
import static java.lang.annotation.ElementType.METHOD;
import static java.lang.annotation.RetentionPolicy.RUNTIME;
import java.lang.annotation.Retention;
import java.lang.annotation.Target;
import javax.inject.Qualifier;

@Qualifier
@Retention(RUNTIME)
@Target({METHOD, FIELD, PARAMETER, TYPE})
public @interface Premium {
}
```

Qualifiers are standard Java annotations, they typically have retention of runtime and can target methods, fields, parameters, or types. The only difference between a qualifier and a standard annotation is that qualifiers are decorated with the @ Qualifier annotation.

Once we have our qualifier in place, we need to use it to decorate the specific subclass or interface implementation.

```
package com.ensode.model;

import com.ensode.qualifier.Premium;
import javax.enterprise.context.RequestScoped;
import javax.inject.Named;

@Named
@RequestScoped
@Premium
public class PremiumCustomer extends Customer {

    private Integer discountCode;

    public Integer getDiscountCode() {
        return discountCode;
    }

    public void setDiscountCode(Integer discountCode) {
        this.discountCode = discountCode;
    }
}
```

Once we have decorated the specific instance we need to qualify, we can use our qualifiers in the client code to specify the exact type of dependency we need.

```java
package com.ensode.controller;

import com.ensode.model.Customer;
import com.ensode.model.PremiumCustomer;
import com.ensode.qualifier.Premium;
import java.util.logging.Level;
import java.util.logging.Logger;
import javax.enterprise.context.RequestScoped;
import javax.inject.Inject;
import javax.inject.Named;

@Named
@RequestScoped
public class PremiumCustomerController {

    private static final Logger logger = Logger.getLogger(
            PremiumCustomerController.class.getName());
    @Inject
    @Premium
    private Customer customer;

    public String saveCustomer() {

        PremiumCustomer premiumCustomer = (PremiumCustomer) customer;

        logger.log(Level.INFO, "Saving the following information \n"
                + "{0} {1}, discount code = {2}",
                new Object[]{premiumCustomer.getFirstName(),
                    premiumCustomer.getLastName(),
                    premiumCustomer.getDiscountCode()});

        //If this was a real application, we would have code to save
        //customer data to the database here.

        return "premium_customer_confirmation";
    }
}
```

Since we used our `@Premium` qualifier to decorate the customer field, an instance of `PremiumCustomer` is injected into that field, since this class is also decorated with the `@Premium` qualifier.

As far as our JSF pages go, we simply access our named bean as usual using its name.

```xml
<?xml version='1.0' encoding='UTF-8' ?>
<!DOCTYPE html PUBLIC "-//W3C//DTD XHTML 1.0 Transitional//EN"
    "http://www.w3.org/TR/xhtml1/DTD/xhtml1-transitional.dtd">
```

```
<html xmlns="http://www.w3.org/1999/xhtml"
    xmlns:h="http://java.sun.com/jsf/html">
  <h:head>
      <title>Create New Premium Customer</title>
  </h:head>
  <h:body>
      <h:form>
          <h3>Create New Customer</h3>
          <h:panelGrid columns="3">
              <h:outputLabel for="firstName" value="First Name"/>
              <h:inputText id="firstName"
                  value="#{premiumCustomer.firstName}"/>
              <h:message for="firstName"/>

              <h:outputLabel for="middleName" value="Middle Name"/>
              <h:inputText id="middleName"
                  value="#{premiumCustomer.middleName}"/>
              <h:message for="middleName"/>

              <h:outputLabel for="lastName" value="Last Name"/>
              <h:inputText id="lastName"
                  value="#{premiumCustomer.lastName}"/>
              <h:message for="lastName"/>

              <h:outputLabel for="email" value="Email Address"/>
              <h:inputText id="email"
                  value="#{premiumCustomer.email}"/>
              <h:message for="email"/>

              <h:outputLabel for="discountCode" value="Discount
              Code"/>
              <h:inputText id="discountCode"
                  value="#{premiumCustomer.discountCode}"/>
              <h:message for="discountCode"/>

              <h:panelGroup/>
              <h:commandButton value="Submit"
                  action="#{premiumCustomerController.
                  saveCustomer}"/>
          </h:panelGrid>
      </h:form>
  </h:body>
</html>
```

In this example, we are using the default name for our bean, which is the class name with the first letter switched to lowercase.

At this point, we are ready to test our application.

After submitting the page we can see the confirmation page.

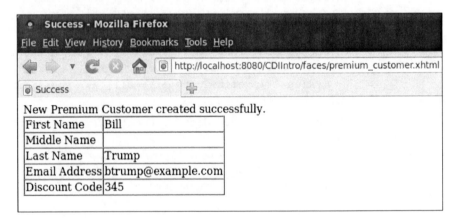

Stereotypes

A CDI stereotype allows us to create new annotations that bundle together several CDI annotations. For example, if we needed to create several CDI named beans with a scope of session, we would have to use two annotations in each of these beans, namely `@Named` and `@SessionScoped`. Instead of having to add two annotations to each of our beans, we could create a stereotype, and then annotate our beans with it.

To create a CDI stereotype in NetBeans, we simply need to create a new file, selecting the **Contexts and Dependency Injection** category and the **Stereotype** file type.

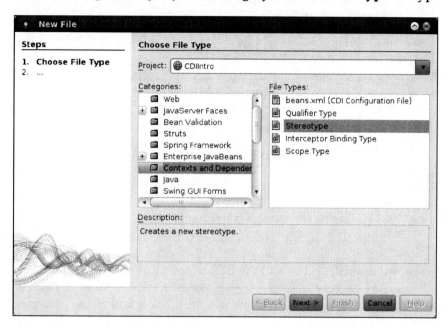

We then need to enter a name and package for our new Stereotype.

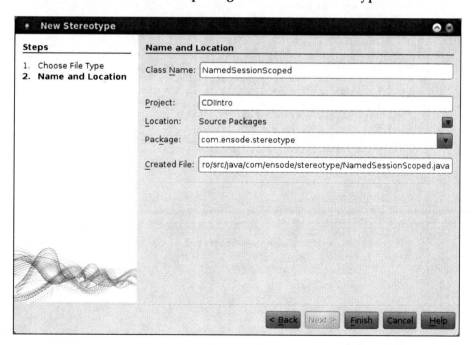

At this point, NetBeans generates the following code:

```
NamedSessionScoped.java ×

1    package com.ensode.stereotype;
2
3    import static java.lang.annotation.ElementType.TYPE;
4    import static java.lang.annotation.ElementType.FIELD;
5    import static java.lang.annotation.ElementType.METHOD;
6    import static java.lang.annotation.RetentionPolicy.RUNTIME;
7    import java.lang.annotation.Retention;
8    import java.lang.annotation.Target;
9    import javax.enterprise.inject.Stereotype;
10
11   @Stereotype
12   @Retention(RUNTIME)
13   @Target({METHOD, FIELD, TYPE})
14   public @interface NamedSessionScoped {
15   }
```

At this point, we simply need to add the CDI annotations that we want the classes
annotated with our stereotype to use. In our case, we want them to be named beans
and have a scope of session, therefore we add the `@Named` and `@SessionScoped`
annotations.

```
NamedSessionScoped.java ×

1    package com.ensode.stereotype;
2
3    import static java.lang.annotation.ElementType.TYPE;
4    import static java.lang.annotation.ElementType.FIELD;
5    import static java.lang.annotation.ElementType.METHOD;
6    import static java.lang.annotation.RetentionPolicy.RUNTIME;
7    import java.lang.annotation.Retention;
8    import java.lang.annotation.Target;
9    import javax.enterprise.context.SessionScoped;
10   import javax.enterprise.inject.Stereotype;
11   import javax.inject.Named;
12
13   @Named
14   @SessionScoped
15   @Stereotype
16   @Retention(RUNTIME)
17   @Target({METHOD, FIELD, TYPE})
18   public @interface NamedSessionScoped {
19   }
20
```

Now we can use our stereotype in our own code.

```
package com.ensode.beans;

import com.ensode.stereotype.NamedSessionScoped;
import java.io.Serializable;

@NamedSessionScoped
public class StereotypeClient implements Serializable {

    private String property1;
    private String property2;

    public String getProperty1() {
        return property1;
    }

    public void setProperty1(String property1) {
        this.property1 = property1;
    }

    public String getProperty2() {
        return property2;
    }

    public void setProperty2(String property2) {
        this.property2 = property2;
    }
}
```

We annotated the above class with our `NamedSessionScoped` stereotype, which is equivalent to using the `@Named` and `@SessionScoped` annotations.

Interceptor Binding Types

One of the advantages of EJBs is that they allow us to easily do **Aspect Oriented Programming (AOP)** via interceptors. CDI allows us to write Interceptor Binding Types, which let us bind interceptors to beans without having the beans depend directly on the interceptor. Interceptor Binding Types are annotations which themselves are annotated with `@InterceptorBinding`.

Creating an interceptor binding type in NetBeans consists of simply creating a new file, selecting the **Contexts and Dependency Injection** category, and the **Interceptor Binding Type** file type.

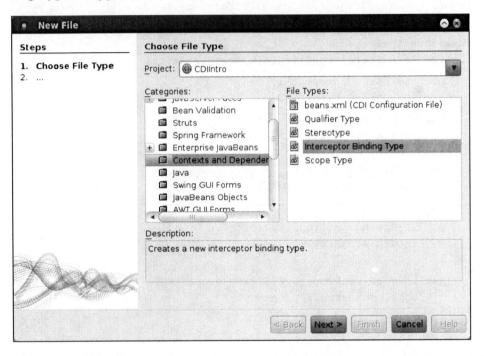

We then need to enter a class name and select or enter a package for our new interceptor binding type.

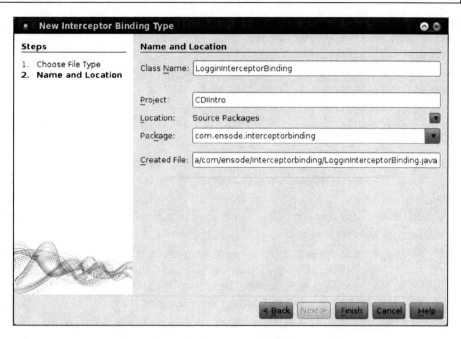

At this point, NetBeans generates the code for our interceptor binding type.

```
package com.ensode.interceptorbinding;

import static java.lang.annotation.ElementType.TYPE;
import static java.lang.annotation.ElementType.METHOD;
import static java.lang.annotation.RetentionPolicy.RUNTIME;
import java.lang.annotation.Inherited;
import java.lang.annotation.Retention;
import java.lang.annotation.Target;
import javax.interceptor.InterceptorBinding;

@Inherited
@InterceptorBinding
@Retention(RUNTIME)
@Target({METHOD, TYPE})
public @interface LoggingInterceptorBinding {
}
```

The generated code is fully functional; we don't need to add anything to it. In order to use our interceptor binding type, we need to write an interceptor and annotate it with our interceptor binding type.

```
package com.ensode.interceptor;

import com.ensode.interceptorbinding.LoggingInterceptorBinding;
```

```
import java.util.logging.Level;
import java.util.logging.Logger;
import javax.interceptor.AroundInvoke;
import javax.interceptor.Interceptor;
import javax.interceptor.InvocationContext;

@LoggingInterceptorBinding
@Interceptor
public class LoggingInterceptor {

    private static final Logger logger = Logger.getLogger(
            LoggingInterceptor.class.getName());

    @AroundInvoke
    public Object logMethodCall(InvocationContext invocationContext)
            throws Exception {
        logger.log(Level.INFO, new StringBuilder("entering ").append(
                invocationContext.getMethod().getName()).append(
                " method").toString());
      Object retVal = invocationContext.proceed();

        logger.log(Level.INFO, new StringBuilder("leaving ").append(
                invocationContext.getMethod().getName()).append(
                " method").toString());

        return retVal;
    }
}
```

As we can see, other than being annotated with our interceptor binding type, the above class is a standard interceptor, just like the ones we use with EJB session beans (refer to *Chapter 7* for details).

In order for our interceptor binding type to work properly, we need to register the above interceptor in `beans.xml`:

```
<?xml version="1.0" encoding="UTF-8"?>
<beans xmlns="http://java.sun.com/xml/ns/javaee"
       xmlns:xsi="http://www.w3.org/2001/XMLSchema-instance"
       xsi:schemaLocation="http://java.sun.com/xml/ns/javaee
       http://java.sun.com/xml/ns/javaee/beans_1_0.xsd">
    <interceptors>
        <class>com.ensode.interceptor.LoggingInterceptor</class>
    </interceptors>
</beans>
```

As can be seen above, all we need to do to register our interceptor is to use the `<interceptor>` tag in `beans.xml`, with one or more nested `<class>` tags containing the fully qualified names of our interceptors.

The final step before we can use our interceptor binding type is to annotate the class to be intercepted with our interceptor binding type.

```
package com.ensode.controller;

import com.ensode.interceptorbinding.LoggingInterceptorBinding;
import com.ensode.model.Customer;
import com.ensode.model.PremiumCustomer;
import com.ensode.qualifier.Premium;
import java.util.logging.Level;
import java.util.logging.Logger;
import javax.enterprise.context.RequestScoped;
import javax.inject.Inject;
import javax.inject.Named;

@LoggingInterceptorBinding
@Named
@RequestScoped
public class PremiumCustomerController {

    private static final Logger logger = Logger.getLogger(
            PremiumCustomerController.class.getName());
    @Inject
    @Premium
    private Customer customer;

    public String saveCustomer() {

        PremiumCustomer premiumCustomer = (PremiumCustomer) customer;

        logger.log(Level.INFO, "Saving the following information \n"
                + "{0} {1}, discount code = {2}",
                new Object[]{premiumCustomer.getFirstName(),
                    premiumCustomer.getLastName(),
                    premiumCustomer.getDiscountCode()});

        //If this was a real application, we would have code to save
        //customer data to the database here.

        return "premium_customer_confirmation";
    }
}
```

At this point we are ready to use our interceptor, after executing the above code, and examining the GlassFish log, we can see our interceptor binding type in action.

```
Output - GlassFish Server 3.1
  INFO: Instantiated an instance of org.hibernate.validator.engine.resolver.JPATraversableResolver.
  INFO: entering saveCustomer method
  INFO: Saving the following information
  Ron Baker, discount code = 7,256
  INFO: leaving saveCustomer method
```

The lines **entering saveCustomer method** and **leaving saveCustomer method** were added to the log by our interceptor, which was indirectly invoked by our interceptor binding type.

Summary

In this chapter, we covered NetBeans support for Contexts and Dependency Injection (CDI), a new Java EE API introduced in Java EE 6. We provided an introduction to CDI, and explained additional functionality that the CDI API provides over standard JSF. We also covered how to disambiguate CDI injected beans via CDI Qualifiers. Additionally, we covered how to group together CDI annotations via CDI Stereotypes. Finally, we saw how CDI can help us with Aspect-Oriented Programming via Interceptor Binding Types.

Messaging with JMS and Message Driven Beans

The **Java Messaging Service (JMS)** is a standard Java EE messaging API that allows loosely coupled, asynchronous communication between Java EE components.

NetBeans includes good support to aid us in creating applications that take advantage of the JMS API, generating a lot of necessary boilerplate code, allowing us to focus on the business logic of our application.

We will cover the following topics in this chapter:

- Introduction to JMS
- Creating an enterprise project to take advantage of JMS
- Creating JMS resources from NetBeans
- Implementing a JMS message producer
- Implementing a JMS message consumer
- Processing JMS messages with message driven Beans

Introduction to JMS

The **Java Messaging Service (JMS)** is a standard Java EE API that allows loosely coupled, asynchronous communication between Java EE components. Applications taking advantage of JMS do not interact directly with each other, instead JMS message producers send messages to a destination (JMS Queue or Topic), and JMS consumers receive messages from the said destinations.

There are two messaging domains that can be used when working with JMS, the **Point To Point (PTP)** messaging, in which a JMS message is processed by only one message receiver, and Publish/Subscribe (pub/sub) messaging, in which all message receivers subscribed to a specific topic receive and process each message for said topic. JMS applications using the PTP messaging domain use message queues as their JMS destinations, where applications using pub/sub use message topics.

The following diagram illustrates the JMS architecture:

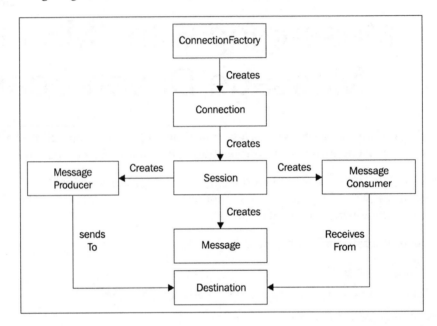

When working with JMS we need to obtain a reference to a connection factory, either via JNDI or via dependency injection. From this connection factory we can create a JMS session, that in turn can be used to create JMS messages.

When developing code to send messages to a JMS destination, we need to create a JMS message producer from the JMS session. In turn, we use this message producer to send messages to the destination.

When developing code to receive messages from a JMS destination, we need to create a message consumer from the JMS session. We can then use this message consumer to retrieve messages from our JMS destination.

Creating the project and JMS resources

We will be creating a new Enterprise Application project for our example.

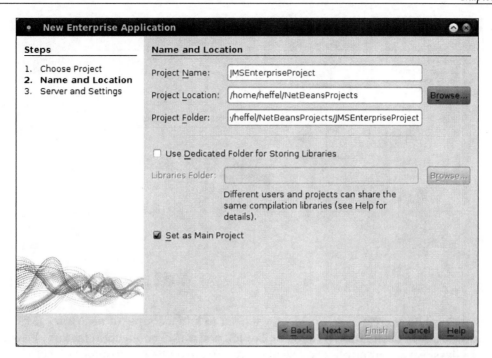

In our example, we will be adding an EJB module and an Application Client module.

Any type of Java EE module can be a JMS message producer and/or consumer by simply invoking methods from the JMS API, we chose to create an EJB module since later in the chapter we will be creating a **Message Driven Bean (MDB)**, that is a type of EJB. We chose an application client since it is one of the simplest modules that can be added to an enterprise application, allowing us to focus on JMS code without having to worry about writing lots of extraneous code. However, in real applications, it is common to have web applications or Session Beans act as JMS message producers, with an MDB acting as the consumer.

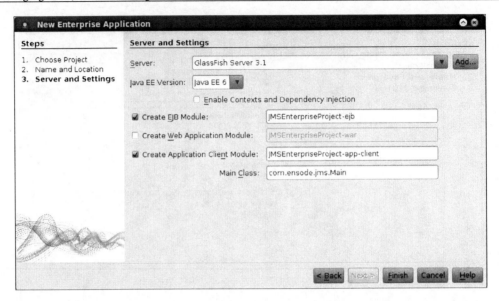

Now that we have created our project, we need to add a couple of necessary JMS resources, a JMS destination (Queue or Topic), and a JMS connection factory. When using GlassFish as our application server, we can create these resources directly from NetBeans.

Creating a JMS destination

JMS destinations are an intermediate location where JMS producers place messages, and JMS consumers retrieve them. When using the **Point To Point (PTP)** Messaging Domain, JMS destinations are message queues, where with the Publish/Subscribe Messaging Domain, the destination is a message topic.

In our example we will be using the PTP messaging domain, therefore we need to create a message queue, and the procedure to create a message topic is almost identical.

In order to create a message queue, we need to click on **File | New File**, select **GlassFish** from the **Categories** list, and **JMS Resource** from the **File Types** list.

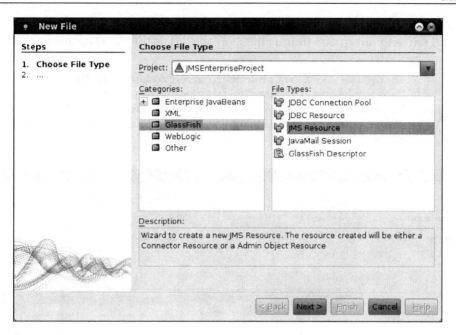

We then need to enter a JNDI name for our queue, in our example, we simply picked the default name `jms/MyQueue`, and accepted the default resource type of **javax.jms.Queue**.

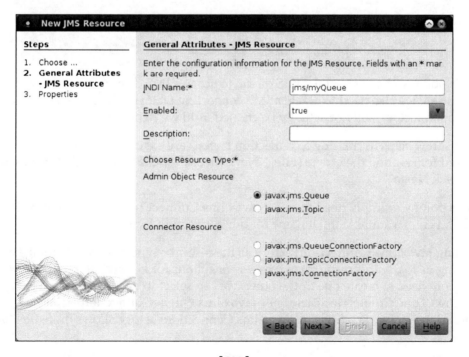

JMS message queues require a `Name` property, in our example we simply chose to use the JNDI name of our queue (minus the `jms/` prefix) as the value of this property.

 The options under the **Connector Resource** section in the **New JMS Resource** wizard are connection factories that can be used to obtain a JMS Queue or Session. With Java EE it is simpler to have the JMS Queue or Session injected directly into the code rather than obtaining it through a connection factory.

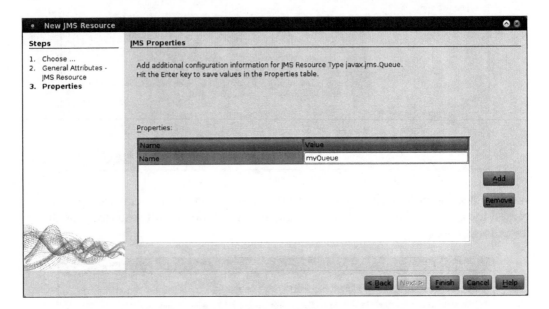

At this point we have created a JMS queue to act as a JMS destination for our application; we also need to create a JMS connection factory. The JMS queue and connection factory will not actually be created until we deploy our project.

The first few steps in creating a connection factory are exactly the same as the ones we used for creating the queue (**File | New File**, select **GlassFish** and **JMS Resource**, then click **Next>**).

At this point we simply need to select **javax.jms.ConnectionFactory** as the resource type and enter a suitable JNDI name for our connection factory.

Selecting **javax.jms.ConnectionFactory** as the resource type has the advantage of allowing us to use this resource to create connections for both queues and topics. If we only need to create one or the other, we can select to create a resource of type **javax.jms.TopicConnectionFactory** or **javax.jms.QueueConnectionFactory** as appropriate. However, choosing javax.jms.ConnectionFactory allows more flexibility.

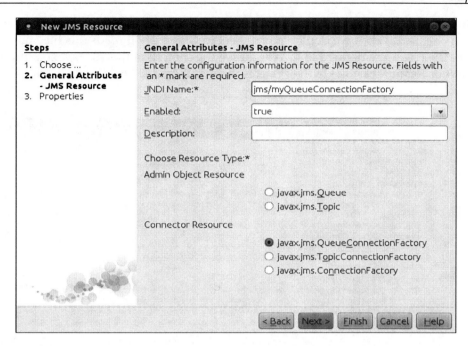

At this point we can simply click on **Finish**, or we can click on **Next** to assign additional properties to our connection factory, however this step is not necessary for connection factories.

NetBeans adds the GlassFish resources we created to a file called `glassfish-resources.xml`. When we deploy our project to GlassFish, it reads this file and creates the resources defined in it. We can see the content of this file by expanding the **Server Resources** node in the Projects view and double-clicking on its name.

```xml
glassfish-resources.xml ×

/home/heffel/NetBeansProjects/2701_code/ch09_src/JMSEnterpriseProject/setup/glassfis

1   <?xml version="1.0" encoding="UTF-8"?>
2   <!DOCTYPE resources PUBLIC "-//GlassFish.org//DTD GlassFish Application Server
    3.1 Resource Definitions//EN" "http://glassfish.org/dtds/glassfish-resources
    1_5.dtd">
3   <resources>
4     <admin-object-resource enabled="true" jndi-name="jms/myQueue" object-type=
    user" res-adapter="jmsra" res-type="javax.jms.Queue">
5       <description/>
6       <property name="Name" value="myQueue"/>
7     </admin-object-resource>
8     <connector-resource enabled="true" jndi-name="jms/myQueueConnectionFactory"
    object-type="user" pool-name="jms/myQueueConnectionFactory">
9       <description/>
10    </connector-resource>
11    <connector-connection-pool associate-with-thread="false" connection-creation
    -retry-attempts="0" connection-creation-retry-interval-in-seconds="10"
    connection-definition-name="javax.jms.QueueConnectionFactory" connection-leak-
    reclaim="false" connection-leak-timeout-in-seconds="0" fail-all-connections="
    false" idle-timeout-in-seconds="300" is-connection-validation-required="false"
    lazy-connection-association="false" lazy-connection-enlistment="false" match-
    connections="true" max-connection-usage-count="0" max-pool-size="32" max-wait-
    time-in-millis="60000" name="jms/myQueueConnectionFactory" ping="false" pool-
    resize-quantity="2" pooling="true" resource-adapter-name="jmsra" steady-pool-
    size="8" validate-atmost-once-period-in-seconds="0"/>
12  </resources>

2 | 166    INS
```

Sending messages to a message destination

Once we have created our connection factory and destination (queue or topic), we need to write some code to send messages to it.

In our example, we will use the application client to send messages to the queue. NetBeans can generate a lot of the necessary boilerplate code automatically. In order to generate this code, the connection factory and destination to be used need to be created in the server, recall we mentioned in the previous section that GlassFish JMS resources created with NetBeans aren't actually created until we deploy our project. In order for these resources to be available to our application client, we need to deploy the project to have these resources created.

After we have deployed our project, we can generate the JMS code opening the main class (`Main.java`) for the application client project, right-clicking on its source, and selecting Insert Code, then selecting **Send JMS Message** from the resulting pop up window.

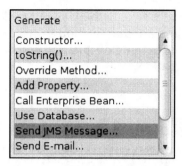

At this point we need to select a message destination and connection factory.

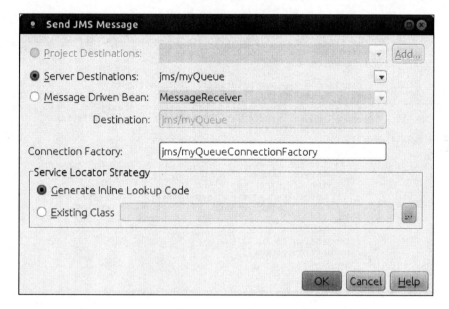

NetBeans detects the different destinations in the server, and provides them in a drop down list. It also makes a best guess at the JNDI name of the connection factory, that, in our case, turns out not to be correct. The above screenshot shows the corrected connection factory JNDI name.

At this point NetBeans generates two methods in our code, a method to send a JMS message to our destination, and another method to create it. Additionally, it injects the necessary resources, the messaging destination and connection factory, into our code via the @Resource annotation.

```
📖 Main.java ×

36
37        private Message createJMSMessageForjmsMyQueue(Session session,
38                Object messageData) throws JMSException {
39            // TODO create and populate message to send
40            TextMessage tm = session.createTextMessage();
41            tm.setText(messageData.toString());
42            return tm;
43        }
44
45        private void sendJMSMessageToMyQueue(Object messageData) throws JMSException {
46            Connection connection = null;
47            Session session = null;
48            try {
49                connection = myQueueFactory.createConnection();
50                session = connection.createSession(false, Session.AUTO_ACKNOWLEDGE);
51                MessageProducer messageProducer = session.createProducer(myQueue);
52                messageProducer.send(createJMSMessageForjmsMyQueue(session,
53                        messageData));
54            } finally {
55                if (session != null) {
56                    try {
57                        session.close();
58                    } catch (JMSException e) {
59                        Logger.getLogger(this.getClass().getName()).log(
60                                Level.WARNING, "Cannot close session", e);
61                    }
62                }
63                if (connection != null) {
64                    connection.close();
65                }
66            }
67        }
```

In our example, the name of the method used to create messages is createJMSMessageForjmsMyQueue() (the exact method name will vary depending on the name of our JMS destination), it returns an instance of a class implementing javax.jms.Message, which all JMS message types must implement, and takes two parameters, an instance of a class implementing javax.jms.Session, and an object containing the message data.

javax.jms.Message has several subinterfaces that are part of the standard Java EE API, in most cases, we use one of the subinterfaces to send messages, instead of using a direct implementation of javax.jms.Message. The following table summarizes all of the standard Java EE subinterfaces:

Subinterface	Description
BytesMessage	Used to send an array of bytes as a message.
MapMessage	Used to send name-value pairs as messages. The names must be String objects, the values must be either primitive types or Java objects.
ObjectMessage	Used to send serializable objects as messages. A serializable object is an instance of any class that implements java.io.Serializable.
StreamMessage	Used to send a stream of Java primitive types as a message.
TextMessage	Used to send a String as a message.

Of the above message types, TextMessage and ObjectMessage are the most frequently used. We will use TextMessage for our example, using other message types is very similar.

Consult the Java EE JavaDoc for details on the APIs for each of the message types. Java EE JavaDoc can be found at http://download. oracle.com/javaee/6/api/.

Notice that the createJMSMessageforjmsMyQueue() method is invoked by the generated sendJMSMessageToMyQueue(), we are expected to invoke sendJMSMessageToMyQueue() as opposed to invoking createJMSMessageForjmsMyqueue() directly. In our example, we do this in the main method of our application.

After adding this invocation, our main() method looks like this:

```
32
33   public static void main(String[] args) throws JMSException {
34       // TODO code application logic here
35       new Main().sendJMSMessageToMyQueue("NetBeans makes JMS trivial!");
36   }
37
```

At this point we have a complete application that will send messages to our message queue. We can deploy the project and execute it, however, we haven't written any code to retrieve messages yet, which is the next step we need to take. However, before moving on, let's go through the generated sendJMSMessageToMyQueue() method so that we can better understand how it works.

The first thing the method does is to obtain a JMS connection by invoking the createConnection() method on the injected instance of javax.jms. ConnectionFactory, and assigning it to a local variable of type javax.jms. Connection.

After the JMS connection is created, the method obtains a JMS session by invoking the `createSession()` method on the `Connection` object. The `createSession()` method has two parameters, the first parameter is a Boolean indicating if the created session is transacted. Transacted sessions allow the code sending messages to a JMS destination to send several messages as part of a transaction. To send several messages as part of a transaction, the JMS client sends messages to the queue as usual, then invokes the `commit()` method on the JMS session. By default, the code generated by NetBeans does not create a transacted JMS session, but we can override this by simply changing the value of the first parameter in `createSession()` to `true`.

The second parameter of the `createSession()` method indicates how JMS messages will be acknowledged by the message receiver. There are three valid values for this parameter, all three are defined as constants in the `javax.jms.Session` interface. The value of the second parameter to `createSession()` is ignored when creating a transacted session.

Acknowledge Mode	Description
`Session.AUTO_ACKNOWLEDGE`	When using this mode, the JMS session will auto-acknowledge message receipt for the client.
`Session.CLIENT_ACKNOWLEDGE`	When using this mode, message receivers must explicitly invoke the `acknowledge()` method defined in `javax.jms.Message` in order to acknowledge receipt of a message.
`Session.DUPS_OK_ACKNOWLEDGE`	When using this mode, the JMS session will lazily acknowledge message receipts on behalf of the JMS client. Using this acknowledge mode may result in some messages being delivered more than once, but it can improve performance by eliminating some of the work the session must do in order to avoid duplicate message deliveries.

Of the three acknowledge modes, `Session.AUTO_ACKNOWLEDGE` is the most commonly used, since it slightly reduces the amount of work to be done by application developers. NetBeans uses this mode by default in the generated code, but we are free to modify the generated code as necessary to meet our requirements.

After creating a JMS session, the next thing the generated code does is to create a JMS message producer by invoking the `createProducer()` method on the JMS session object. This method takes a JMS destination as its sole parameter, unsurprisingly, in the generated code the injected message queue is sent as a parameter to this method.

The last thing this method does is to actually send the message to the message queue. This is done by invoking the `send()` method on the `javax.jms.MessageProducer` instance obtained in the previous line. This method takes an instance of a class implementing `javax.jms.Message` or one of its subinterfaces as a parameter, in the generated code, the generated method to create the message (`createJMSMessageForjmsMyQueue()` in our example) is invoked inline, since this method's return value is of the appropriate type.

Notice that most of the body of the generated method to send JMS messages is enclosed in a `try`/`finally` block. Most of the lines inside the `try` block have the potential of throwing a `JMSException`, if this happens, the code attempts to close the JMS session and connection, which is the exact same thing that needs to be done if the code ends normally, therefore it makes sense to put this code in the `finally` block.

Although it is possible to write standalone applications that can retrieve messages from a messaging destination, most Java EE applications rely on message driven beans for this task, and NetBeans makes it very easy to generate message driven beans.

Processing JMS messages with message driven Beans

In order to create a message driven bean, we need to right-click on our EJB project and select **File | New**, then select the **Enterprise JavaBeans** category and the **Message-Driven Bean** file type.

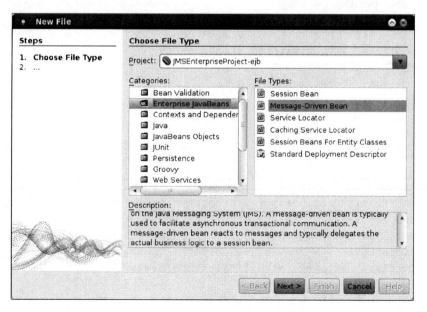

In the resulting dialog window, we need to enter a name, package, and select a JMS destination for the message driven bean.

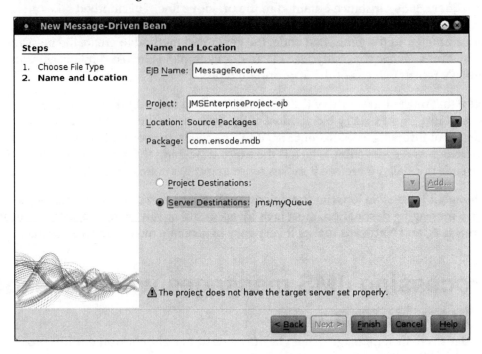

Once we have entered all the required information, our message driven bean is created in the specified package.

```
package com.ensode.mdb;

import javax.ejb.ActivationConfigProperty;
import javax.ejb.MessageDriven;
import javax.jms.Message;
import javax.jms.MessageListener;

/**
 *
 * @author heffel
 */
@MessageDriven(mappedName = "jms/myQueue", activationConfig = {
    @ActivationConfigProperty(propertyName = "acknowledgeMode",
    propertyValue = "Auto-acknowledge"),
    @ActivationConfigProperty(propertyName = "destinationType",
    propertyValue = "javax.jms.Queue")})
public class MessageReceiver implements MessageListener {

    public MessageReceiver() {
```

```
    }
    @Override
    public void onMessage(Message message) {
    }
}
```

In the generated code, all we need to do is implement the body of the onMessage()
method, and deploy our project. The onMessage() method will process any
messages on the JMS destination our message-driven bean is receiving messages
from.

We can write any arbitrary code in the onMessage() method, the possibilities are
endless, however, this method is typically used to save data from the message into a
database, or to write some output into a log. In our example, we will simply send the
contents of the message to the stdout log of our application server.

```
public void onMessage(Message message) {
    TextMessage textMessage = (TextMessage) message;
    try {
        System.out.println("Received message:" +
            textMessage.getText());
    } catch (JMSException ex) {
        Logger.getLogger(
            MessageReceiverBean.class.getName()).log(
            Level.SEVERE, null, ex);
    }
}
```

Notice that we had to cast the message parameter to the actual subinterface that was
sent to the message destination, which in our case is javax.jms.TextMessage. To
obtain the message contents, we invoked the getText() method of TextMessage,
this method throws JMSException, because of this, we had to wrap its invocation in
a try/catch block.

> NetBeans will remind us that we need to catch JMSException by
> underlining the offending code with a wiggly red line, by hitting
> *Alt+Enter* at the offending line we can have NetBeans generate the try/
> catch block automatically.

At this point we are ready to try our application. We can do so by simply right-clicking on our **Enterprise Application Project** and selecting **Run**, at this point the application will be deployed, and the application client project will be executed, sending a message to our message queue. Our EJBs will also be deployed, and the application server will automatically assign one to process the message sent to the queue. We can see the output of the message driven bean in the application server log.

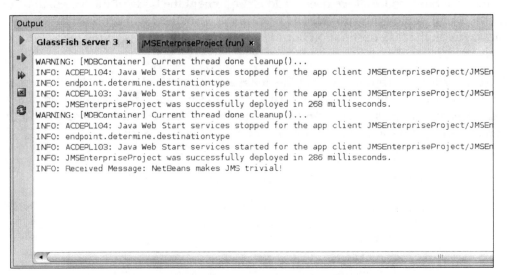

As we can see, NetBeans automates most of the "grunt work" needed to write applications taking advantage of the JMS API, leaving us to only write the business logic part that is specific to our application.

Before moving on, let's discuss the code that NetBeans generates in our Message Driven Beans. Notice that the generated class is decorated with the @MessageDriven annotation, this annotation marks our class as a Message Driven Enterprise JavaBean.

The mappedName attribute of the @MessageDriven annotation should contain the JNDI name of the JMS destination (queue or topic) that our message driven bean will be assigned to.

The value of the activationConfig property must be an array of @ActivationConfigProperty annotations. The @ActivationConfigProperty annotation is used to specify values for certain properties, it has a propertyName attribute used to specify the property name, and a propertyValue attribute used to specify the property value.

When developing message driven beans, we use `@ActivationConfigProperty` annotations to specify the acknowledge mode of the bean (see explanation in the previous section). The destination type of the JMS destination the bean is assigned to, can be `javax.jms.Queue` when using point to point messaging domain, or `javax.jms.Topic` when using the publish/subscribe messaging domain.

In addition to the annotations, we should also notice that the generated message driven bean implements `javax.jms.MessageListener`, which has a single method, `onMessage()`, all message driven beans must implement this interface.

Summary

In this chapter we covered how to develop messaging applications using the JMS API with NetBeans. We talked about how to configure the application server by adding JMS resources directly from NetBeans. We also covered how NetBeans can generate most of the code necessary to send a JMS message, leaving the application developers to simply "fill in the blanks", and write only the business logic part that is specific to our application. Similarly, we covered how NetBeans can generate most of the code necessary to receive a JMS message from a Message Driven Bean, again leaving only the business logic part of our application to be written by hand.

10
SOAP Web Services with JAX-WS

Web services allow us to develop functionality that can be accessed across a network. What makes web services different from other similar technologies such as EJBs is that they are language and platform independent, that is to say, for example, a web service developed in Java may be accessed by clients written in other languages, and vice versa.

In this chapter we will cover the following topics:

- Introduction to web services
- Creating a simple web service
- Creating a web service client
- Exposing EJBs as web services

Introduction to web services

Web services allow us to write functionality that can be accessed across a network in a language- and platform-independent way.

There are two different approaches that are frequently used to develop web services, the first approach is to use the **Simple Object Access Protocol (SOAP)**, the second approach is to use the **Representational State Transfer (REST)** protocol. NetBeans supports creating web services using either approach. SOAP web services are covered in this chapter. RESTful web services are covered in the next chapter.

When using the SOAP protocol, web service operations are defined in an XML document called a **Web Services Definition Language (WSDL)** file. After creating the WSDL, implementation of web services is done in a proper programming language such as Java. The process of creating a WSDL is complex and error prone, fortunately, when working with Java EE, a WSDL can be automatically generated from a web service written in Java when this web service is deployed to the application server. Additionally, if we have a WSDL file available, and need to implement the web service operations in Java, NetBeans can automatically generate most of the Java code for the implementation, creating a class with method stubs for each web service operation. All we need to do is to implement the actual logic for each method, all the "plumbing" code is automatically generated.

Creating a simple web service

In this section, we will develop a web service that performs conversion of units of length. Our web service will have an operation that will convert inches to centimeters, and another operation to do the opposite conversion (centimeters to inches).

In order to create a web service, we need to create a new web application project, in our example, the project name is `UnitConversion`. We can create the web service by right-clicking on our project and selecting **File | New File**, then selecting the **Web Services** category and **Web Service** as our file type.

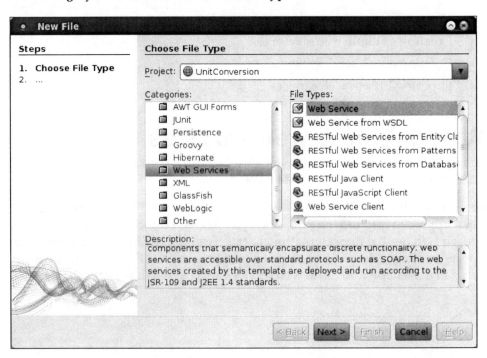

After clicking **Next>**, we need to enter a name and package for our web service.

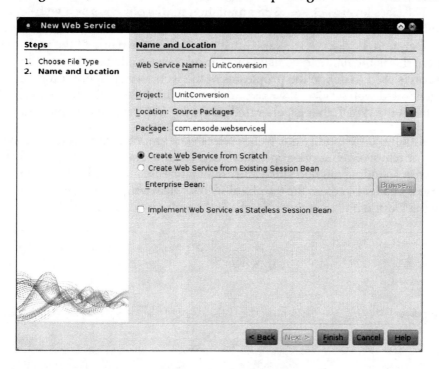

After clicking **Finish**, our web service is created, the source code for our web service is automatically opened.

```java
/*
 * To change this template, choose Tools | Templates
 * and open the template in the editor.
 */

package com.ensode.webservices;

import javax.jws.WebService;
import javax.jws.WebMethod;
import javax.jws.WebParam;

/**
 *
 * @author heffel
 */
@WebService(serviceName="UnitConversion")
public class UnitConversion {

    /** This is a sample web service operation */
    @WebMethod(operationName="hello")
    public String hello(@WebParam(name="name") String txt) {
        return "Hello "+txt+" !";
    }
}
```

As we can see, NetBeans automatically generates a simple "Hello World" web service. The class level `@WebService` annotation marks our class as a web service. The method level `@WebMethod` annotation marks the annotated method as a web service operation; its `operationName` attribute defines the name of the web service operation, this is the name to be used by the web service clients. The `@WebParam` annotation is used to define the properties of the web service operation parameters. In the generated web service, the `name` attribute is used to specify the name of the parameter in the WSDL that is generated when the web service is deployed.

NetBeans allows us to modify our web services via a graphical interface. We can simply add and/or remove web service operations and parameters by pointing and clicking, and the corresponding method stubs and annotations are automatically added to our web service's code. To access the graphical web service designer, we simply need to click on the **Design** button at the top right of the web service source code.

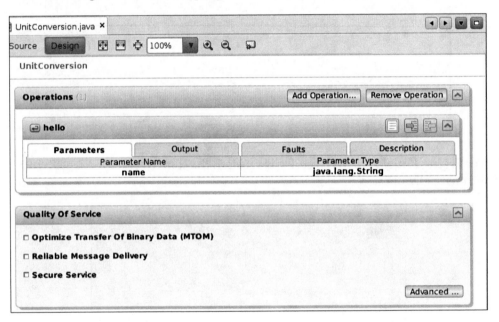

The first thing we need to do is to remove the automatically generated operation, all we need to do to accomplish this is to click on the **Remove Operation** button.

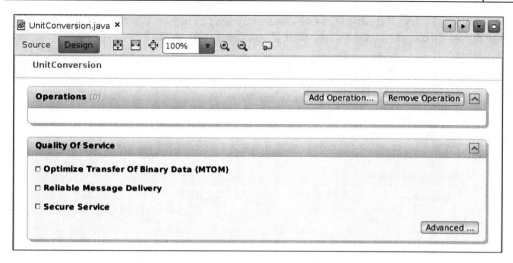

To add a web service operation, we simply need to click on the **Add Operation...** button and fill in the blanks in the resulting window.

Our web service will have two operations, one to convert from inches to centimeters and another one to convert centimeters to inches, both of these operations will take a single parameter of type double, and return a double value. After clicking on the **Add Operation...** button we can enter the required information for the inchesToCentimeters operation.

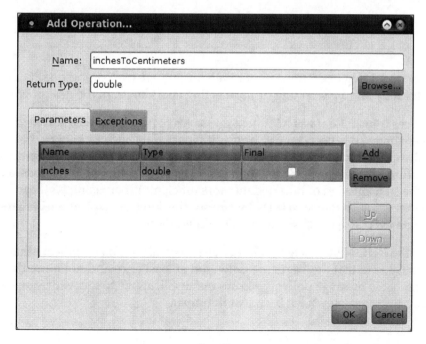

We then need to do the same for the `centimetersToInches` operation (not shown), after doing so our design window will show the newly added operations.

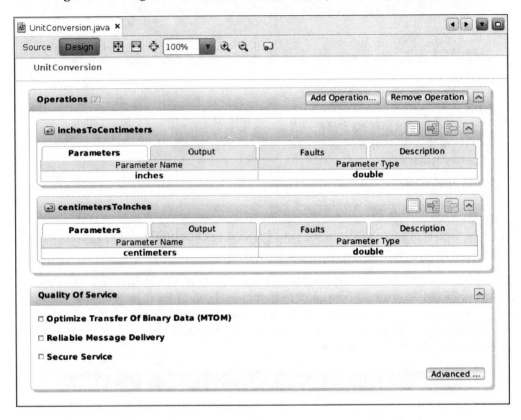

In addition to adding operations to our web service, we can control quality of service settings for it by simply selecting or unselecting checkboxes in the design window.

Web services transmit data as XML text messages between the web service and its client. Sometimes, it is necessary to transmit binary data such as images. Binary data is normally inlined in the SOAP message, by using **MTOM (Message Transmission Optimization Mechanism)**, binary data is sent as an attachment to the message, making the transmission of binary data more efficient. When using NetBeans, we can indicate that we wish to use MTOM by simply checking the **Optimize Transfer Of Binary Data (MTOM)** checkbox in the design window.

Checking the **Reliable Message Delivery** checkbox allows us to indicate that we want to make sure that messages are delivered at least once and not more than once. Enabling reliable message delivery allows our applications to recover from situations where our messages may have been lost in transit.

Clicking on the **Secure Service** checkbox results in security features; such as encrypting messages between the client and server; and requiring client authentication, to be enabled for our web service.

Web service security can be configured by clicking on the **Advanced ...** button and selecting the appropriate security options in the resulting window.

We can see the generated method stubs by clicking on the **Source** tab.

```java
6    package com.ensode.webservices;
7
8    import javax.jws.WebService;
9    import javax.jws.WebMethod;
10   import javax.jws.WebParam;
11
12   /**
13    *
14    * @author heffel
15    */
16   @WebService(serviceName="UnitConversion")
17   public class UnitConversion {
18
19       /**
20        * Web service operation
21        */
22       @WebMethod(operationName = "inchesToCentimeters")
23       public double inchesToCentimeters(@WebParam(name = "inches")
24       double inches) {
25           //TODO write your implementation code here:
26           return 0.0;
27       }
28
29       /**
30        * Web service operation
31        */
32       @WebMethod(operationName = "centimetersToInches")
33       public double centimetersToInches(@WebParam(name = "centimeters")
34       double centimeters) {
35           //TODO write your implementation code here:
36           return 0.0;
37       }
38   }
```

Now all we need to do is to replace the generated body of the methods in the class with the "real" bodies, deploy our application, and our web service will be good to go. In our case, all we need to do is divide the inches by 2.54 to convert from inches to centimeters, and multiply the centimeters by 2.54 to convert them to inches.

Once we have replaced the method bodies with the actual required functionality, we are ready to deploy our web service, which can be done by right-clicking on our project and selecting **Deploy**.

Testing our web service

At this point we should notice a **Web Services** node in our **Projects** window.
If we expand it we should see our newly developed web service.

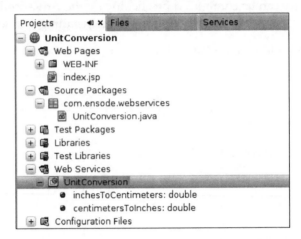

If we deploy our web service to the GlassFish application server included with
NetBeans, we can test it by simply right-clicking on it in the **Projects** window and
selecting **Test Web Service**.

Here we can test our web service's methods by simply entering some values in the text fields and clicking on the appropriate button. For example, entering 2.54 in the second text field and clicking on the button labeled **centimetersToInches** results in the following page being displayed in the browser:

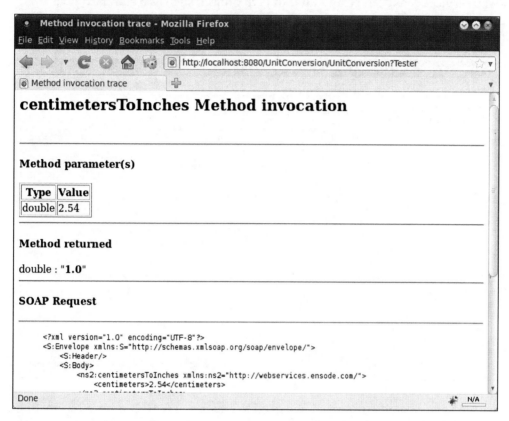

At the top of the page we can see the parameters that were passed to the method, along with the return value. At the bottom of the page we can see the "raw" SOAP request and response.

Developing a client for our web service

Now that we have developed our web service and tested it to verify that it works properly, we are going to create a simple client that will invoke our web service. A web services client can be any kind of Java project, such as a standard Java application, a Java ME application, a web application, or an enterprise project. To keep our client code simple we will create a Java Application project for our client.

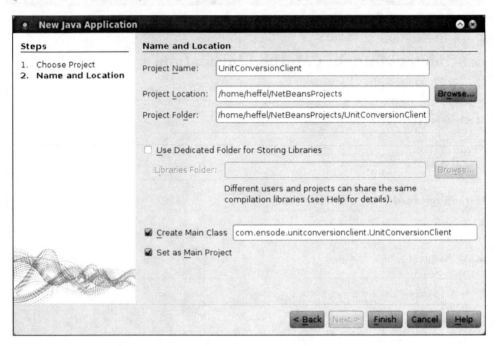

Once we have created our project, we need to create a new web service by creating a new file, selecting the **Web Services** category and the **Web Service Client** file type.

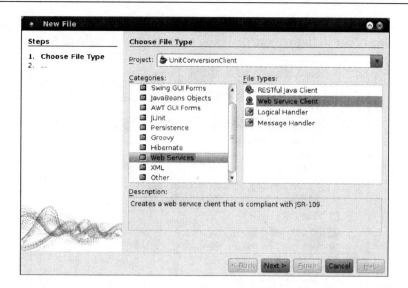

In the next step in the wizard, we need to select the radio button labeled **Project** if it is not selected already, then click on **Browse** and select one of the web services we created in our web services project. The URL for the generated WSDL file for the web service we selected will automatically be added to the corresponding text field.

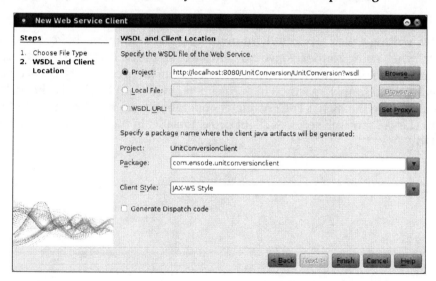

Notice that we can develop web service clients for web services we didn't develop ourselves. In order to do this we simply select the **Local File** radio button to use a WSDL file in our hard drive, or the **WSDL URL** radio button to use a WSDL that is published online.

At this point, a new node labeled **Web Service References** is added to our project. Expanding this node all the way reveals the operations we defined in our web services project.

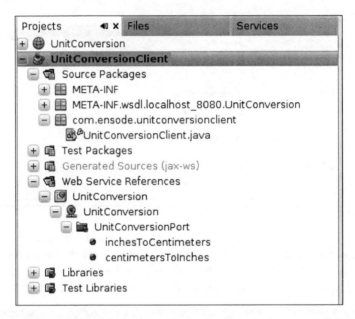

Typically, writing a web services client involves some amount of "boilerplate" code, however, when using NetBeans, we can simply drag the web service operation we wish to invoke to our code. This results in generating all necessary boilerplate code, and leaving us to simply specify which parameters we want to send to the web service. Dragging the **inchesToCentimeters** operation from the **Projects** window to the main class of our web services client project results in the following code being generated:

```
UnitConversionClient.java ×

 5    package com.ensode.unitconversionclient;
 6
 7  /**
 8    *
 9    * @author heffel
10    */
11    public class UnitConversionClient {
12
13  /**
14    * @param args the command line arguments
15    */
16    public static void main(String[] args) {
17        // TODO code application logic here
18    }
19
20    private static double inchesToCentimeters(double inches) {
21        com.ensode.unitconversionclient.UnitConversion_Service service =
22            new com.ensode.unitconversionclient.UnitConversion_Service();
23        com.ensode.unitconversionclient.UnitConversion port =
24            service.getUnitConversionPort();
25        return port.inchesToCentimeters(inches);
26    }
27    }
```

As we can see, a method called `inchesToCentimeters()` (the name of the web service operation we dragged to the source code) is automatically added. This method in turn invokes a couple of methods in a class called `UnitConversion_Service`. This class (and several others) is automatically generated when we drag the web service operation to our code. We can see the generated classes by expanding the **Generated Sources (jax-ws)** node in our project window.

The `getUnitConversionPort()` method of `UnitConversion_Service` returns an instance of the `UnitConversion` class that is generated from the WSDL and is similar to the identically named class we wrote in our web service project. The method generated when we drag the web service operation to our code invokes this method, then invokes the `inchesToCentimeters()` method on the `UnitConversion` instance that is returned. All we need to do is invoke the generated method from the main method in our code. After making this simple modification, our code now looks like this:

```java
package com.ensode.unitconversionclient;

/**
 *
 * @author heffel
 */
public class UnitConversionClient {

    /**
     * @param args the command line arguments
     */
    public static void main(String[] args) {
        System.out.println("Result = " + inchesToCentimeters(1));
    }

    private static double inchesToCentimeters(double inches) {
        com.ensode.unitconversionclient.UnitConversion_Service service =
                new com.ensode.unitconversionclient.UnitConversion_Service();
        com.ensode.unitconversionclient.UnitConversion port =
                service.getUnitConversionPort();
        return port.inchesToCentimeters(inches);
    }
}
```

At this point, we are ready to execute our web services client code; we should see the following output in the console:

```
Output - UnitConversionClient (run)
init:
Deleting: /home/heffel/NetBeansProjects/UnitConversionClient/build/built-jar.properties
deps-jar:
Updating property file: /home/heffel/NetBeansProjects/UnitConversionClient/build/built-jar.prope
wsimport-init:
wsimport-client-UnitConversion:
files are up to date
wsimport-client-generate:
compile:
run:
Result = 2.54
BUILD SUCCESSFUL (total time: 1 second)
```

Exposing EJBs as web services

In our previous web service example, we saw how we can expose a **Plain Old Java Object (POJO)** as a web service by packaging it in a web application and adding a few annotations to it. This makes it very easy to create web services deployed in a web application.

When working with an EJB module project, we can have stateless session beans exposed as web services, this way they can be accessed by clients written in languages other than Java. Exposing stateless session beans as web services has the effect of allowing our web services to take advantage of all the features available to EJBs, such as transaction management and aspect-oriented programming.

There are two ways we can expose a session bean as a web service, when creating a new web service in an EJB module project, the web service will automatically be implemented as a stateless session bean. Additionally, existing session beans in an EJB module project can be exposed as a web service.

Implementing new web services as EJBs

In order to implement a new web service as an EJB, we simply need to create the web service in an EJB module project by right-clicking on the project and selecting **New | Web Service**.

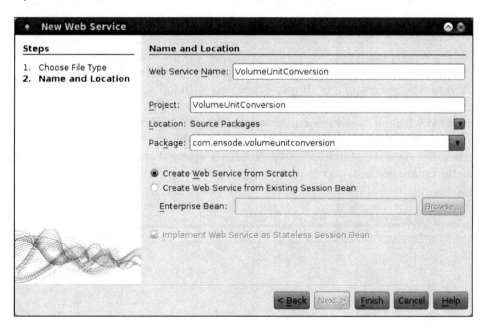

In the web services wizard, we need to enter a name for our web service, a package where our web service implementation code will be created, and select the **Create Web Service From Scratch** radio button, then click **Finish** to generate our web service. At this point we should see the web service source code.

```java
/*
 * To change this template, choose Tools | Templates
 * and open the template in the editor.
 */

package com.ensode.volumeunitconversion;

import javax.jws.WebService;
import javax.jws.WebMethod;
import javax.jws.WebParam;
import javax.ejb.Stateless;

/**
 *
 * @author heffel
 */
@WebService(serviceName="VolumeUnitConversion")
@Stateless()
public class VolumeUnitConversion {

    /** This is a sample web service operation */
    @WebMethod(operationName="hello")
    public String hello(@WebParam(name="name") String txt) {
        return "Hello "+txt+" !";
    }
}
```

Notice that the generated session bean does not implement neither a local nor remote business interface, it is simply decorated with the @WebService annotation, its methods are decorated with the @WebMethod annotation, and each parameter is decorated with the @WebParam annotation. The only difference between the generated code for this web service and the one for the previous example is that the generated class is a stateless session bean, therefore it can take advantage of EJB transaction management, aspect-oriented programming, and other EJB features.

Just as with regular web services, a web service implemented as a session bean can be designed using the NetBeans visual web service designer. In our example, after removing the automatically generated operation and adding two operations, our web service visual designer looks like this:

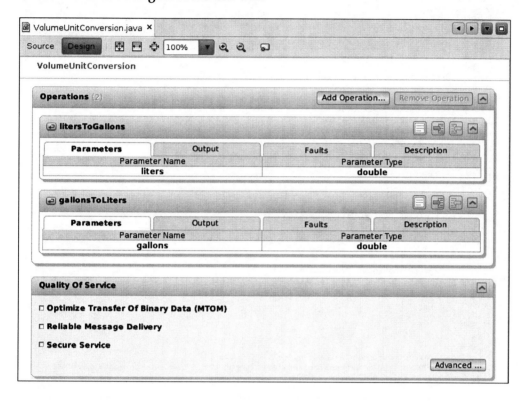

Clicking on the **Source** tab reveals the newly generated methods, along with all appropriate annotations.

```
VolumeUnitConversion.java ×

Source   Design

1  /*
2   * To change this template, choose Tools | Templates
3   * and open the template in the editor.
4   */
5  package com.ensode.volumeunitconversion;
6
7  import javax.jws.WebService;
8  import javax.jws.WebMethod;
9  import javax.jws.WebParam;
10 import javax.ejb.Stateless;
11
12 /**
13  *
14  * @author heffel
15  */
16 @WebService(serviceName = "VolumeUnitConversion")
17 @Stateless()
18 public class VolumeUnitConversion {
19
20     /**
21      * Web service operation
22      */
23     @WebMethod(operationName = "litersToGallons")
24     public double litersToGallons(@WebParam(name = "liters") double liters) {
25         return liters * 0.26417;
26     }
27
28     /**
29      * Web service operation
30      */
31     @WebMethod(operationName = "gallonsToLiters")
32     public double gallonsToLiters(@WebParam(name = "gallons") double gallons) {
33         return gallons * 3.7854;
34     }
```

Once we deploy our project, our web service can be accessed by clients just like any other web service. It makes no difference to the client that our web service was implemented as a session bean.

Exposing existing EJBs as web services

The second way we can expose EJBs as web services is to expose an existing EJB as a web service. In order to do this, we need to create a web service as usual by going to **File | New | Web Service**, then enter a name and a package for our web service and select the **Create Web Service from Existing Session Bean** radio button, then we need to select the session bean to expose as a web service by clicking on the **Browse...** button and selecting the appropriate bean.

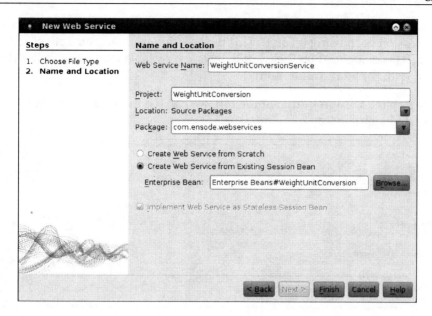

When we click on **Finish,** our new web service is created and its source code is automatically opened.

```java
6    package com.ensode.webservices;
7
8    import com.ensode.ejb.WeightUnitConversion;
9    import javax.ejb.EJB;
10   import javax.jws.WebMethod;
11   import javax.jws.WebParam;
12   import javax.jws.WebService;
13   import javax.ejb.Stateless;
14
15   /**
16    *
17    * @author heffel
18    */
19   @WebService(serviceName="WeightUnitConversionService")
20   @Stateless()
21   public class WeightUnitConversionService {
22       @EJB
23       private WeightUnitConversion ejbRef;// Add business logic
24       // "Insert Code > Add Web Service Operation")
25
26       @WebMethod(operationName = "kilosToPounds")
27       public double kilosToPounds(@WebParam(name = "kilos")
28       double kilos) {
29           return ejbRef.kilosToPounds(kilos);
30       }
31
32       @WebMethod(operationName = "poundsToKilos")
33       public double poundsToKilos(@WebParam(name = "pounds")
34       double pounds) {
35           return ejbRef.poundsToKilos(pounds);
36       }
37
38   }
```

As we can see, creating a web service from an existing session bean results in a new stateless session bean being created. This new session bean acts as a client for our existing EJB (as evidenced by the `ejbRef` instance variable in our example, which is annotated with the `@EJB` annotation).

By clicking on the **Design** button at the top, we can see the visual designer for our newly created web service.

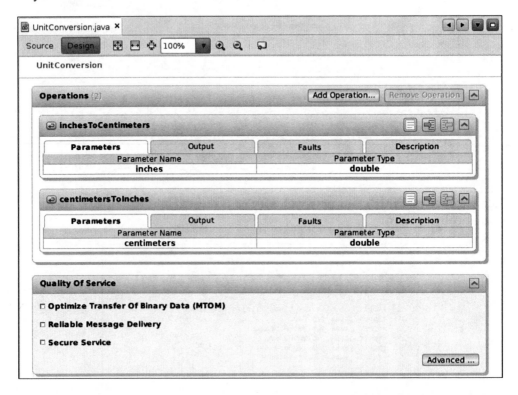

EJBs can also be exposed as web services from a web application project, in which case the generated web service will be a POJO annotated with the `@WebService`, `@WebMethod`, and `@WebParam` annotations, with pass-through methods invoking the corresponding methods on the EJB being exposed as a web service.

Creating a web service from an existing WSDL

Normally, creating SOAP web services requires the creation of a **Web Services Definition (WSDL)** file. The process of creating a WSDL is complex and error prone, but thankfully Java EE frees us from having to create a WSDL file by hand, since it gets generated automatically whenever we deploy a web service into our application server.

However, sometimes we have a WSDL file available, and we need to implement its operations in Java code. For these cases, NetBeans provides a wizard that creates a Java class with method stubs from an existing WSDL.

In order to do so, we need to create a new file, select the **Web Services** category, and **Web Service from WSDL** as the file type.

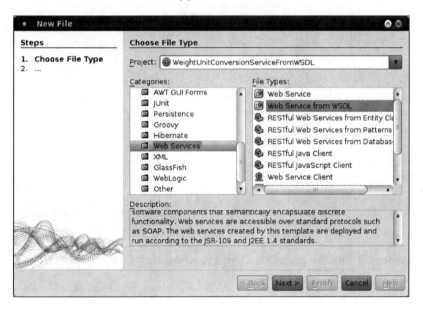

We then need to enter a name, package and existing WSDL for our web service.

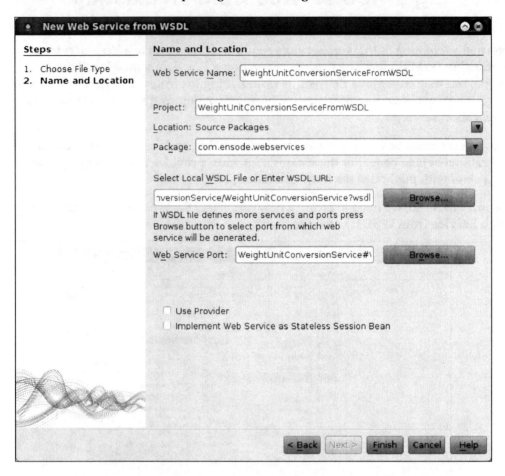

A web service will then be generated with method stubs for all operations defined in the WSDL.

```
WeightUnitConversionServiceFromWSDL.java  ×

 Source   Design      🖾  ▣▾  ▣▾    Q  ⬱  ⬱  🖳    ⬱  ⬱  ⬱    ⬱ ⬱   ◉  ▣    🗎  ⬛

  4   L  */
  5      package com.ensode.webservices;
  6
  7 ⊟  import javax.jws.WebService;
  8
  9 ⊟  /**
 10      *
 11      * @author heffel
 12   L  */
 13      @WebService(serviceName = "WeightUnitConversionService",
         portName = "WeightUnitConversionServicePort",
 14      endpointInterface = "com.ensode.webservices.WeightUnitConversionService", targ↵
 15      etNamespace = "http://webservices.ensode.com/",
         wsdlLocation = "WEB-INF/wsdl/WeightUnitConversionServiceFromWSDL/localhost_808↵
 16      0/WeightUnitConversionService/WeightUnitConversionService.wsdl")
         public class WeightUnitConversionServiceFromWSDL {
 17
 18          public double kilosToPounds(double kilos) {
 19 ⊟            //TODO implement this method
 20              throw new UnsupportedOperationException("Not implemented yet.");
 21          }
 22   L
 23          public double poundsToKilos(double pounds) {
 24 ⊟            //TODO implement this method
 25              throw new UnsupportedOperationException("Not implemented yet.");
 26          }
 27   L  }
```

At this point we simply need to add the method bodies for all the generated methods.

In this example, we used the WSDL that was generated from our previous example, which is redundant since we already have implementations for all the operations. However, the procedure illustrated here applies to any WSDL file, either in the local file system or deployed in a server.

Summary

In this chapter, we explored NetBeans' support for Web Service development, including how to expose a POJO's methods as web services and how NetBeans automatically adds the required annotations to our web services.

We covered how NetBeans aids us in creating web service clients by generating most of the required boilerplate code, leaving us to simply initialize any parameters to be passed to our web service's operations.

Additionally we covered how to expose EJB methods as web service operations, and how NetBeans supports and makes it easy to expose both new and existing EJBs as web services.

Finally, we saw how NetBeans can help us implement a web service from an existing WSDL file, located either on our local file system or deployed on a server, by generating method stubs from said WSDL.

11
RESTful Web Services with JAX-RS

Representational State Transfer (REST) is an architectural style in which web services are viewed as resources and can be identified by **Uniform Resource Identifiers (URIs)**.

Web services developed using the REST style are known as RESTful web services. Java EE 6 adds support to RESTful web services through the addition of the Java API for RESTful Web Services (JAX-RS). JAX-RS has been available as a standalone API for a while, it became part of Java EE in version 6 of the specification.

One very common use of RESTful web services is to act as a frontend to a database, that is, RESTful web service clients can use a RESTful web service to perform **CRUD (Create, Read, Update, Delete)** operations in a database. Since this is such a common use case, NetBeans includes outstanding support for this, allowing us to create RESTful web services that act as a database frontend with a few simple mouse clicks.

Here are some of the topics we will cover in this chapter:

- Generating RESTful web services from an existing database
- Testing RESTful web services using tools provided by NetBeans
- Generating a RESTful web service client code for our RESTful web services

Generating a RESTful web service from an existing database

To create a RESTful web service from an existing database, in a web application project, we simply need to select **File | New**, then pick the **Web Services** category and the **RESTful Web Services From Database** file type.

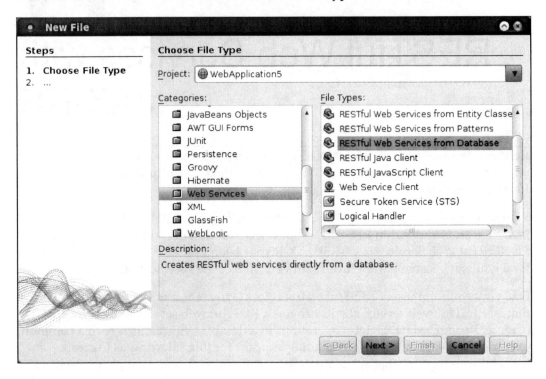

In the next step in the wizard, we need to pick a datasource and select one or more tables to generate our web service. In our example, we will generate a web service for the CUSTOMER table of the customerdb database.

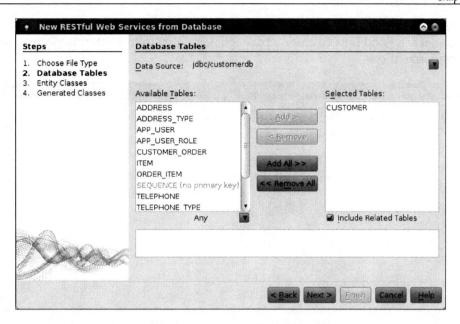

In the next step in the wizard, we need to enter a package for our web service code.

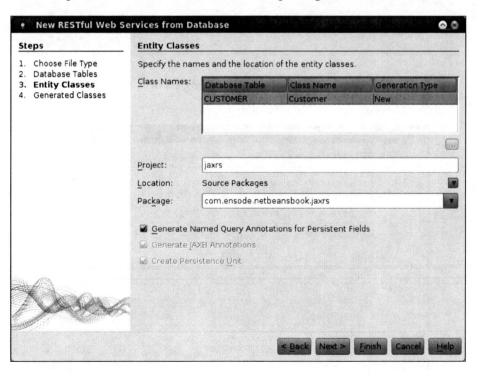

We then need to pick a **Resource Package,** or simply accept the default value of service, it is a good idea to enter a package name that follows standard package naming conventions.

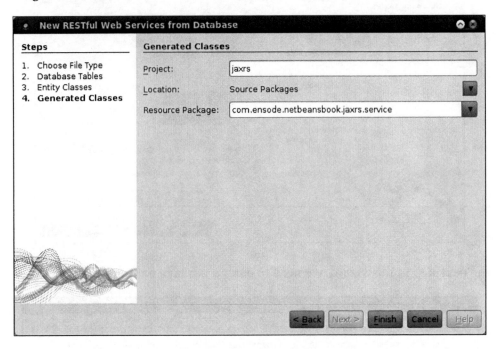

When we click on **Finish,** a window pops up asking us how we want to register REST resources.

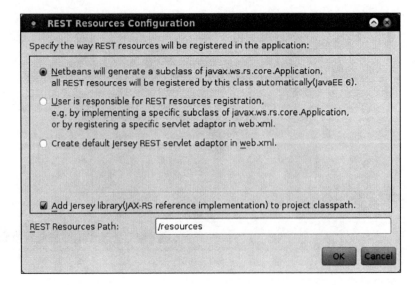

We are presented with three options:

- Generate a subclass of `javax.ws.rs.core.Application`
- Do nothing, then manually write some code or configuration to register JAX-RS resources
- Generate a `web.xml` deployment descriptor with the appropriate configuration

In most cases we want to pick the first option since one of the major benefits of Java EE 6 over previous versions is reduced reliance on configuration files such as `web.xml`. The **do nothing** option requires us to manually configure our RESTful web services, and the `web.xml` option uses the older way of configuring JAX-RS via this deployment descriptor.

 In most cases, the **Add Jersey Library (JAX-RS reference implementation) to project classpath** checkbox should be checked, since this option automatically adds the required JAX-RS libraries to our project.

Analyzing the generated code

The wizard discussed in the previous section creates a JPA entity for each chosen table, plus an `AbstratFacade` class and a Facade class for each generated JPA entity. The generated code follows the Facade design pattern, in essence, each Facade class is a wrapper for JPA code.

 See `http://en.wikipedia.org/wiki/Facade_pattern` for more information on the Facade design pattern.

The generated Facade classes are deployed as RESTful web services and can be accessed as such:

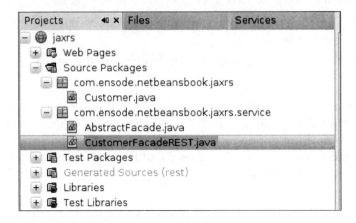

The AbstractFacade class serves as a parent class for all other Facade classes:

```java
package com.ensode.netbeansbook.jaxrs.service;

import java.util.List;
import javax.persistence.EntityManager;

public abstract class AbstractFacade<T> {
    private Class<T> entityClass;

    public AbstractFacade(Class<T> entityClass) {
        this.entityClass = entityClass;
    }

    protected abstract EntityManager getEntityManager();

    public void create(T entity) {
        getEntityManager().persist(entity);
    }

    public void edit(T entity) {
        getEntityManager().merge(entity);
    }

    public void remove(T entity) {
        getEntityManager().remove(getEntityManager().merge(entity));
    }

    public T find(Object id) {
        return getEntityManager().find(entityClass, id);
    }

    public List<T> findAll() {
        javax.persistence.criteria.CriteriaQuery cq =
```

```
            getEntityManager().getCriteriaBuilder().createQuery();
        cq.select(cq.from(entityClass));
        return getEntityManager().createQuery(cq).getResultList();
    }

    public List<T> findRange(int[] range) {
        javax.persistence.criteria.CriteriaQuery cq =
            getEntityManager().getCriteriaBuilder().createQuery();
        cq.select(cq.from(entityClass));
        javax.persistence.Query q =
    getEntityManager().createQuery(cq);
        q.setMaxResults(range[1] - range[0]);
        q.setFirstResult(range[0]);
        return q.getResultList();
    }

    public int count() {
        javax.persistence.criteria.CriteriaQuery cq =
            getEntityManager().getCriteriaBuilder().createQuery();
        javax.persistence.criteria.Root<T> rt = cq.from(entityClass);
        cq.select(getEntityManager().getCriteriaBuilder().count(rt));
        javax.persistence.Query q =
    getEntityManager().createQuery(cq);
        return ((Long) q.getSingleResult()).intValue();
    }

}
```

As we can see, `AbstractFacade` has an `entityClass` variable that gets set to the appropriate type via generics by its child classes. It also has methods to create, edit, remove, find, and count entities. The body of these methods is standard JPA code and should be familiar by now.

As we mentioned earlier, the wizard generates a Facade for each generated JPA entity, in this example we picked a single table (CUSTOMER), therefore a single JPA entity was created, the Facade class for this JPA entity is called `CustomerFacadeRest`.

```
package com.ensode.netbeansbook.jaxrs.service;

import com.ensode.netbeansbook.jaxrs.Customer;
import java.util.List;
import javax.ejb.Stateless;
import javax.persistence.EntityManager;
import javax.persistence.PersistenceContext;
import javax.ws.rs.Consumes;
import javax.ws.rs.DELETE;
import javax.ws.rs.GET;
```

```java
import javax.ws.rs.POST;
import javax.ws.rs.PUT;
import javax.ws.rs.Path;
import javax.ws.rs.PathParam;
import javax.ws.rs.Produces;

@Stateless
@Path("com.ensode.netbeansbook.jaxrs.customer")
public class CustomerFacadeREST extends AbstractFacade<Customer> {
    @PersistenceContext(unitName = "jaxrsPU")
    private EntityManager em;

    @java.lang.Override
    protected EntityManager getEntityManager() {
        return em;
    }

    public CustomerFacadeREST() {
        super(Customer.class);
    }

    @POST
    @Override
    @Consumes({"application/xml", "application/json"})
    public void create(Customer entity) {
        super.create(entity);
    }

    @PUT
    @Override
    @Consumes({"application/xml", "application/json"})
    public void edit(Customer entity) {
        super.edit(entity);
    }

    @DELETE
    @Path("{id}")
    public void remove(@PathParam("id")
    Integer id) {
        super.remove(super.find(id));
    }

    @GET
    @Path("{id}")
    @Produces({"application/xml", "application/json"})
    public Customer find(@PathParam("id")
    Integer id) {
        return super.find(id);
    }
```

```
@GET
@Override
@Produces({"application/xml", "application/json"})
public List<Customer> findAll() {
    return super.findAll();
}

@GET
@Path("{from}/{to}")
@Produces({"application/xml", "application/json"})
public List<Customer> findRange(@PathParam("from")
Integer from, @PathParam("to")
Integer to) {
    return super.findRange(new int[]{from, to});
}

@GET
@Path("count")
@Produces("text/plain")
public String countREST() {
    return String.valueOf(super.count());
}

}
```

As evident by the `@Stateless` annotation, the generated class is a stateless session bean. The `@Path` annotation is used to identify the **Uniform Resource Identifier (URI)** that our class will serve requests for. As we can see, several of the methods in our class are annotated with the `@POST`, `@PUT`, `@DELETE`, and `@GET` annotations. These methods will be automatically invoked when our web service responds to the corresponding HTTP requests. Notice that several of the methods are annotated with the `@Path` annotation as well, the reason for this is that some of these methods require a parameter, for example, when we need to delete an entry from the CUSTOMER table, we need to pass the primary key of the corresponding row as a parameter. The format of the value attribute of the `@Path` annotation is "`{varName}`", the text between the curly braces is known as a **path parameter**. Notice that the method has corresponding parameters that are annotated with the `@PathParam` annotation.

Testing our RESTful web service

Once we deploy our project, we can make sure that the web service was deployed successfully by expanding the **RESTful Web Services** node on our project, right-clicking on our RESTful web service and selecting **Test Resource Uri**.

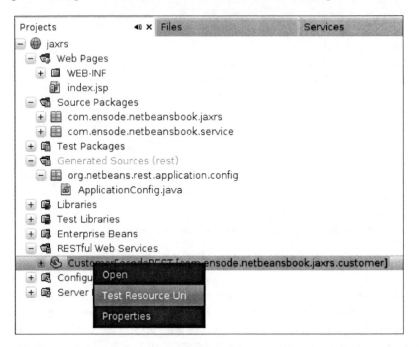

This action will invoke the `findAll()` method in our service (since it is the only method that doesn't require a parameter), the generated XML response will automatically open in the browser.

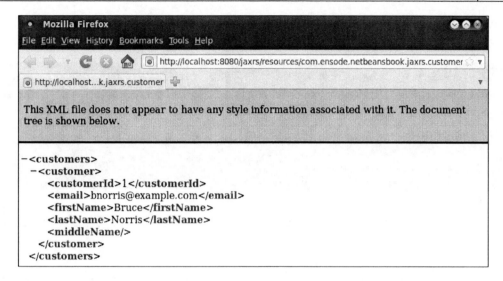

There is only one row in the CUSTOMER table of our database, the XML response for our web service displays the data in this row.

We can also easily test other methods in our web service by right-clicking on the project and selecting **Test RESTful Web Services**.

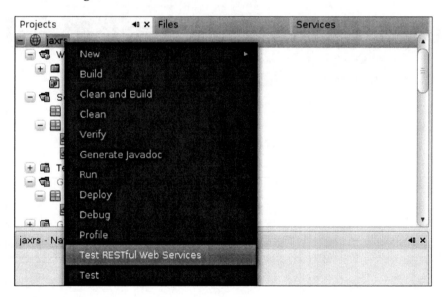

After doing this, a page similar to the following will automatically open in the browser:

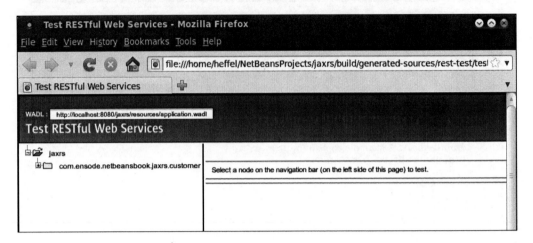

By clicking on our web service at the left, and then selecting **GET(application/xml)** from the drop down menu labeled **Choose method to test**, then clicking on **Test** results in an HTTP GET request being sent to our RESTful web service returns an XML response.

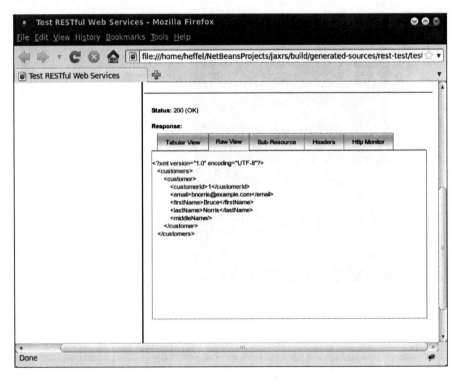

Unsurprisingly, the XML we see here is identical to the one that we saw earlier.

Our RESTful web service can produce or consume either XML or JSON (JavaScript Object Notation). This can be seen in the values for each of the @Produces and @Consumes annotations in our code.

If we can see the JSON representation of the result of the findAll() method, all we need to do is select **GET(application/json)** and click on the **Test** button.

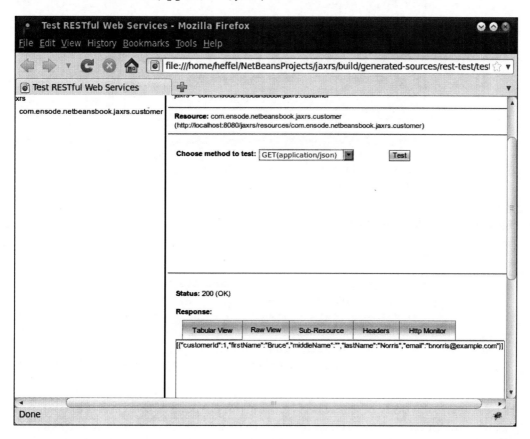

We can also insert, read, or modify a single record by selecting the appropriate HTTP request and passing the appropriate parameters. The corresponding method in our RESTful web service will be automatically called.

Now that we have verified our RESTful web service was deployed successfully, the next step is to implement a client application that uses our service. But before doing so let's take a look at the NetBeans generated `ApplicationConfig` class, which can be seen by expanding the **Generated Sources (rest)** node in the project view.

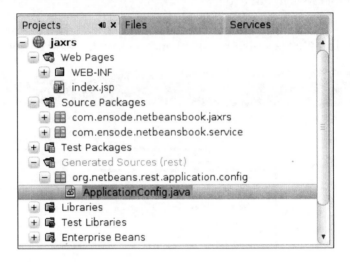

The source code for this class looks like this:

```
package org.netbeans.rest.application.config;
/**
 * This class is generated by the Netbeans IDE,
 * and registers all REST root resources created in the project.
 * Please, DO NOT EDIT this class !
 */
@javax.ws.rs.ApplicationPath("resources")
public class ApplicationConfig extends javax.ws.rs.core.Application {
}
```

As we can see, the body of this class is empty, the purpose of this class is to configure JAX-RS, and therefore no actual code needs to be generated. The only requirement is that the class extends `javax.ws.rs.core.Application` and for the class to be annotated with the `@javax.ws.rs.ApplicationPath` annotation. This annotation is used to specify the base URI of all paths specified by the `@Path` annotation in our RESTful web services classes. NetBeans by default uses a path named `resources` for all RESTful web services.

Developing a RESTful web service client

NetBeans provides a wizard that can automatically generate client code that invokes our RESTful web service methods via the corresponding HTTP requests.

To generate this client code, we simply need to click on **File | New File**, then select the **Web Services** category and **RESTful Java Client** as the file type.

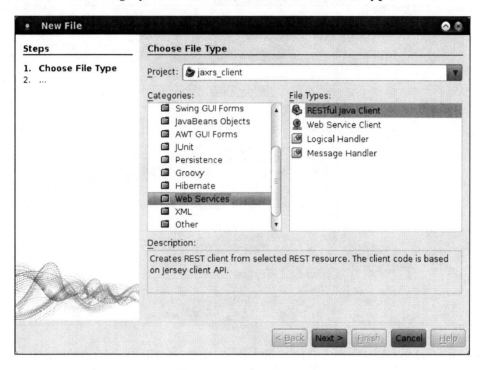

In the next step in the wizard, we need to enter a class name and a package name for our JAX-RS client.

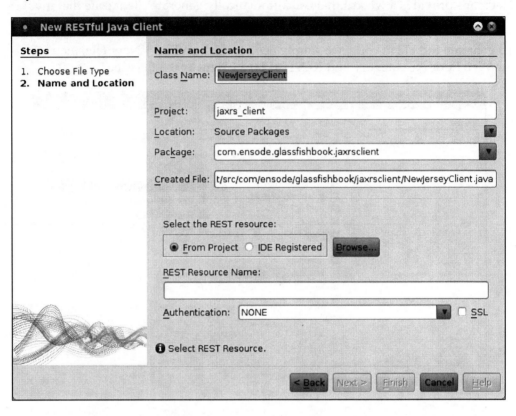

We then need to select the RESTful web service that our client will consume, in our case we need to select the **From Project** radio button under **Select the REST resource**, then click on the button labeled **Browse....**

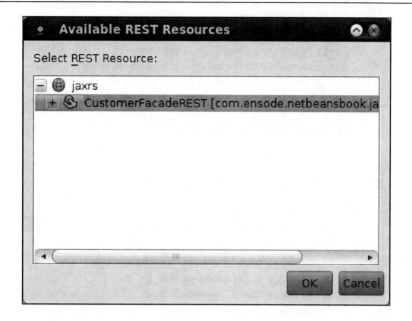

We then simply need to select the RESTful web service we developed earlier.

At this point, NetBeans generates the following code:

```
package com.ensode.glassfishbook.jaxrsclient;

import com.sun.jersey.api.client.Client;
import com.sun.jersey.api.client.UniformInterfaceException;
import com.sun.jersey.api.client.WebResource;

/** Jersey REST client generated for REST resource:CustomerFacadeREST
[com.ensode.netbeansbook.jaxrs.customer]<br>
 *   USAGE:<pre>
 *         NewJerseyClient client = new NewJerseyClient();
 *         Object response = client.XXX(...);
 *         // do whatever with response
 *         client.close();
 *   </pre>
 * @author heffel
 */
public class NewJerseyClient {
    private WebResource webResource;
    private Client client;
    private static final String BASE_URI =
        "http://localhost:8080/jaxrs/resources";

    public NewJerseyClient() {
        com.sun.jersey.api.client.config.ClientConfig config = new
            com.sun.jersey.api.client.config.DefaultClientConfig();
```

```
        client = Client.create(config);
        webResource =
            client.resource(BASE_URI).path(
            "com.ensode.netbeansbook.jaxrs.customer");
    }
    public void remove(String id) throws UniformInterfaceException {
        webResource.path(java.text.MessageFormat.format("{0}",
            new Object[]{id})).delete();
    }
    public String countREST() throws UniformInterfaceException {
        WebResource resource = webResource;
        resource = resource.path("count");
        return resource.accept(
            javax.ws.rs.core.MediaType.TEXT_PLAIN).get(String.class);
    }
    public <T> T findAll_XML(Class<T> responseType)
        throws UniformInterfaceException {
        WebResource resource = webResource;
        return resource.accept(
        javax.ws.rs.core.MediaType.APPLICATION_XML).get(responseType);
    }
    public <T> T findAll_JSON(Class<T> responseType)
        throws UniformInterfaceException {
        WebResource resource = webResource;
        return resource.accept(
            javax.ws.rs.core.MediaType.APPLICATION_JSON).get(
            responseType);
    }
    public void edit_XML(Object requestEntity)
        throws UniformInterfaceException {
        webResource.type(
        javax.ws.rs.core.MediaType.APPLICATION_XML).
put(requestEntity);
    }
    public void edit_JSON(Object requestEntity)
        throws UniformInterfaceException {
        webResource.type(
            javax.ws.rs.core.MediaType.APPLICATION_JSON).put(
            requestEntity);
    }
    public void create_XML(Object requestEntity)
        throws UniformInterfaceException {
        webResource.type(
            javax.ws.rs.core.MediaType.APPLICATION_XML).post(
            requestEntity);
```

```
    }
    public void create_JSON(Object requestEntity)
        throws UniformInterfaceException {
        webResource.type(
            javax.ws.rs.core.MediaType.APPLICATION_JSON).post(
            requestEntity);
    }
    public <T> T findRange_XML(Class<T> responseType, String from,
        String to) throws UniformInterfaceException {
        WebResource resource = webResource;
        resource = resource.path(
            java.text.MessageFormat.format("{0}/{1}",
            new Object[]{from, to}));
        return resource.accept(
            javax.ws.rs.core.MediaType.APPLICATION_XML).get(
                responseType);
    }
    public <T> T findRange_JSON(Class<T> responseType,
        String from, String to) throws UniformInterfaceException {
        WebResource resource = webResource;
        resource = resource.path(
            java.text.MessageFormat.format("{0}/{1}",
            new Object[]{from, to}));
        return resource.accept(
            javax.ws.rs.core.MediaType.APPLICATION_JSON).get(
            responseType);
    }
    public <T> T find_XML(Class<T> responseType, String id)
        throws UniformInterfaceException {
        WebResource resource = webResource;
        resource = resource.path(java.text.MessageFormat.format("{0}",
            new Object[]{id}));
        return resource.accept(
            javax.ws.rs.core.MediaType.APPLICATION_XML).get(
            responseType);
    }
    public <T> T find_JSON(Class<T> responseType, String id)
        throws UniformInterfaceException {
        WebResource resource = webResource;
        resource = resource.path(java.text.MessageFormat.format("{0}",
            new Object[]{id}));
        return resource.accept(
            javax.ws.rs.core.MediaType.APPLICATION_JSON).get(
            responseType);
    }
```

```
        public void close() {
            client.destroy();
        }

    }
```

As we can see, NetBeans generates wrapper methods for each of the methods in our RESTful web service. NetBeans generates two versions of each method, one that produces and/or consumes XML, and another one that produces and/or consumes JSON (JavaScript Object Notation). As we can see, each method uses generics so that we can set the return type of these methods at run time.

The easiest and most straightforward way of using these methods is to use Strings, for example, we can invoke the **find_XML(Class<T> responseType, String id)** as follows:

```
public class Main {
    public static void main(String[] args) {
        NewJerseyClient newJerseyClient = new NewJerseyClient();
        String response = newJerseyClient.find_XML(
            String.class, "1");
        System.out.println("response is: " + response);
        newJerseyClient.close();
    }

}
```

The above invocation will return a String containing an XML representation of the values in the row with ID of 1 in the database, executing the above code we should see the following output:

```
response is: <?xml version="1.0" encoding="UTF-8" standalone
="yes"?><customer><customerId>1</customerId><email>bnorris@
example.com</email><firstName>Bruce</firstName><lastName>Norris</
lastName><middleName></middleName></customer>
```

We can then parse and manipulate this XML as usual.

Additionally, we can send data to our web service in XML format, all we need to do is create a String with the appropriate XML and pass it to one of the generated methods. For example, we could insert a row into the database by using the following code:

```
package com.ensode.glassfishbook.jaxrsclient;
public class Main1 {
    public static void main(String[] args) {
        NewJerseyClient newJerseyClient = new NewJerseyClient();
```

```
        String xml = "<?xml version=\"1.0\" encoding=\"UTF-8\"
standalone=\"yes\"?>"
            + "<customer>"
            + "<customerId>2</customerId>"
            + "<email>jjones@example.com</email>"
            + "<firstName>John</firstName>"
            + "<lastName>Jones</lastName>"
            + "<middleName>Jason</middleName>"
            + "</customer>";
        newJerseyClient.create_XML(xml);

        newJerseyClient.close();
    }
}
```

In the client code above, we generate XML formatted so that our RESTful web service can understand it, then pass it to the `create_XML()` method in the generated client class. This class in turn invokes our web service which inserts a row in the database.

We can verify that the data was inserted successfully by querying the database.

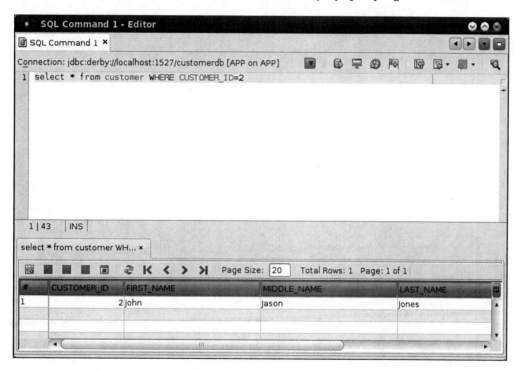

As we can see, the data in the database matches the data in the XML string we generated.

Summary

In this chapter, we covered some of the powerful RESTful web service generation capabilities that NetBeans offers. We saw how NetBeans allows us to easily generate a RESTful web service from an existing database schema. We also saw how we can easily test our web services using tools provided by NetBeans and GlassFish. Additionally, we saw how to generate a web service client with a few clicks of the mouse. Finally we saw how we can invoke our web service functionality with a few simple method calls.

A
Debugging Enterprise Applications with the NetBeans Debugger

Debuggers help us test and debug applications. NetBeans includes a debugger that can help us seamlessly debug all of our Java applications, including enterprise applications. In this appendix we will cover the NetBeans debugger, highlighting features that make our lives as Java EE developers easier.

Debugging enterprise applications

Typically debugging enterprise Java EE applications is a somewhat complicated process, our application server needs to be started in the "debug mode". The procedure for doing this is different depending on the application server, but typically involves passing some command line parameters to the shell script or executable that starts the application server. Our code must also be compiled with debugging enabled; this is usually done by either setting a parameter on the IDE or passing some arguments to the `javac` executable. Also, our debugger must be "attached" to the application server so that it can "see" the code running in a separate JVM.

Thankfully all of the steps described in the previous paragraph are automated when using NetBeans with the bundled GlassFish application server. When using this combination, all we need to do is open our Enterprise Application Project then right-click on it and select **Debug**, at this point the application server is started in debug mode (or restarted in debug mode if it was already running in standard mode), the application is deployed and the debugger is automatically attached to the application server.

We will use a simple application involving JSF, CDI, and JPA to illustrate NetBeans debugging capabilities.

When persisting data in JPA entities, we either need to set the primary key explicitly when inserting a new row in the database, or we need to set automatic primary key generation using the `@GeneratedValue` annotation. In our example we will use neither approach, this will make our application break when inserting new rows. Here is the relevant code for the JPA entity:

```
package com.ensode.nbbook.buggywebapp.entity;

import java.io.Serializable;
import javax.persistence.Basic;
import javax.persistence.Column;
import javax.persistence.Entity;
import javax.persistence.Id;
import javax.persistence.NamedQueries;
import javax.persistence.NamedQuery;
import javax.persistence.Table;
import javax.validation.constraints.NotNull;
import javax.validation.constraints.Size;
import javax.xml.bind.annotation.XmlRootElement;
```

```
@Entity
@Table(name = "CUSTOMER")
public class Customer implements Serializable {
    private static final long serialVersionUID = 1L;
    @Id
    @Basic(optional = false)
    @NotNull
    @Column(name = "CUSTOMER_ID")
    private Integer customerId;
    @Size(max = 20)
    @Column(name = "FIRST_NAME")
    private String firstName;
    @Size(max = 20)
    @Column(name = "MIDDLE_NAME")
    private String middleName;
    @Size(max = 20)
    @Column(name = "LAST_NAME")
    private String lastName;
    @Size(max = 30)
    @Column(name = "EMAIL")
    private String email;
    public Customer() {
    }
    public Customer(Integer customerId) {
        this.customerId = customerId;
    }
    //getters and setters omitted for brevity.
}
```

Notice that the above JPA entity does not use the `@GeneratedValue` annotation, therefore the value for its primary key needs to be explicitly set before persisting its data.

The following CDI Named bean acts as a controller in our example application, it has a method that is meant to persist data in an instance of the `Customer` JPA entity.

```
package com.ensode.nbbook.buggywebapp.controller;

//imports omitted for brevity

@Named
@RequestScoped
@Stateful
public class CustomerController {

    @PersistenceContext(unitName = "BuggyWebAppPU")
```

```java
    private EntityManager em;
    @Inject
    private CustomerModel customerModel;
    public String createCustomer() {
        Customer customer = entityFromModel(customerModel);
        try {
            persist(customer);
            return "confirmation";
        } catch (Exception e) {
            Logger.getLogger(getClass().getName()).log(
                Level.SEVERE, "exception caught", e);
            return "error";
        }
    }

    public void persist(Object object) {
        try {
            em.persist(object);
        } catch (Exception e) {
            Logger.getLogger(getClass().getName()).log(
                Level.SEVERE, "exception caught", e);
            throw new RuntimeException(e);
        }
    }

    private Customer entityFromModel(CustomerModel customerModel) {
        Customer customer = new Customer();
        customer.setFirstName(customerModel.getFirstName());
        customer.setLastName(customerModel.getLastName());
        return customer;
    }
    public CustomerModel getCustomerModel() {
        return customerModel;
    }
    public void setCustomerModel(CustomerModel customerModel) {
        this.customerModel = customerModel;
    }
    public EntityManager getEm() {
        return em;
    }
    public void setEm(EntityManager em) {
        this.em = em;
    }
}
```

Notice that nowhere in the above code is the primary key property in the Customer JPA entity set. Since we are not using automatic primary key generation, and we are not explicitly setting the primary key value, our application will throw an exception when attempting to persist an instance of the Customer JPA entity.

If we examine the GlassFish log in the NetBeans output window, we can see the following line:

```
at com.ensode.nbbook.buggywebapp.controller.CustomerController.creat
eCustomer(CustomerController.java:35)
```

The above line is telling us that an exception occurred on line 35 of `CustomerController.java`. Therefore we need to pause our application's execution just before that line is executed so that we can inspect the values of all relevant variables at that point.

One central feature of debuggers is the ability to pause execution of the application being debugged by adding **breakpoints** to it. When a line of code where a breakpoint has been placed is about to be executed, the application pauses, allowing us to inspect the values of all instance and method scoped variables in the class where the breakpoint was placed. In NetBeans, placing a breakpoint in a line is very simple, all we need to do is click on the left margin of the source editor right next to the line where the breakpoint will be added, at this point the line will be highlighted in red plus a red square icon will be placed in the left margin.

To display line numbers, right-click on the left margin and click on the checkbox labeled **Show Line Numbers**.

```
CustomerController.java ×

26
27        @PersistenceContext(unitName = "BuggyWebAppPU")
28        private EntityManager em;
29        @Inject
30        private CustomerModel customerModel;
31
32 ⊟      public String createCustomer() {
33            Customer customer = entityFromModel(customerModel);
34            try {
                    persist(customer);
36                return "confirmation";
37            } catch (Exception e) {
38                Logger.getLogger(getClass().getName()).log(Level.SEVERE, "exception caught", e);
39                return "error";
40            }
41        }
```

At this point we are ready to debug our application, which we can do by simply right-clicking on our project and selecting **Debug**. Doing this causes our application to be deployed and executed as in debug mode.

We need to test our application as usual in order to get to the point where it is failing. In our example application we simply need to execute the code until it attempts to persist our JPA entity.

Looking at the editor, we will see that the line containing the breakpoint is now highlighted in green, plus an arrow has been placed on the left side margin.

```
CustomerController.java ×

25        public class CustomerController {
26
27        @PersistenceContext(unitName = "BuggyWebAppPU")
28        private EntityManager em;
29        @Inject
30        private CustomerModel customerModel;
31
32 ⊟      public String createCustomer() {
33            Customer customer = entityFromModel(customerModel);
34            try {
                    persist(customer);
36                return "confirmation";
37            } catch (Exception e) {
38                Logger.getLogger(getClass().getName()).log(Level.SEVERE, "exception caught", e);
39                return "error";
40            }
41        }
```

These changes indicate the current line in the execution path. Once the execution has been paused, we can execute the code line-by-line in order to pin point exactly where the problem is happening. There are two ways we can execute each line, we can either **step over** the line, or **step into** it, the difference being when we step over, we will not go "into" any method calls, simply going "over" the line. When we step into it, we actually navigate inside any method calls that are being invoked in the current line.

In our example, stepping over the current line would skip the line that is actually persisting the data, therefore the most appropriate course of action is to step into the current line.

In NetBeans, we can step over the current line by pressing *F7* or clicking on the icon:

Doing so will take us to the method being invoked in the current line, execution will pause at this point, the next line to be executed will be highlighted in green and an arrow will be placed next to it in the left margin.

```
CustomerController.java ×

30    private CustomerModel customerModel;
31
32    public String createCustomer() {
33        Customer customer = entityFromModel(customerModel);
34        try {
35            persist(customer);
36            return "confirmation";
37        } catch (Exception e) {
38            Logger.getLogger(getClass().getName()).log(Level.SEVERE, "exception caught", e);
39            return "error";
40        }
41    }
42
43    public void persist(Object object) {
44        try {
45            em.persist(object);
46        } catch (Exception e) {
47            Logger.getLogger(getClass().getName()).log(Level.SEVERE, "exception caught", e);
48            throw new RuntimeException(e);
49        }
```

Since there is only one executable line in this method, we know that stepping over this line will cause the exception. We can inspect any local variables in the current class and method by looking at the **Local Variables** window.

The **Local Variables** window can be opened by going to **Window | Debugging | Local Variables** or by pressing *Alt+Shift+1* on windows and Linux systems, and *Ctrl+Shift+1* on Mac OS X systems.

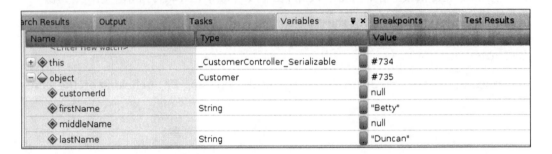

Name	Type	Value
`<Enter new watch>`		
+ ◈ this	_CustomerController_Serializable	#734
− ◇ object	Customer	#735
◈ customerId		null
◈ firstName	String	"Betty"
◈ middleName		null
◈ lastName	String	"Duncan"

By expanding the node corresponding to our `customer` object, we can see the values of all of its properties. At this point we should notice that the `customerId` property is null, which results in the code attempting to insert a new row with a null primary key. At this point we have discovered the problem. Now that the problem is known, fixing the code is trivial, in our example, the easiest way to fix it is to add the `@GeneratedValue` annotation to the `customerId` property of our entity bean.

Summary

In this appendix we covered how to debug enterprise applications using NetBeans, we saw how NetBeans makes debugging remote applications deployed to an application server as simple as debugging standard Java applications.

We also saw how we can add breakpoints to pause execution of our applications and either step into or step over each line.

Additionally we saw how we can inspect the values of all variables in scope by looking at the **Local Variables** window.

B

Identifying Performance Issues with the NetBeans Profiler

Sometimes we run into performance problems in some of our applications. At times, identifying the code to be optimized may be trivial, but sometimes it is not easy. Profilers are tools that can help us pinpoint performance problems in our code. NetBeans comes with a very good profiler that we can use with our Java EE applications.

Profiling our application

All we need to do in order to profile our application is right-click on it in the **Projects** window and select **Profile**. At that point, the following window will pop up:

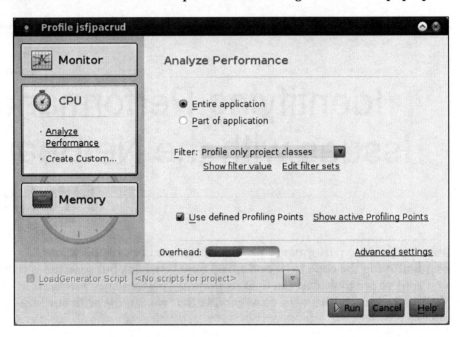

As we can see, there are several aspects of our application we can profile, such as memory allocation and CPU usage. One of the most useful features of the NetBeans profiler is the ability to report how long each method invocation in our application is taking, this information is provided when we profile CPU usage.

In order to start profiling, we simply click on the **Run** button. At this point the application server will be started in profiling mode, and our application will be deployed and executed. After a few seconds the Profiler control panel will open.

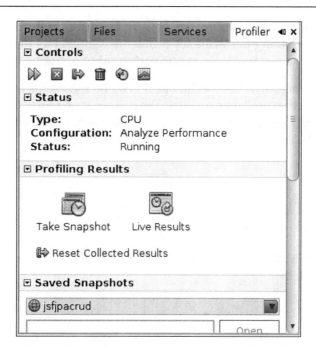

At this point we can see how long each method is taking and how many times each method has been executed by simply clicking on the **Live Results** button.

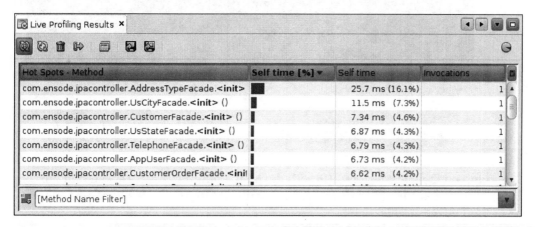

The **Live Profiling Results** window displays every method invocation, along with the percentage of total time in the application that the method is using, and the number of milliseconds the method takes to complete, it also shows how many times each method has been invoked.

As we can see, the NetBeans profiler can be very helpful in pinpointing areas of our application that are having performance problems, allowing us to easily identify these areas so that we can better focus our performance optimization efforts.

Although this information is very valuable, it is by no means the only information we can obtain from the NetBeans profiler. We can see how much memory our application is using by simply opening the **VM Telemetry Overview** window by clicking on the **VM Telemetry** icon on the Profiling control panel.

After clicking the VM Telemetry Icon, the **VM Telemetry** window opens. This window has three tabs:

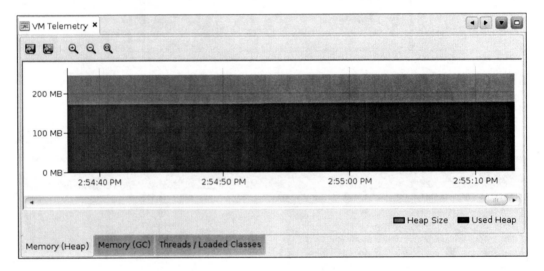

The graph on the left tab shows (in red) the total amount of heap allocated in our application's Java Virtual Machine. Additionally, it also shows the total amount of heap used by our application.

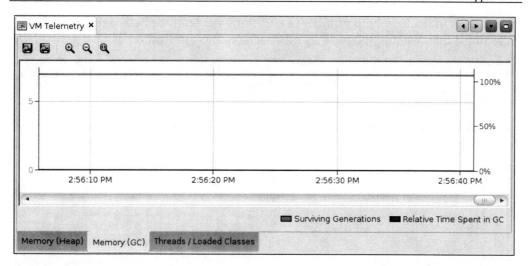

The graph in the middle tab is useful for detecting "memory leaks" (Java has garbage collection, therefore in theory memory leaks are impossible. However, if we keep references to objects that are no longer needed they are never garbage collected, therefore a memory leak is possible). The purple line in the middle graph indicates the amount of time the JVM spends doing garbage collection. The red line indicates **Surviving Generations**. A **generation** is a set of objects that were created within two garbage collection intervals. A surviving generation is a generation that survived one or more garbage collections. We can force our application to garbage collect by clicking on the icon in the Profiling control panel:

If the graph indicates a high number of surviving generations between garbage collections, then we might have a memory leak in our application.

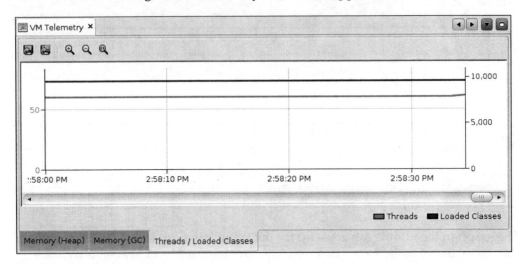

The graph on the right tab of the **VM Telemetry Overview** window indicates the number of active threads and the number of loaded classes in our application.

Summary

The NetBeans profiler is a very valuable tool in identifying performance problems in our applications. It provides several useful tools to aid us in identifying poorly performing code, as well as allow us to easily monitor memory usage and object allocation in our applications. More information about the NetBeans profiler can be found at http://profiler.netbeans.org/.

Index

Thank you for buying
Java EE 6 Development with NetBeans 7

About Packt Publishing

Packt, pronounced 'packed', published its first book "*Mastering phpMyAdmin for Effective MySQL Management*" in April 2004 and subsequently continued to specialize in publishing highly focused books on specific technologies and solutions.

Our books and publications share the experiences of your fellow IT professionals in adapting and customizing today's systems, applications, and frameworks. Our solution based books give you the knowledge and power to customize the software and technologies you're using to get the job done. Packt books are more specific and less general than the IT books you have seen in the past. Our unique business model allows us to bring you more focused information, giving you more of what you need to know, and less of what you don't.

Packt is a modern, yet unique publishing company, which focuses on producing quality, cutting-edge books for communities of developers, administrators, and newbies alike. For more information, please visit our website: www.packtpub.com.

About Packt Open Source

In 2010, Packt launched two new brands, Packt Open Source and Packt Enterprise, in order to continue its focus on specialization. This book is part of the Packt Open Source brand, home to books published on software built around Open Source licences, and offering information to anybody from advanced developers to budding web designers. The Open Source brand also runs Packt's Open Source Royalty Scheme, by which Packt gives a royalty to each Open Source project about whose software a book is sold.

Writing for Packt

We welcome all inquiries from people who are interested in authoring. Book proposals should be sent to author@packtpub.com. If your book idea is still at an early stage and you would like to discuss it first before writing a formal book proposal, contact us; one of our commissioning editors will get in touch with you.

We're not just looking for published authors; if you have strong technical skills but no writing experience, our experienced editors can help you develop a writing career, or simply get some additional reward for your expertise.

Java EE 5 Development with NetBeans 6

ISBN: 978-1-847195-46-3   Paperback: 400 pages

Develop professional enterprise Java EE applications quickly and easily with this popular IDE

1. Use features of the popular NetBeans IDE to improve Java EE development

2. Careful instructions and screenshots lead you through the options available

3. Covers the major Java EE APIs such as JSF, EJB 3 and JPA, and how to work with them in NetBeans

NetBeans IDE 7 Cookbook

ISBN: 978-1-84951-250-3   Paperback: 308 pages

Over 70 highly focused practical recipes to maximize your output with NetBeans

1. Covers the full spectrum of features offered by the NetBeans IDE

2. Discover ready-to-implement solutions for developing desktop and web applications

3. Learn how to deploy, debug, and test your software using NetBeans IDE

4. Another title in Packt's Cookbook series giving clear, real-world solutions to common practical problems

Please check **www.PacktPub.com** for information on our titles

Java EE 6 with GlassFish 3 Application Server

ISBN: 978-1-849510-36-3   Paperback: 488 pages

A practical guide to install and configure the GlassFish 3 Application Server and develop Java EE 6 applications to be deployed to this server

1. Install and configure the GlassFish 3 Application Server and develop Java EE 6 applications to be deployed to this server

2. Specialize in all major Java EE 6 APIs, including new additions to the specification such as CDI and JAX-RS

3. Use GlassFish v3 application server and gain enterprise reliability and performance with less complexity

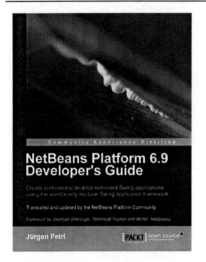

NetBeans Platform 6.9 Developer's Guide

ISBN: 978-1-849511-76-6   Paperback: 288 pages

Create professional desktop rich-client Swing applications using the world's only modular Swing application framework

1. Create large, scalable, modular Swing applications from scratch

2. Master a broad range of topics essential to have in your desktop application development toolkit, right from conceptualization to distribution

3. Pursue an easy-to-follow sequential and tutorial approach that builds to a complete Swing application

Please check **www.PacktPub.com** for information on our titles

Lightning Source UK Ltd.
Milton Keynes UK
UKOW020733070613

211896UK00004B/154/P